IMAGES
of America
ROANOKE

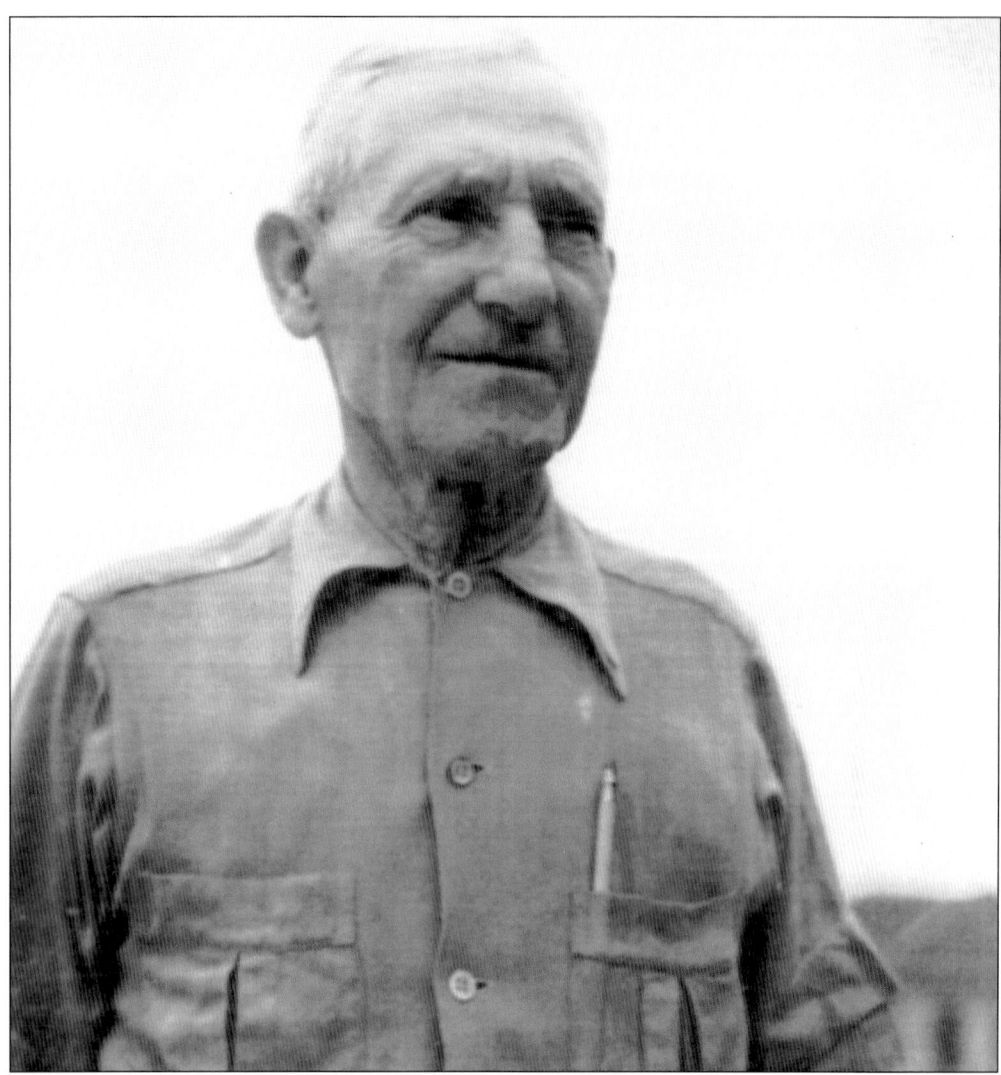

Hugh Jenkins came to Roanoke from Tennessee in May 1904. He quickly aligned himself with prominent people such as rancher Berry Hood, who gave him his first job. Jenkins married Hood's daughter, Hattie, on July 2, 1905, and received the Hood's family home on Oak Street as a wedding gift. Jenkins built a hardware and lumber store in 1916 at the corner of Oak and Rusk Streets. (Courtesy of City of Roanoke.)

ON THE COVER: The individuals pictured in this c. 1908 photograph are thought to be members of the Ballew family, who lived in a residence near the town's old water well. Pictured here are, from left to right, Ella Ballew (Prewitt), approximately 16 years old, and Zera Ballew, approximately 18 years old. Both were Sheriff George Thomas Ballew's daughters from his first marriage to Mattie. The small boy, about four years old, is Eddie, Ballew's son with his second wife, Brice. The adult man and older boy standing are unidentified. (Courtesy of Emily Ragsdale.)

IMAGES
of America
ROANOKE

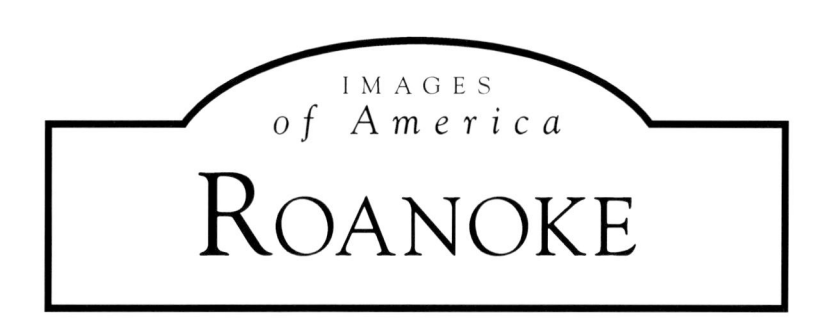

Wanda Smith and Ann French Clark

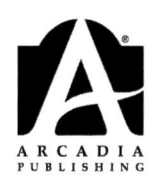

ARCADIA
PUBLISHING

Copyright © 2010 by Wanda Smith and Ann French Clark
ISBN 978-0-7385-8458-4

Published by Arcadia Publishing
Charleston, South Carolina

Printed in the United States of America

Library of Congress Control Number: 2009941023

For all general information contact Arcadia Publishing at:
Telephone 843-853-2070
Fax 843-853-0044
E-mail sales@arcadiapublishing.com
For customer service and orders:
Toll-Free 1-888-313-2665

Visit us on the Internet at www.arcadiapublishing.com

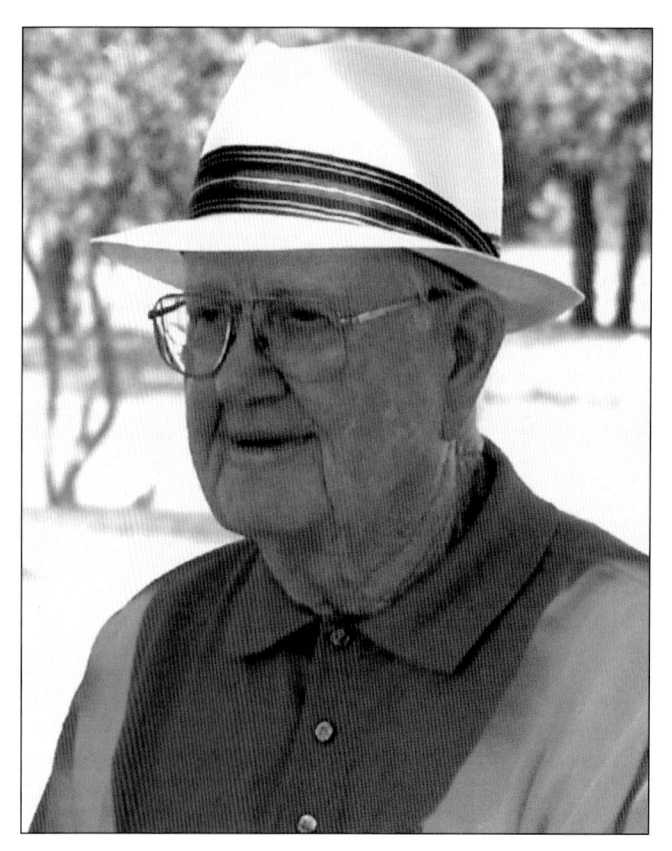

Professional golfer Byron Nelson, although not a native of the city, moved to Roanoke in 1945 with his wife, Louise. Nelson's golf feats are legendary—he won 11 consecutive tournaments and a record 18 total golf events in 1945. Nelson died in 2006 and was awarded the Congressional Gold Medal posthumously, which was accepted by his widow, Peggy, whom Nelson married after his first wife died. (Courtesy of Metroport Meals on Wheels.)

Contents

Acknowledgements		6
Introduction		7
1.	The Railroad and Early Settlement	9
2.	People and Places	45
3.	Out and About	73
4.	Schools and Churches	99
5.	Farms and Ranches	117

Acknowledgments

The photographs displayed in this book reflect the struggles and triumphs of a small community and a group of determined citizens. Museum employees Heidi McCullough (manager) and Stacy Lotz (curator) were most supportive of this effort. Amy Radford, marketing director for the City of Roanoke, offered helpful advice and assistance. The images contained here were primarily collected from current and former residents, with the exception of the two introductory pictures of Hugh Jenkins (City of Roanoke) and Byron Nelson (Metroport Meals on Wheels). Unfortunately, it is impossible to assemble a photographic collection that recognizes all those who have had important roles in the development of the city. The majority of the photographs are from the collections of Hise Seagraves Jr. (HSC), Alberta Lincecum, and Emily Ragsdale, whose families all arrived in Roanoke in the 1800s, and without them this book would not be possible.

    Thank you to the Roanoke Visitor Center and Museum (RVCM) for loaning pictures from its collection. We would also like to thank Inez and Henry "Mc" Howe, Vertalee and John Coleman, Cozette Harris, Pat Turner, Vance McDonald, and Calvin Peterson, not only for donating pictures, but also for helping us identify individuals and buildings. A special thanks to Gary Alexander for making the Hise Seagraves Jr. collection available, which contributed significantly to this effort. Toni Clark Beckett deserves, besides thanks, an award for patience and perseverance as she scanned pictures, typed, and offered editing suggestions.

Introduction

In 1881, the town of Roanoke, Texas, was platted from the D. O. (David) Hoover survey by the Texas and Pacific Railroad. The railroad came to this part of Texas at the behest of residents who had arrived in three waves of wagon trains led by Charles and Louis Medlin, who had embarked from North Carolina, buying and selling land along the way. Hoover, a surveyor, came to the area in 1853 with the William Royal Kelsay family, and his name is on the original plat of Roanoke, which was filed in Denton County on July 1, 1881.

The original settlers were seeking land grants from the government of Texas, which required a potential landowner to patent the land and then live on it for a specified period of time before they were actually considered landowners.

There are still Texas Land Grants in existence, signed by Gov. Sam Houston. One grant, given to William Royal Kelsay, began when he received a preemption certificate on February 18, 1861, legally confirming that he possessed the 160 acres where he and his family had lived since 1853. This was a time, just before the Civil War, rife with stress for citizens, since the residents in North Texas were not interested in seceding from the United States, as slavery was not an issue or economic necessity to them. There were few slave owners in this part of Texas, even though Mary Medlin had 10 slaves. The rest of the state of Texas thought differently. Sam Houston was adamantly opposed to the idea of seceding from the Union, but his opposition was fruitless when the rest of the state voted to leave the United States on February 1, 1861. However, by March 16, 1861, Sam Houston was removed from office.

The Kelsay land grant is now displayed at the University of North Texas in Denton, and another grant, found in the papers of Hugh Wilson Jenkins, can be seen at the Roanoke Visitor Center and Museum.

Some of the early families who arrived in the Medlin settlement, in addition to the Medlins, Hoovers, and Kelsays, bore names such as Hallford, Allen, Foster, Anderson, Throop, Loving, Harris, Dunham, Crowley, Eads, Graham, Deavenport, Freeman, Bush, and Bartwell. Some of these families became prominent in Elizabethtown and Justin, as well as in Roanoke.

By the time the 1870 census was taken, Denton County had 7,251 residents, 6,751 of who were white and 500 who were listed as colored. In 1880, the population count in Denton County more than doubled, probably connected to the anticipated railroad, which was coming to the area.

The railroad provided settlers with a reliable resource for receiving and shipping goods. The railroads' ability to quickly move people across the country usurped the popularity of the much slower and more dangerous wagon trains.

Though the early families, particularly the Medlins, had a significant impact on the area, there were others who arrived in the late 1800s and early 1900s who managed to leave their mark on the community as well. For example, William Patterson built the first store in 1882 and the first private residence as well. Berry Hood and Samuel Reynolds were cattlemen who acquired land, as well as mentoring newcomers who needed jobs but had little training in the cattleman occupation.

Thomas Brand traveled to Roanoke with some of his neighbors from Kentucky. He quickly acquired land and owned the Eureka Hotel, which was well situated next to the Silver Spur Saloon. The saloon was built by Robert and Burrell Snead, sons of Mary Counsel Medlin and John Snead. Brand also erected a furniture store in 1906. Through the years, the furniture store building held many businesses, most notably Noah's Grocery for years, which was owned first by Monroe Noah and then by his son James Noah. The two generations of Noahs also owned the same house on Walnut Street; both the grocery and home are still standing. The 1906 building on Oak Street, once the grocery, is now known as Babe's Restaurant.

In the late 1800s, a new wave of residents arrived to become the businessmen and leaders of the community. On March 27, 1885, Byram Seagraves and his children, two boys and two girls, stepped off the train in Roanoke at the newly completed railroad. The elder Seagraves began a medical practice, even though he was not educated as a physician. Some later historians postulated that perhaps he served as a medic in a war.

When Byram's sons, Hise and James, were old enough, they were partners in a commercial venture that combined dry goods, lumber, and hardware. Later Hise and James parted ways in commerce when James sold his part of the business to Hugh Jenkins, and his brother Hise concentrated only on the dry-goods segment of the business. Hise owned the business for more than 40 years and was one of the most prominent and influential citizens of Roanoke.

James Seagraves was a cobbler and something of an eccentric in town, as he carved his own tombstone, which he kept in his backyard. At one point he used it as a step at his house. The tombstone now rests where he intended, over his grave at the Oddfellow Cemetery, now in the town of Westlake.

Hugh Jenkins, another important figure in Roanoke's history, arrived in 1904. Jenkins kept handwritten notes of the life and times in Roanoke. His description of first seeing Roanoke includes a detailed account of the wooden well, which was in the middle of Oak Street, powered by a windmill. The windmill had a trough for horses at its base. Jenkins embraced modern ideas, including the idea that motor cars were the wave of the future. He purchased a Hupmobile in Dallas and had it delivered to Roanoke, complete with someone to teach him how to drive. As others bought automobiles, Jenkins imported gasoline in barrels to sell.

In 1910, when Roanoke had 400 residents, there was what old-timers refer to as "the great fire" that destroyed a good portion of the buildings on the west side of Oak Street when a hastily arranged bucket brigade was unable to put out the fire. Even though the fire was a setback, it did not deter the community from rebuilding and continuing to add businesses and services.

In the early 1930s, Hugh Jenkins, the owner of a hardware and lumber store, was the leader of a group called the Committee for the Community. This group, with input from citizens, decided that it wanted a more modern water system and that Roanoke needed to incorporate as a city, which took effect in 1933. It took several years for the water system to be fully operational, complete with a 150-foot-tall water tower situated at the corner of Main and Oak Streets, not far from where the original wooden tower stood. The 1933 tower is still an imposing sight in old town Roanoke, though it is no longer operational.

Today Roanoke enjoys an enviable location near major cities such as Fort Worth and Dallas, which offer entertainment, sports venues, and educational opportunities at Southern Methodist and Texas Christian Universities. The University of Texas at Arlington is within commuting distance, as are the University of North Texas and Texas Woman's University in Denton.

In 2009, Roanoke was named the "Unique Dining Capital of Texas," with many restaurants within the city limits. The city also boasts several festivals each year: Celebrate Roanoke in October and a Christmas event in December. With 10,000 visitors in October 2008 for Celebrate Roanoke, visitors flock to these events. Roanoke citizens are justifiably proud of their community and the rich mix of historical and new properties.

One
The Railroad and Early Settlement

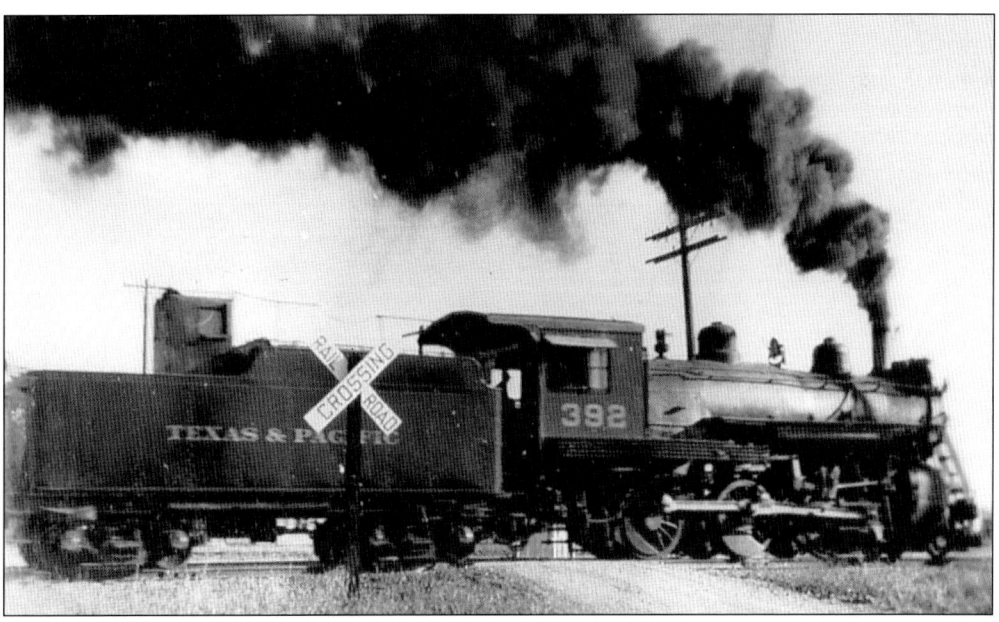

The Texas and Pacific Railroad came to this part of Texas, now known as Roanoke, in the early 1880s, primarily because residents who lived in the area, including cattleman Samuel Reynolds, lobbied the company. Railroad officials established a town south of the original settlement, with the majority of the land bought from Samuel Reynolds, who had arrived by wagon train with Louis and Charles Medlin from Missouri in the mid-1800s. (Courtesy of Alberta Lincecum.)

10

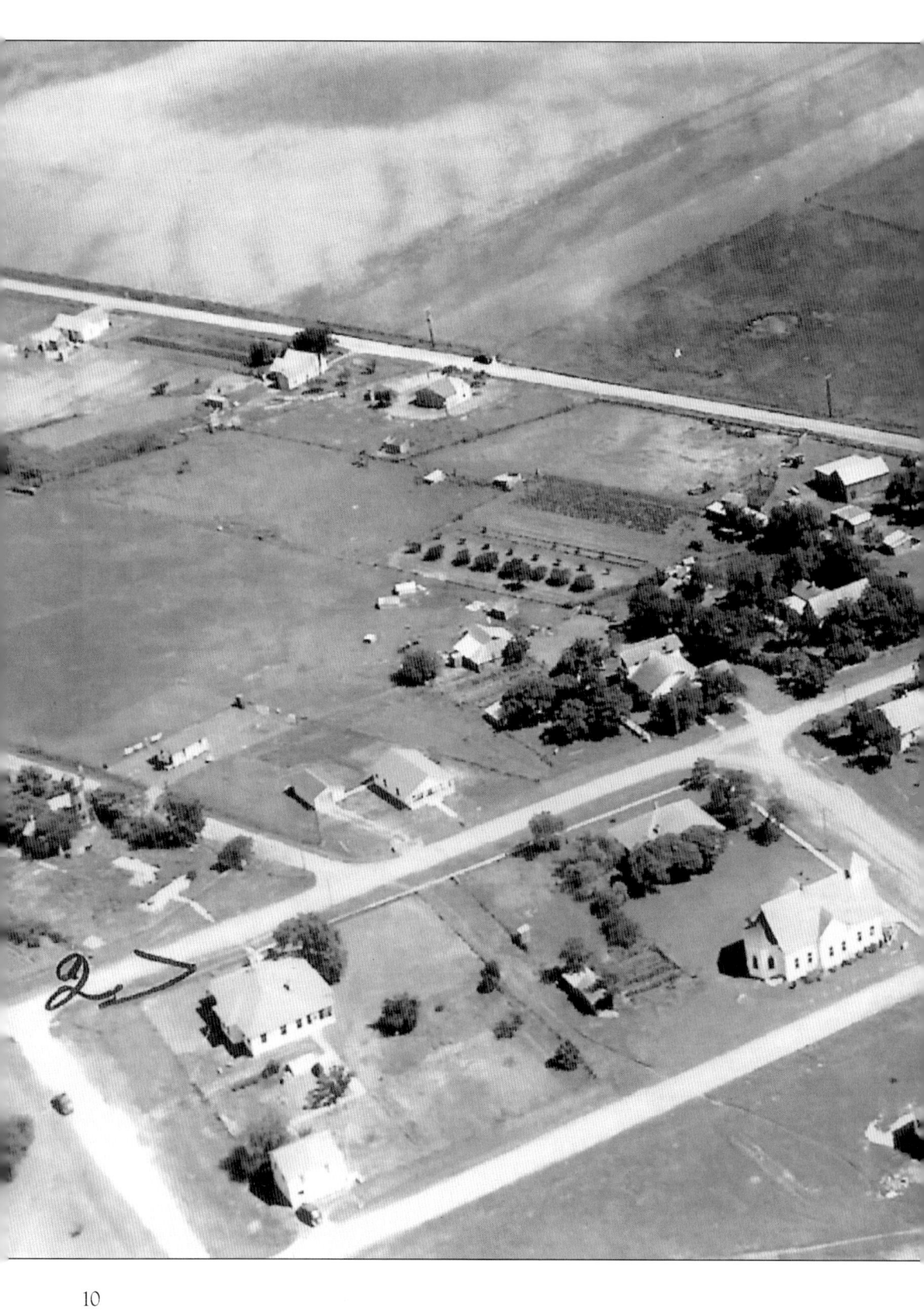

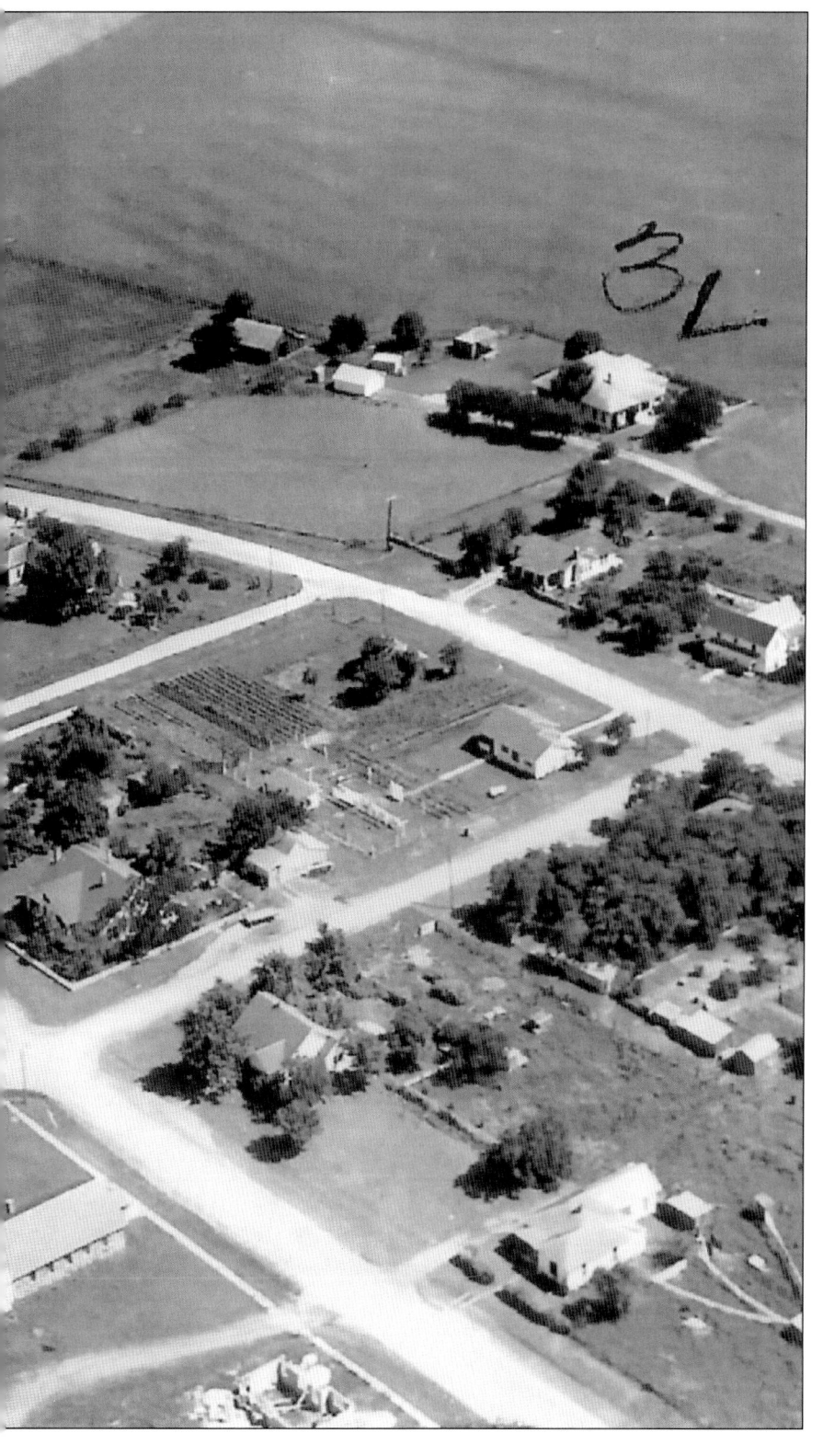

This eastern aerial view of Roanoke primarily features individual homesites, though in the center (bottom third) of the photograph is the First Methodist Church, with the Church of Christ across the side street. The Methodist church, built in the early 1900s, was moved to a new location east of Lois and Dorman Streets. Highway construction caused it to be sold and moved again to Trophy Club, where it is used as a wedding chapel. (Courtesy of Vertalee and John Coleman.)

11

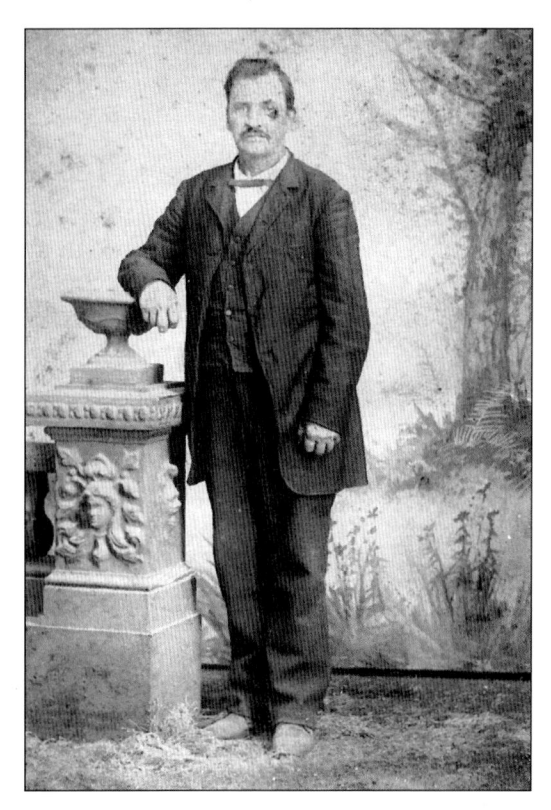

William Owen Medlin, pictured in the mid- to late-1800s photograph at left, was born on August 31, 1838, in Cole County, Missouri. He married Amanda Elizabeth White on July 20, 1865. He was the father of 14 children. The photograph below shows the granddaughter of the Medlins, Mary Elizabeth Luttrell. Mary distinguished herself as a school athlete, and later in life she became a noted historian in Denton County by documenting the burials in the Medlin Cemetery, securing a Texas Historical Marker for the cemetery, and serving as a resource for many who were researching the history of the Roanoke area. (Both, courtesy of the Mary Carpenter Estate.)

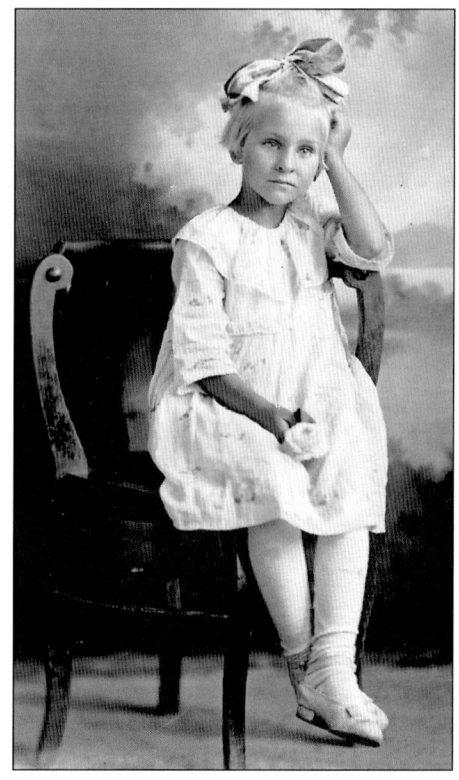

Henry Mack Luttrell and his wife, Mittie Viola Medlin, are pictured in these 1940s photographs. One of their children, Mary Elizabeth, is pictured on the preceding page along with Mittie's father, William O. Medlin. Mittie Viola was named after Mittie Ann Medlin, who died in childbirth and was the first person buried in the family cemetery. The Luttrells lived on a farm with a creek running through it, which was often the site of baptisms. In fact, the *Roanoke Weekly News* of 1908 reported that a crowd estimated to be 1,300 people gathered at the site when 37 people were baptized, including Claud Raibourn, John Seagraves, Clint Yancey, Una Brand, Margaret Francisco, Charles Medlin, T. M. Medlin, Winnie Belle Pickett, and others. The mass baptism was a result of a Baptist revival. (Both, courtesy of the Mary Carpenter Estate.)

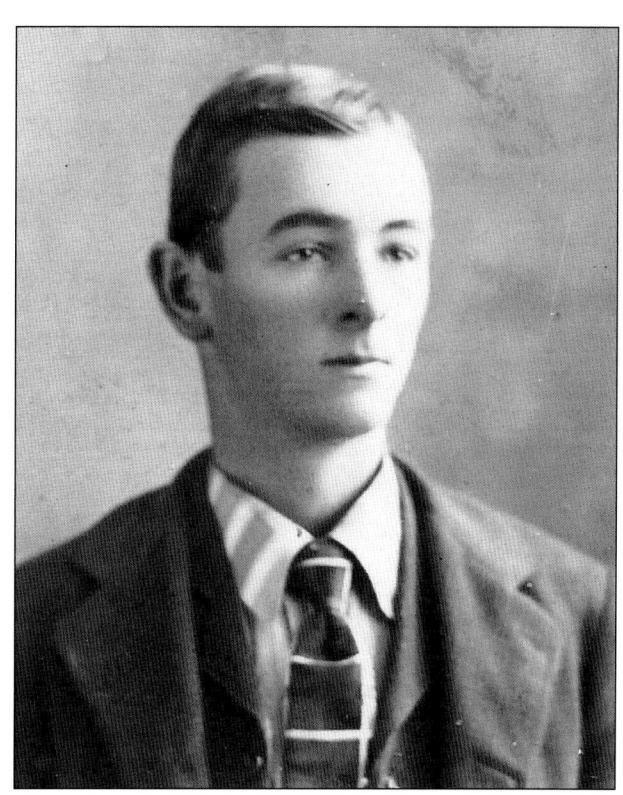

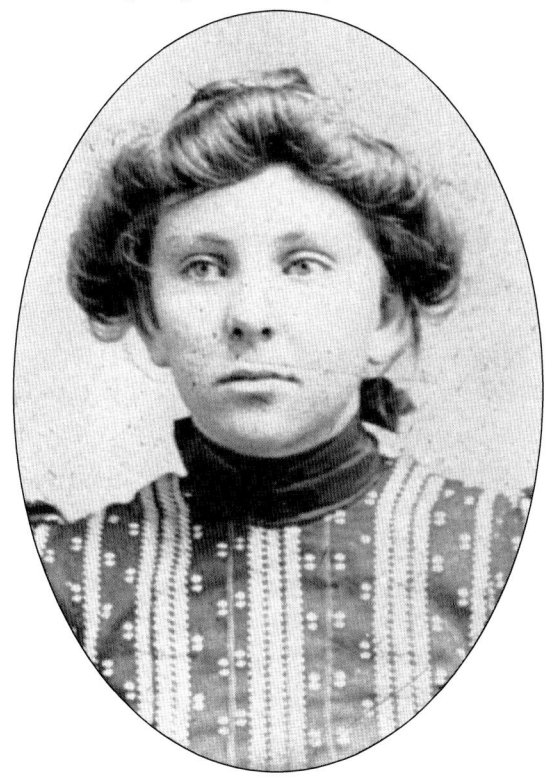

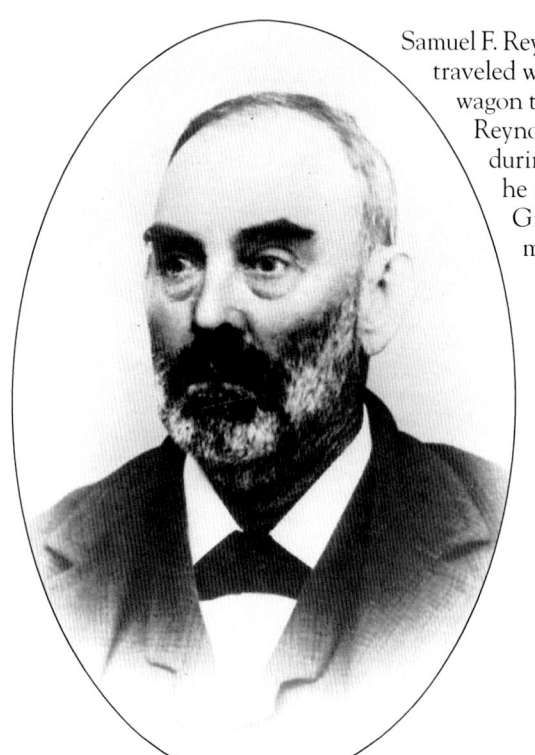

Samuel F. Reynolds, born on September 6, 1832, in Missouri, traveled with his father, Cage, to the Roanoke area in a wagon train led by Louis and Charles Medlin in 1847. Reynolds served in Company E, 29th Texas Calvary during the Civil War. After his first wife's death, he married her sister, Malinda Catherine "Cass" Gillespie, who brought three children to the marriage. (Courtesy of HSC.)

William G. Patterson established the first general store in Roanoke in 1882 and also built the first private residence east of the railroad tracks. He owned a dry-goods store on the west side of Oak Street. His daughter, Ida Cade, took over his business when he returned to Missouri, and the business was called Cade's Dry Goods. Ida's husband, John R., sold caskets in the rear of the store. (Courtesy of HSC.)

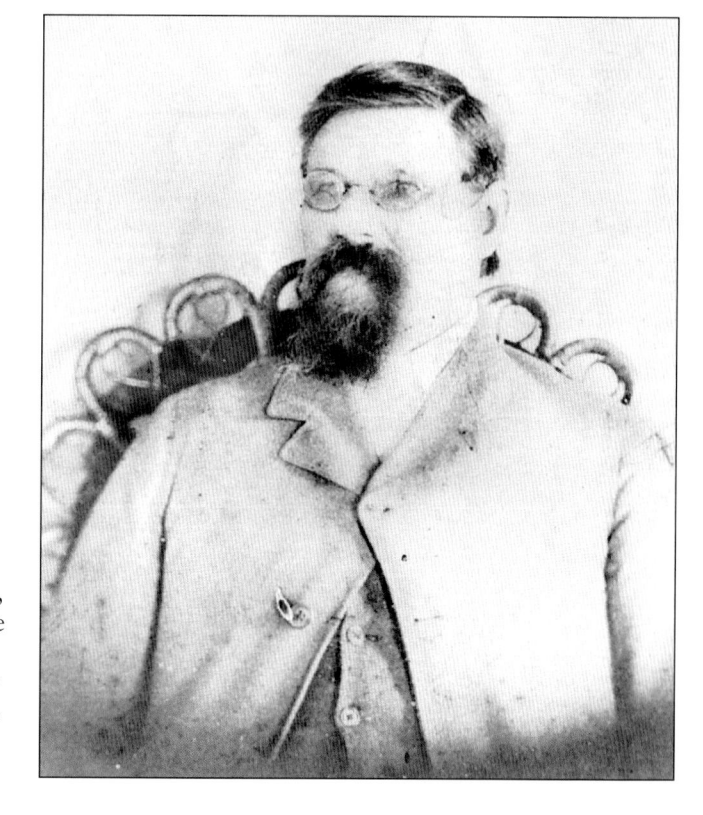

Baxter Ragsdale (seated, left), born in Roanoke in 1885, is shown here with his mother, Charity, and brothers, Willie (standing, left) and Harry. His mother had appendicitis, making a wagon trip to a hospital in Fort Worth a necessity; unfortunately she died at the hospital. Baxter owned a mechanic shop with two generators on Oak Street, which supplied electricity to the town of Roanoke until 1962, when the distribution system was acquired by Texas Power and Light. (Courtesy of Emily Ragsdale.)

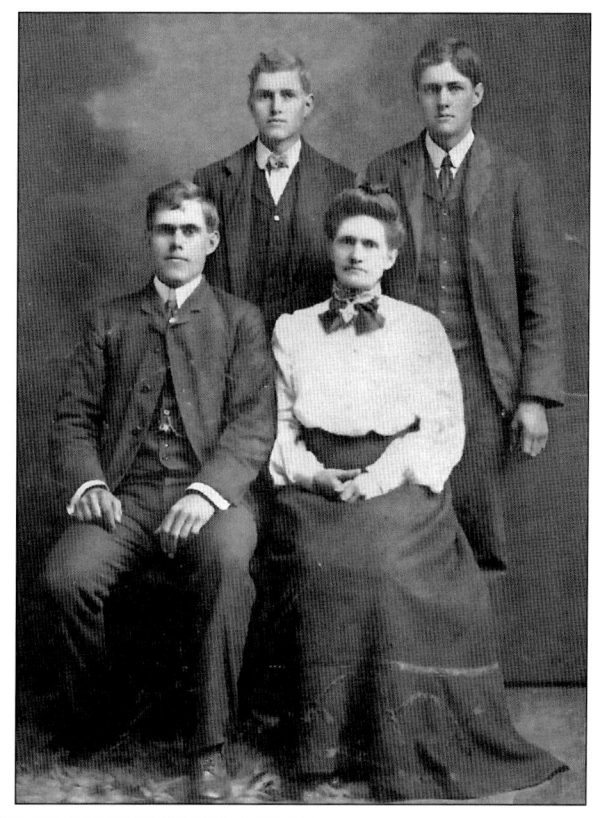

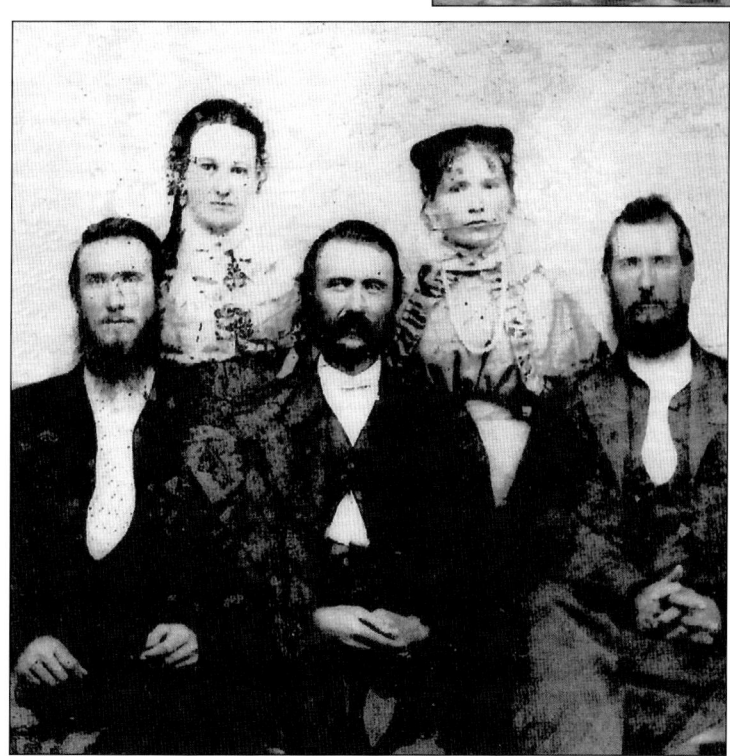

None of the Brands in this picture are identified; however, during the early days in this area, Thomas Richard Brand and his wife, Mary Elizabeth Smith, lived in Garden Valley and later in Roanoke next to the Berry Hood family. The Brands arrived by train in Dallas in 1877, with their long-time neighbors from Kentucky, the Litseys and Smiths, some of whom were kin to Mary, whose father was Capt. John L. Smith. The Brands owned the Eureka Hotel. (Courtesy of Alberta Lincecum.)

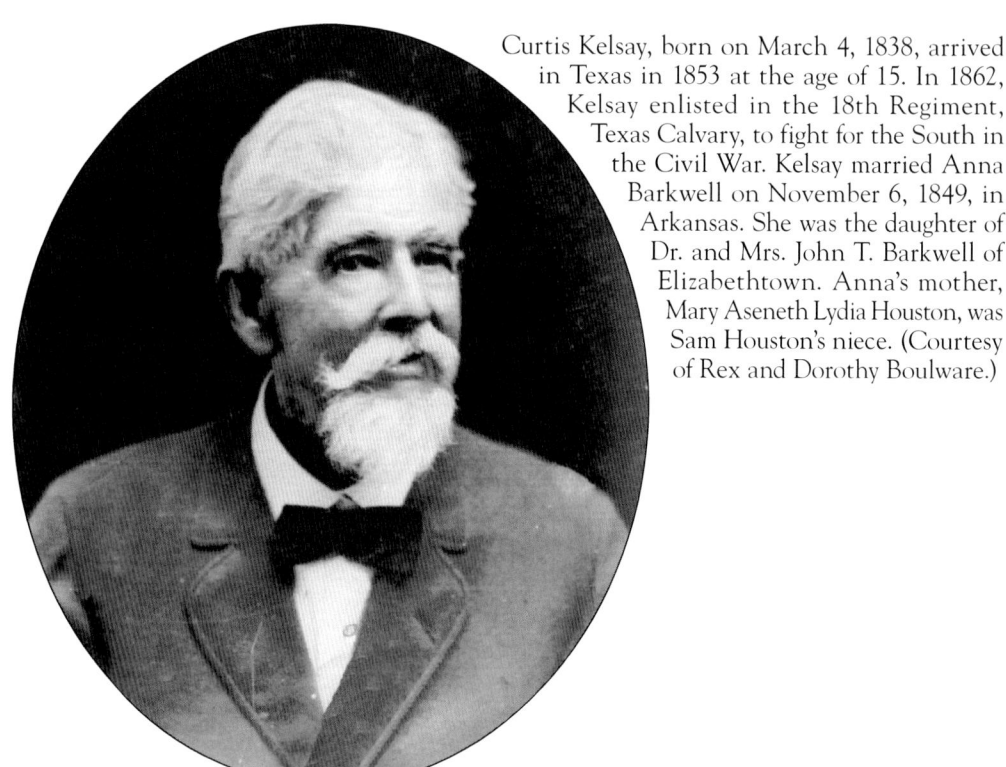

Curtis Kelsay, born on March 4, 1838, arrived in Texas in 1853 at the age of 15. In 1862, Kelsay enlisted in the 18th Regiment, Texas Calvary, to fight for the South in the Civil War. Kelsay married Anna Barkwell on November 6, 1849, in Arkansas. She was the daughter of Dr. and Mrs. John T. Barkwell of Elizabethtown. Anna's mother, Mary Aseneth Lydia Houston, was Sam Houston's niece. (Courtesy of Rex and Dorothy Boulware.)

Pictured here are, from left to right, (first row) Ernest Manire and Lucy Manire, his mother; (second row) Dru, Nannie, and Ella Manire. After the death of her first husband, Phillip Manire, Lucy married Martin VanBuren Elsea. (Courtesy of William Manire.)

16

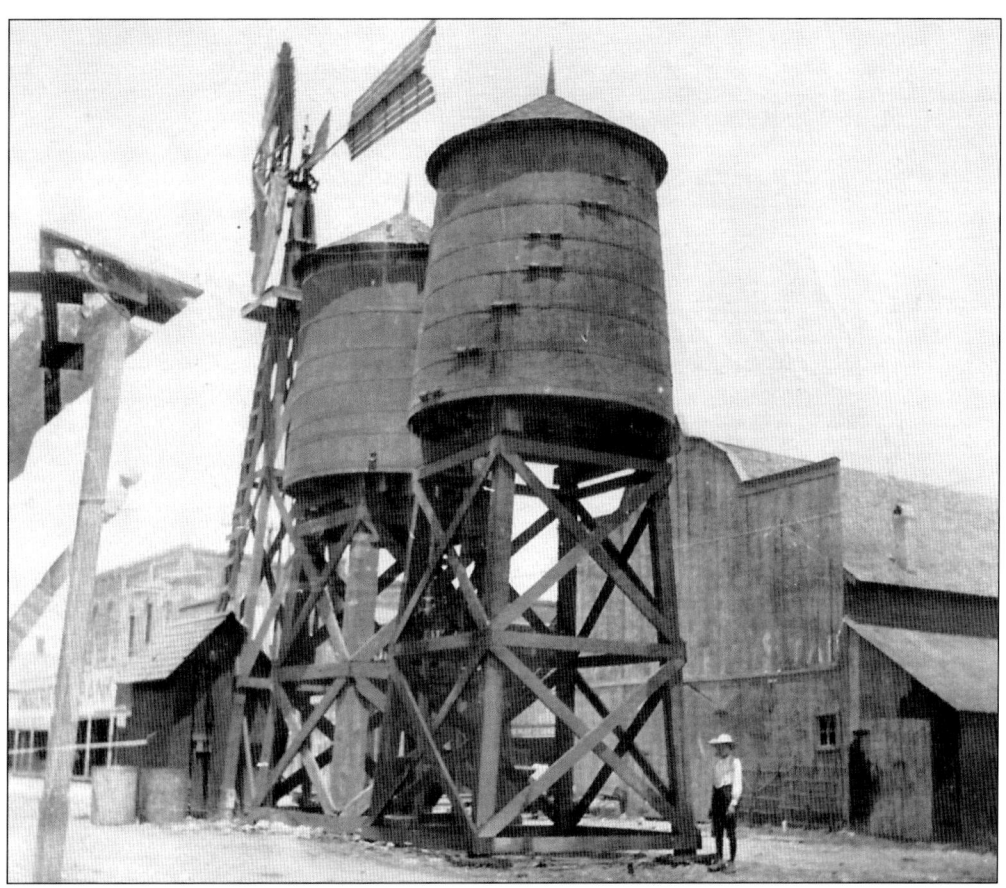

Built in 1882, the first wooden well was located in the center of Oak Street, east of Welborn and Cade's Dry Goods store. Another source showed the well as being built in 1885, which can also be true as the well was relocated to the north end of old downtown near the rock saloon. In any event, when Hugh Jenkins came to Roanoke in 1905, one of the wells was still in existence. Jenkins described it in a handwritten narrative as being two wooden tanks on approximately 16-foot-tall wooden legs with a windmill on the north side of the tanks to pump the water. There was also a trough for horses close to the tanks. (Both, courtesy of Alberta Lincecum.)

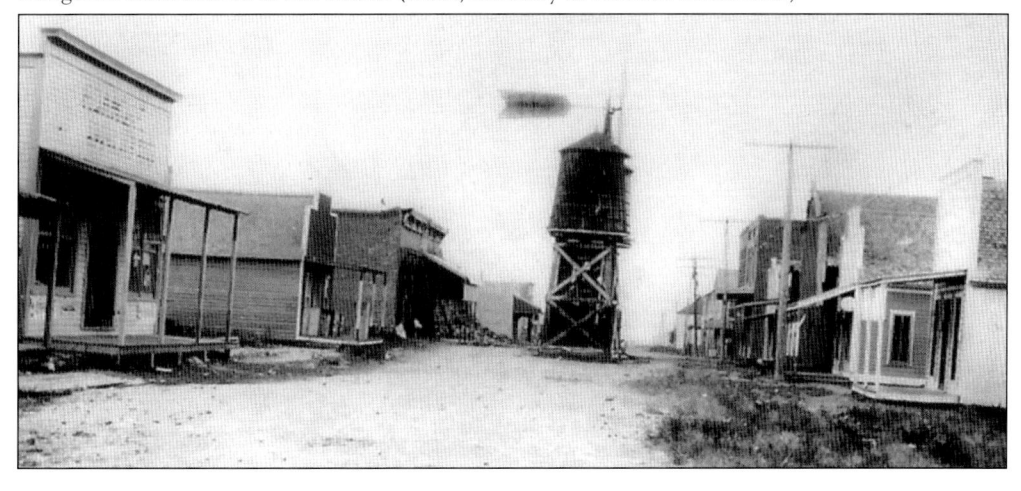

17

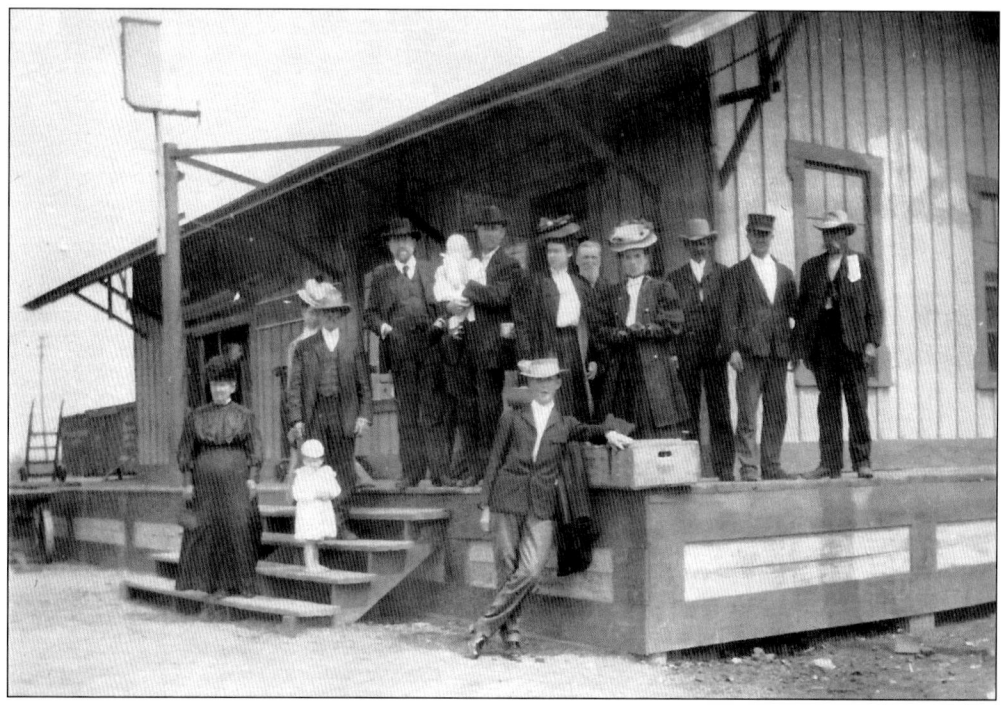

The travelers in the picture above are all unidentified; however, they demonstrate the importance and formality of rail travel. The depot, shown in the 1950s photograph below, was torn down by Joe Bass, who built two houses from the depot lumber. The sign "Roanoke," which was saved, now hangs in the Roanoke Visitor Center and Museum. Stationmasters were John Cade, Lee Bowen Bent, Ben Turk Hambright, Hinton Cade, and Howard G. McDonald. McDonald was the longest-serving stationmaster, with 32 years. (Above, courtesy of Alberta Lincecum; below, courtesy of HSC.)

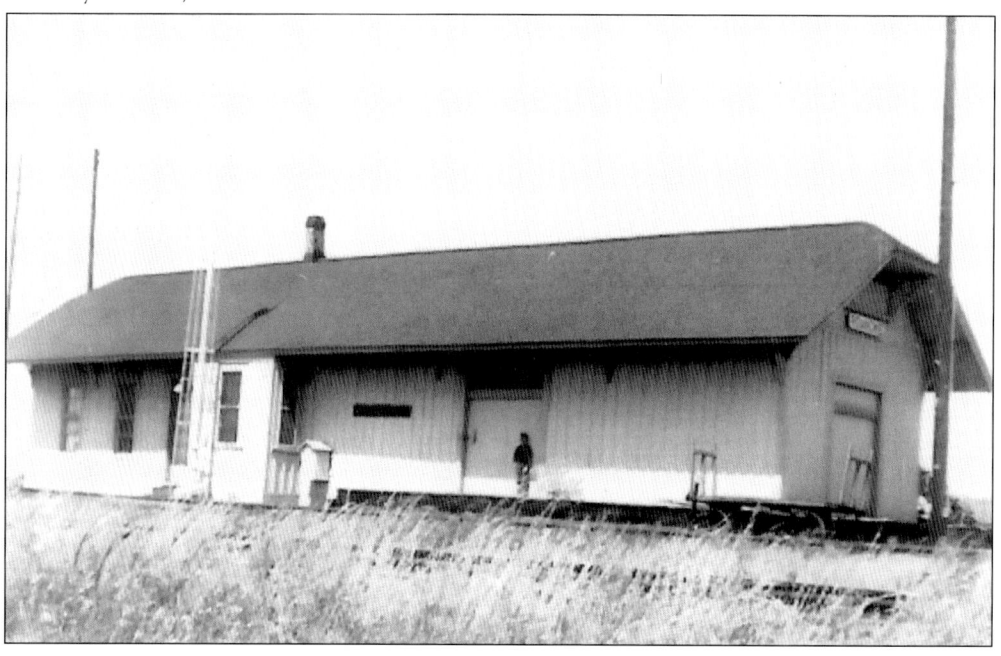

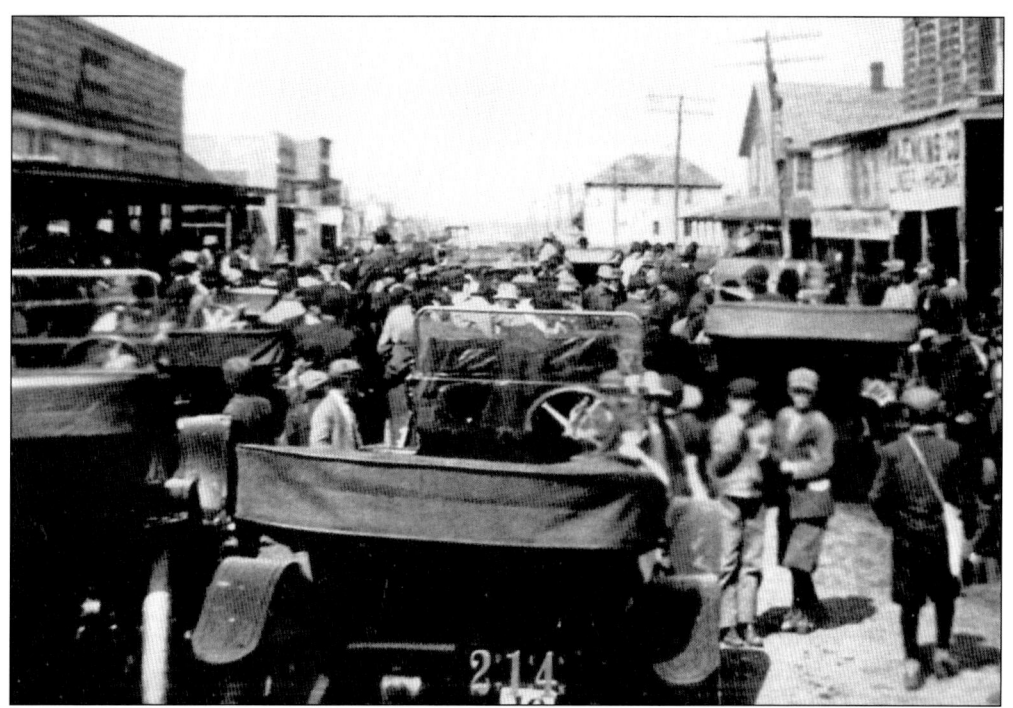

Both of the 1920s photographs on this page feature Trade Days, which were an integral part of Roanoke life well into the 1940s. This was an occasion for people from area farms and ranches to come into town to buy and trade goods, and also to visit and have fun. For example, there were prizes for the best and ugliest cakes. The children enjoyed sack races or climbed a greased pole, hoping to claim the dollar at the top, and even chased a greased pig. (Both, courtesy of Alberta Lincecum.)

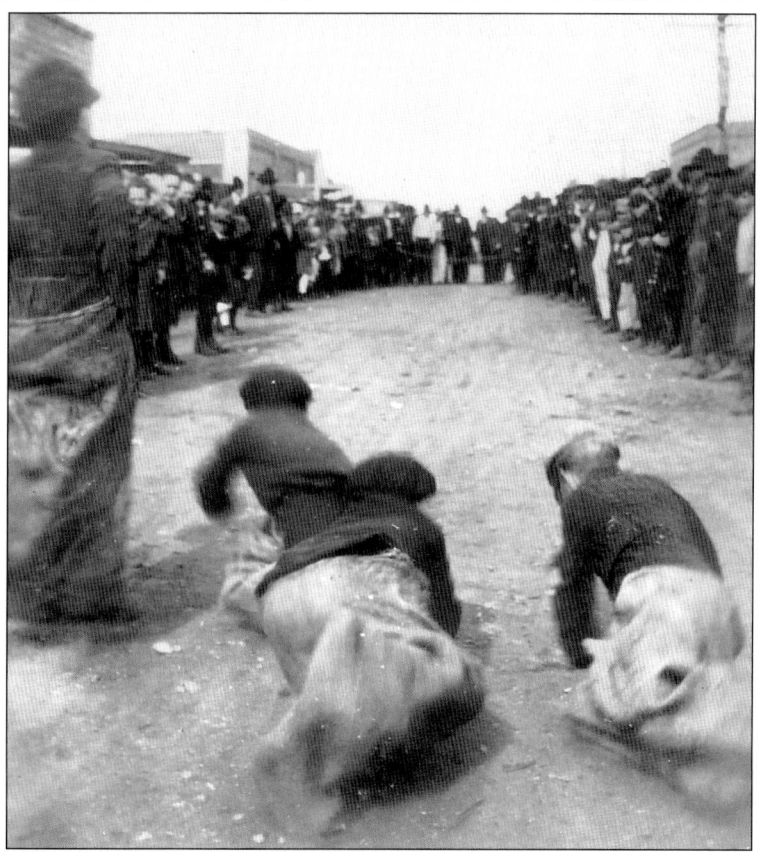

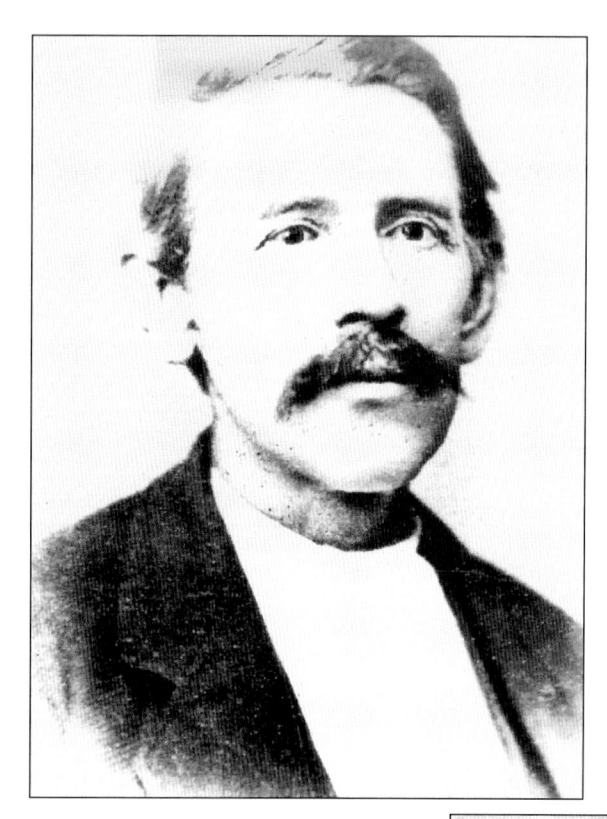

John Chisum, a cattle king who became a legend, brought his mulatto slave, Jensie, to Denton County in 1857. He had acquired her for a sum of approximately $1,500 from Francis Towry, a man who needed money to finance his trip to California to join the Gold Rush. Jensie and Chisum had two daughters, Harriet and Almeady. Though Chisum never married her, he took care of Jensie. Chisum owned 10 slaves, though he professed not to believe in slavery. He did not join the Confederate army and avoided being conscripted into it by hiding out in the woods. His daughter Almeady married cattleman John Dolford "Bob" Jones. (Courtesy of Dr. Bobby Jones.)

Leazure Alvis Jones (right), born on May 28, 1822, was the father of John Dolford "Bob" Jones. The elder Jones left his Caucasian wife, Mary Brown, in Arkansas but brought four children when he moved to Texas. The children were daughter Rochelle and sons Blake, Dick, and Jinks. Also, Elizabeth, Leazure's slave and Bob's mother came with them. According to Eugie, John "Bob" Jones and Almeady Chisum's daughter, her parents met at one of the many dances hosted by John Chisum at his ranch. (Courtesy of Dr. Bobby Jones.)

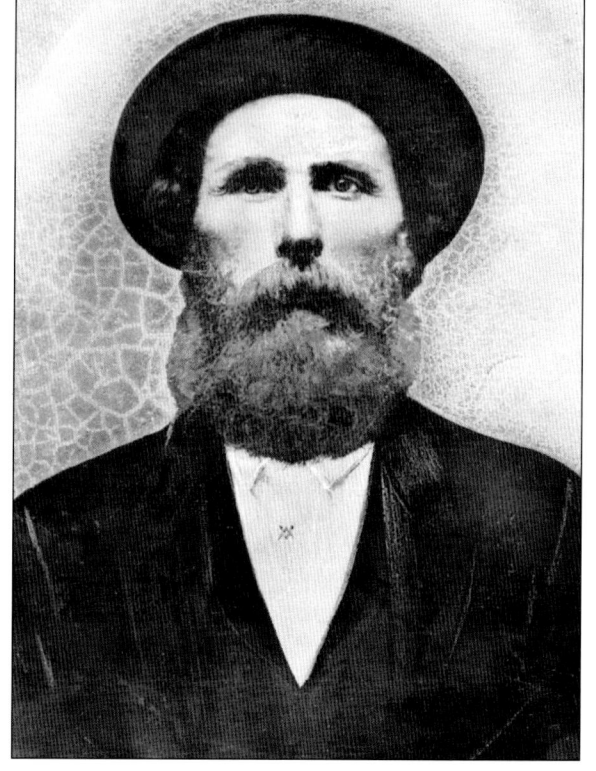

Bob Jones (at right) and Almeady Chisum (below), the daughter of John Chisum, met at a dance, but there is a question of whether it was in Bonham or at Chisum's ranch. Their daughter, Eugie Thomas, once told an interviewer that her father, Bob, was an excellent dancer, and many young women were attracted to him, but he was only interested in Almeady. He made trips to Bonham on horseback from Roanoke to see her. She finally agreed to a trip to his area if he came by wagon and brought his sister, Georgia Ann, presumably as a chaperone. The third time he visited Almeady he married her at her sister, Harriet's, house. They had 10 children, six girls and four boys. The Jones family sponsored a family picnic on June 19, the day Texas learned of the emancipation of slaves. This picnic was open to the community and was enjoyed by everyone, regardless of race. (Both, courtesy of Dr. Bobby Jones.)

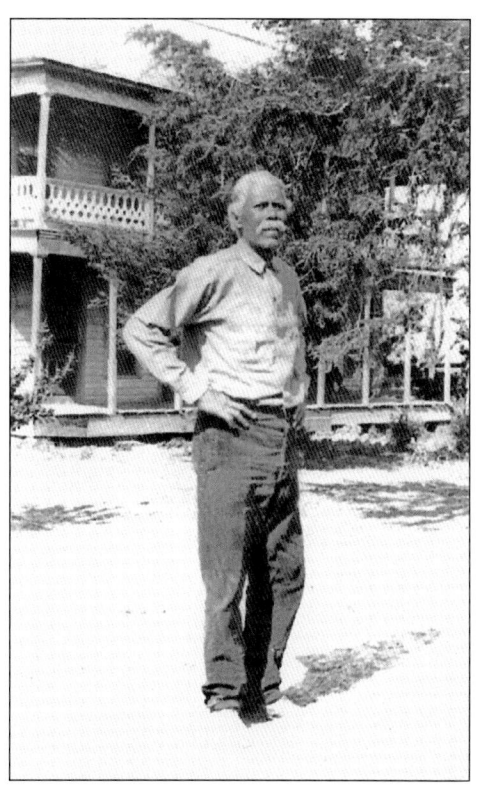

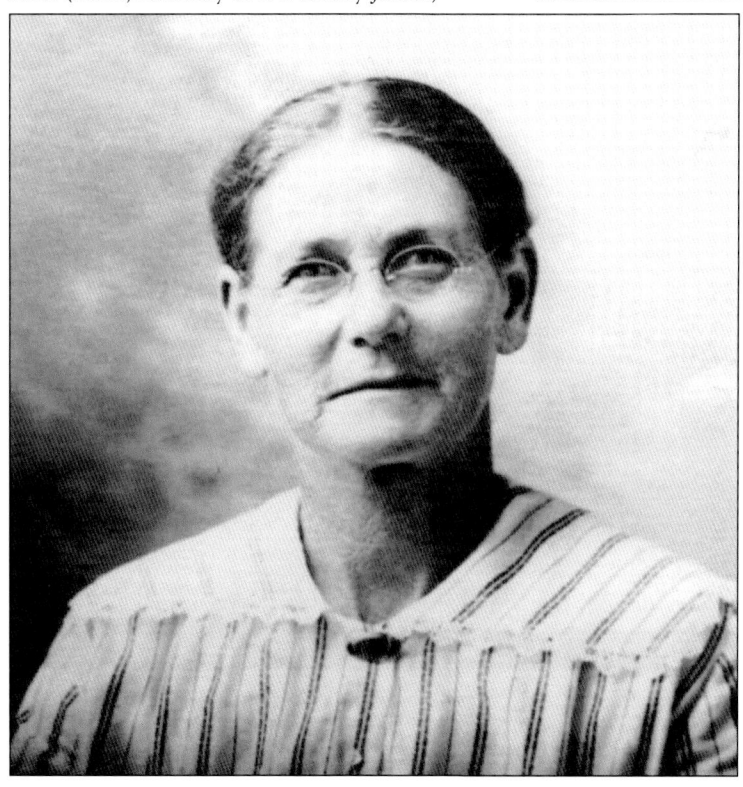

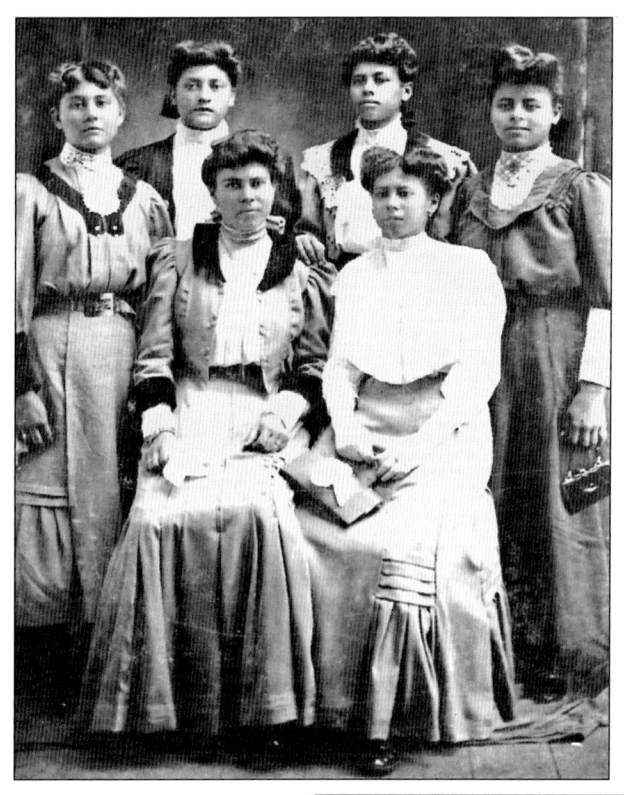

These lovely young women are the daughters of Almeady and John Dolford "Bob" Jones. Identified by their married names are, from left to right, (first row) Artie Clay and Virgie Evans; (second row) Venora Meeks, Alice Frentwell, Eugie Thomas, and Emma Frentwell. One of their brothers (pictured below), John Emory Jones, was born on October 28, 1898. Emory and his brother Jinks owned and operated a livestock auction barn and café east of Roanoke on Highway 114. In fact, their cafe is often considered the first completely integrated cafe in Texas. (Both, courtesy of Dr. Bobby Jones.)

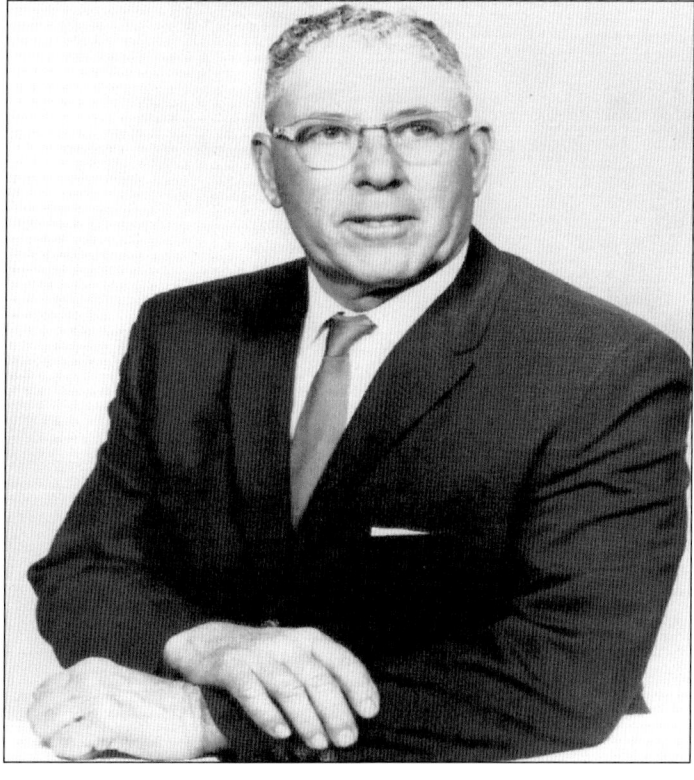

In this c. 1897 photograph, 17-year-old Virgie Jones is wearing a dress that she and her older sister, Alice, made for the 1897 Dallas fair. The dress was made of brown-and-white striped flannelette, trimmed with black velvet ribbon. Virgie was one of the six daughters of Bob and Almeady Jones who lived in Roanoke. Virgie and James T. Evans (shown below) are pictured with two of their five children, Lorene and Glenn. Virgie and James were married on September 2, 1906. Virgie was the first of the Jones girls to marry. They were wed on the front porch of the Jones's home (as were all of the others to follow). Except for the first several years of their marriage, they lived on what is now Bob Jones Road and farmed 250 acres. (Both, courtesy of Marie Grigsby.)

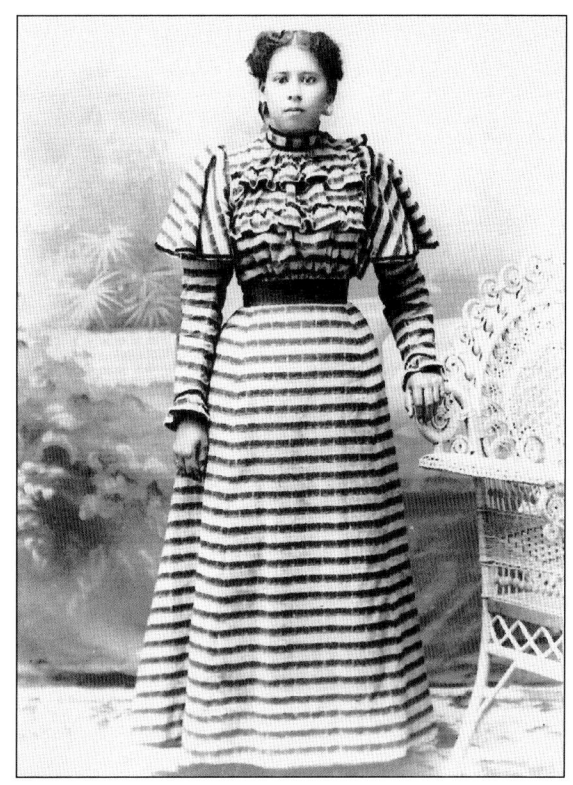

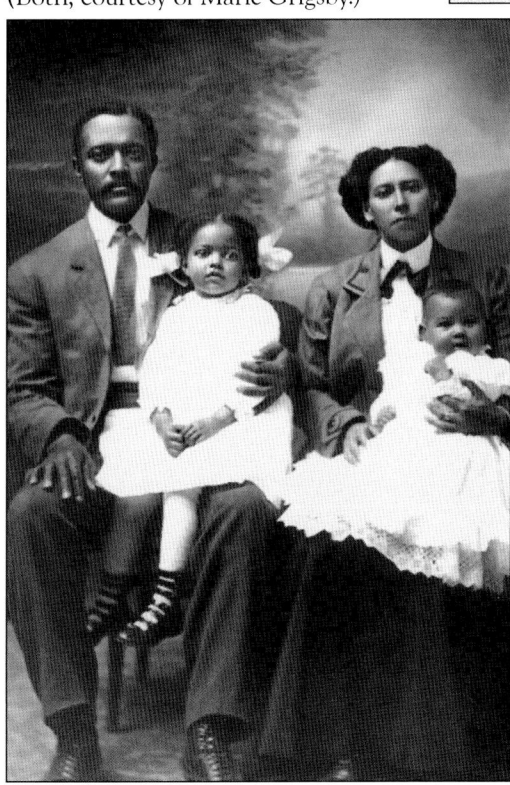

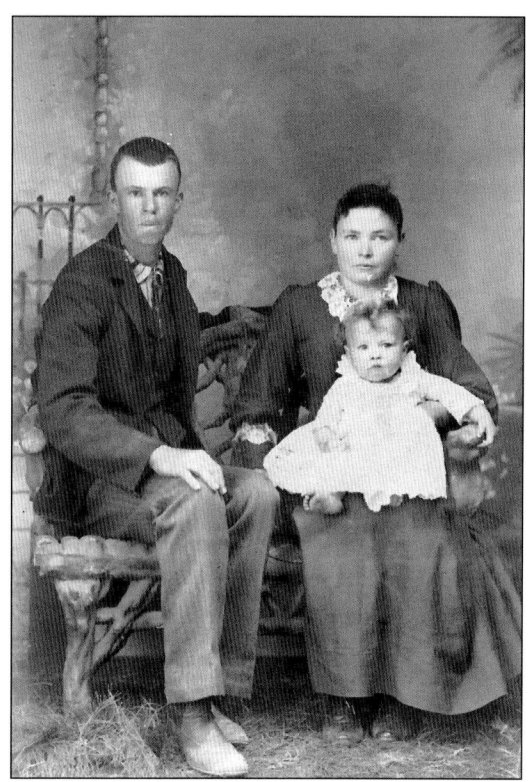

Ben Warder Yancey, his wife, Della Sandifer, and their son, Clint, are shown here in a studio portrait. The Yanceys had three other children who lived to adulthood, Bessie Warder, Mary Jo, and Hannah. The family lived on a farm at the southwest corner of Farm Road 1171. Ben Yancey was a member of the Roanoke Masonic Lodge. Clint and Bessie were unable to attend college; however, Mary and Hannah graduated from the College of Industrial Arts, which is now known as Texas Woman's University. Clint worked at the Continental State Bank prior to moving to Grapevine and working in the bank there. The Dallas/Fort Worth International Airport absorbed Clint's farm. (Courtesy of Ann Clark.)

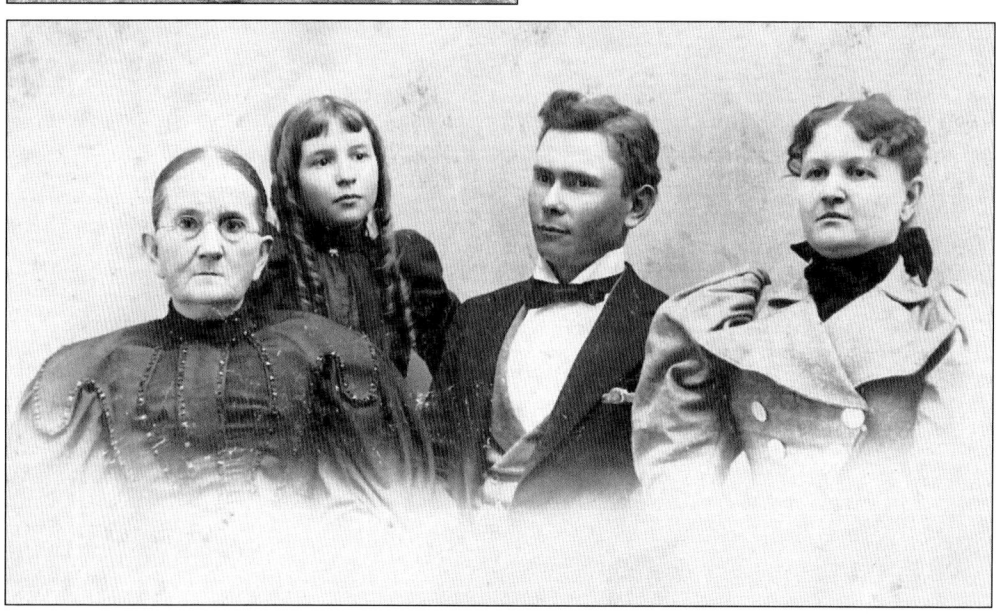

This picture depicts the Eliphalet "Lifey" Brand family. Brand (third from left) was known as E. C. or Lifey, and his wife was Sofia Terrell (far right). The others in this picture are unidentified, though the young girl may be Roselle, the Brands' first daughter. He was in charge of the Continental State Bank in Roanoke during the early years. Later he moved to Hamlin, then Sweetwater, Texas. In the Depression years, he was the Texas banking commissioner credited with saving Texas banks from failure. (Courtesy of Alberta Lincecum.)

This studio portrait (right) of Jack Medlin and his wife, Loula, was most likely taken shortly after their marriage. The Medlins are shown below years later, after their grandson John Medlin White had come to live with them when his parents, Cora Louise Medlin and Dawson White, divorced. Jack Medlin owned a gin, which was destroyed by an explosion in 1910. Another gin was built on the foundation. He also owned the weekly newspaper in Roanoke, which he sold to the Usry family. (Both, courtesy of John Medlin White.)

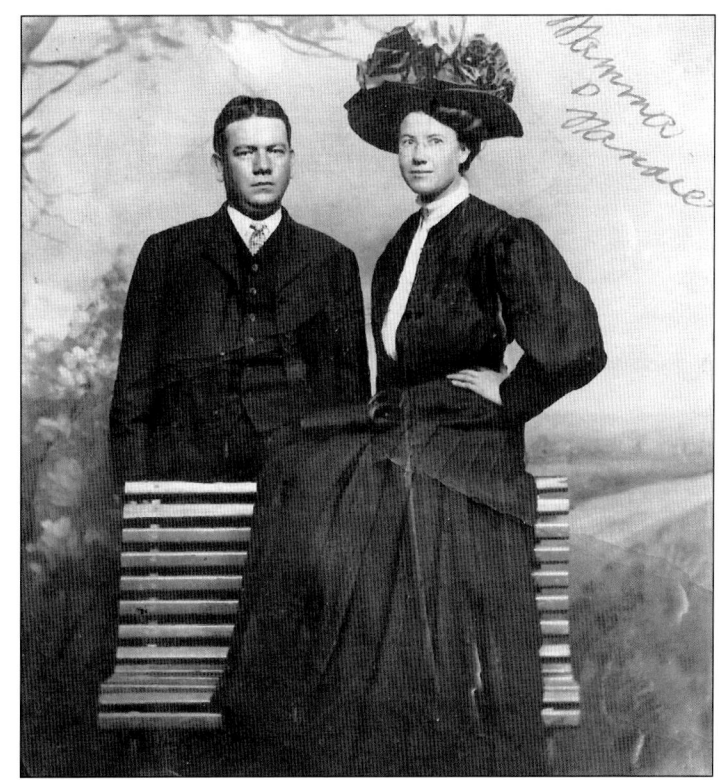

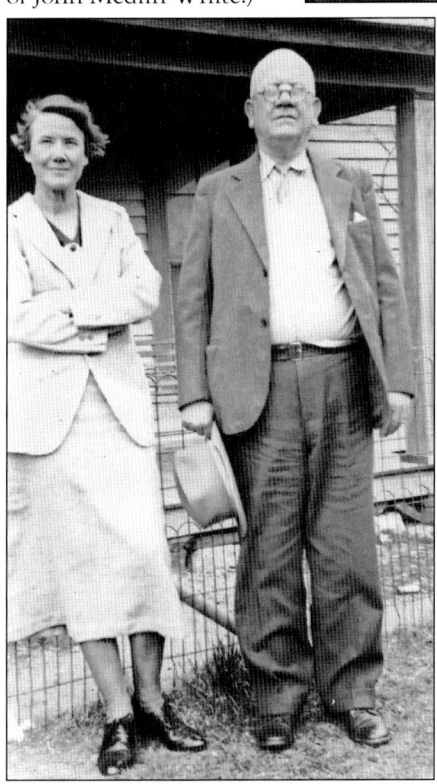

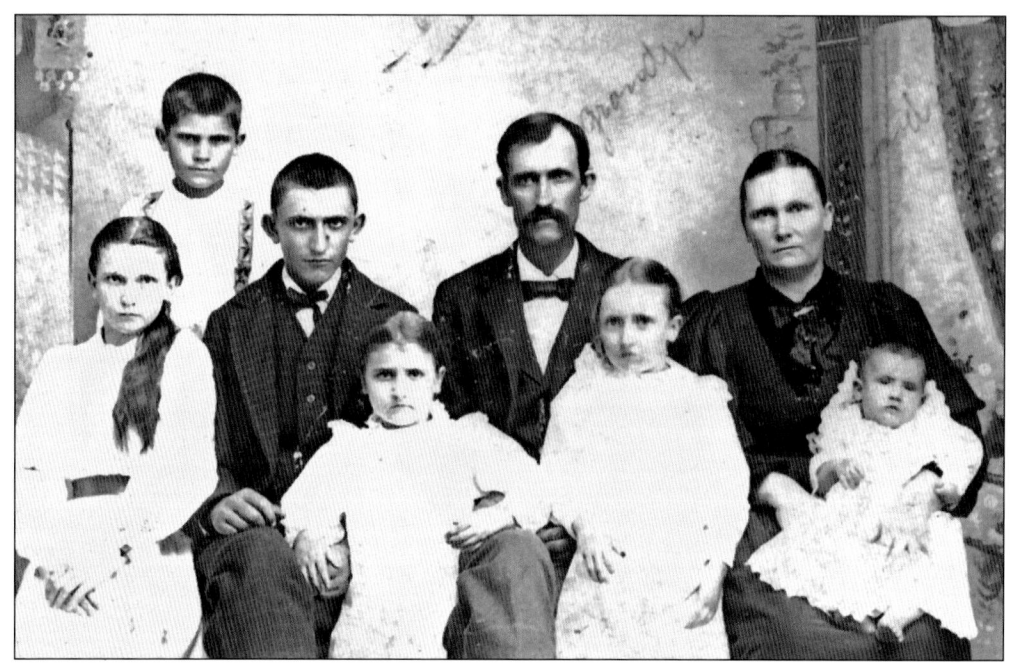

The John and Margaret Ann Medlin family are pictured in this c. 1898 photograph. From left to right are (first row) Minnie, Lizzie, and Lillie (baby); (second row) Lou, Charles, and their parents, John and Margaret; (third row) Jim. Little is known about this family other than they were a part of the extended Medlin clan. (Courtesy of Barbara Langford.)

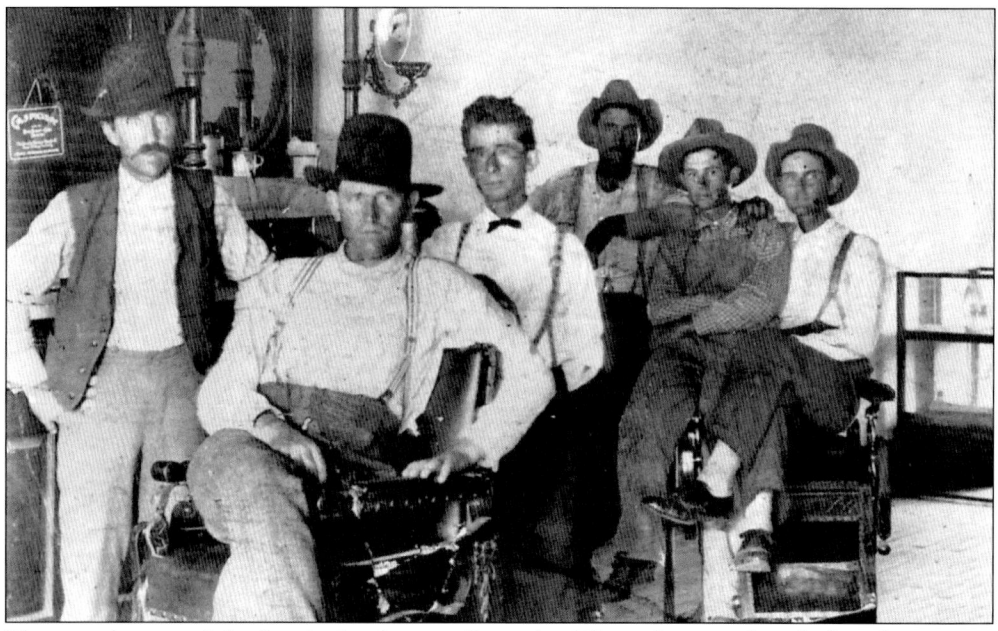

This may be one of the first barbershops in Roanoke. The only men identified in this picture are Murdoch Howell, seated in front, and behind him to the right, Wilson Smith. According to local historians, there was a tub in the back of the shop that was kept busy on Saturday nights when ranch hands lined up to bathe. Howell and Smith were both barbers. Smith also gained local notoriety as a jockey at local tracks. (Courtesy of RVCM.)

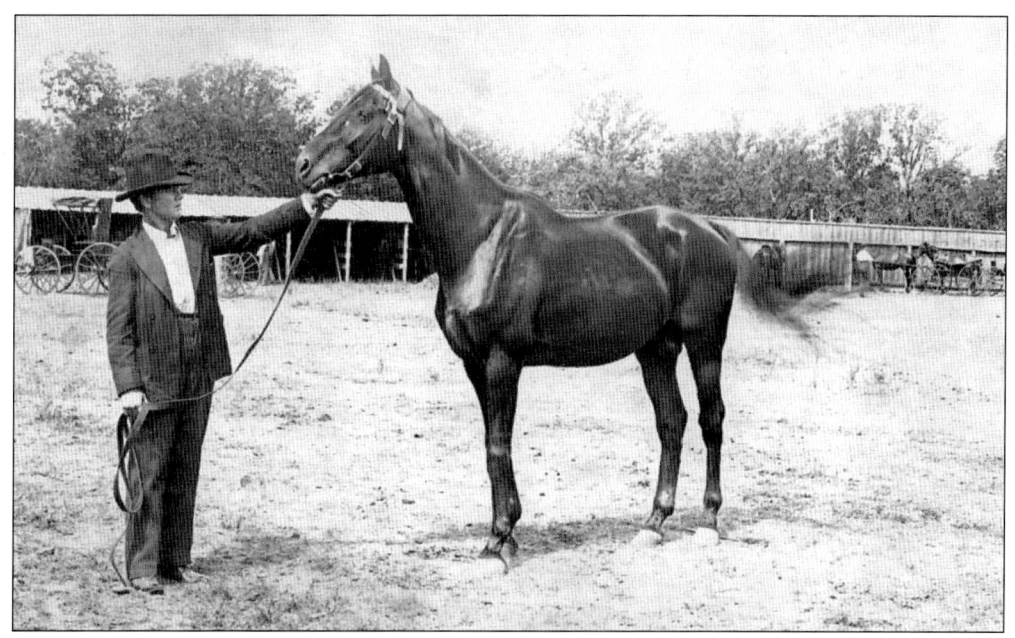

This photograph is of Jack Medlin with one of his father, James Medlin's, thoroughbred horses. The elder Medlin owned a large farm east of Roanoke in what is now the town of Trophy Club. His barn was the culmination of studying barns across the United States prior to building his own. Unfortunately, a modern-day owner had the structure destroyed even though area residents labored to save it. (Courtesy of HSC.)

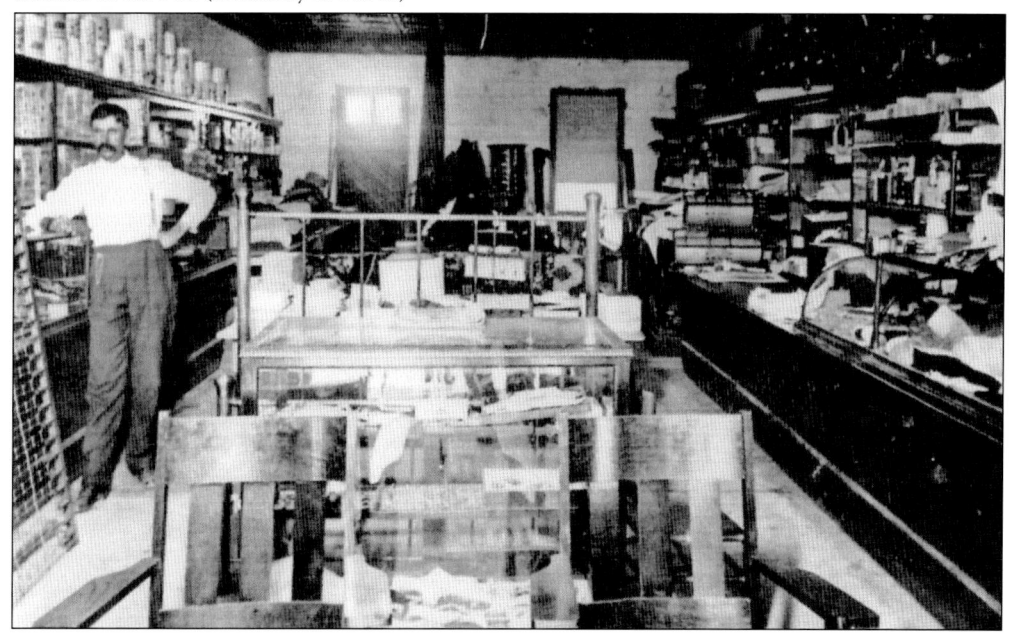

This early-1909 photograph of William Prewitt, known as "Walking Willie," was taken in his general store on Oak Street. His merchandise included piece goods, hats, trimmings, clothing patterns, and clothing supplies. His wife, Willie, was a partner and buyer for the store. Prewitt also sold farm real estate. He had a car at times, but sometimes he could not afford one. He often walked or hitchhiked to his destination. (Courtesy of Inez and Henry "Mc" Howe.)

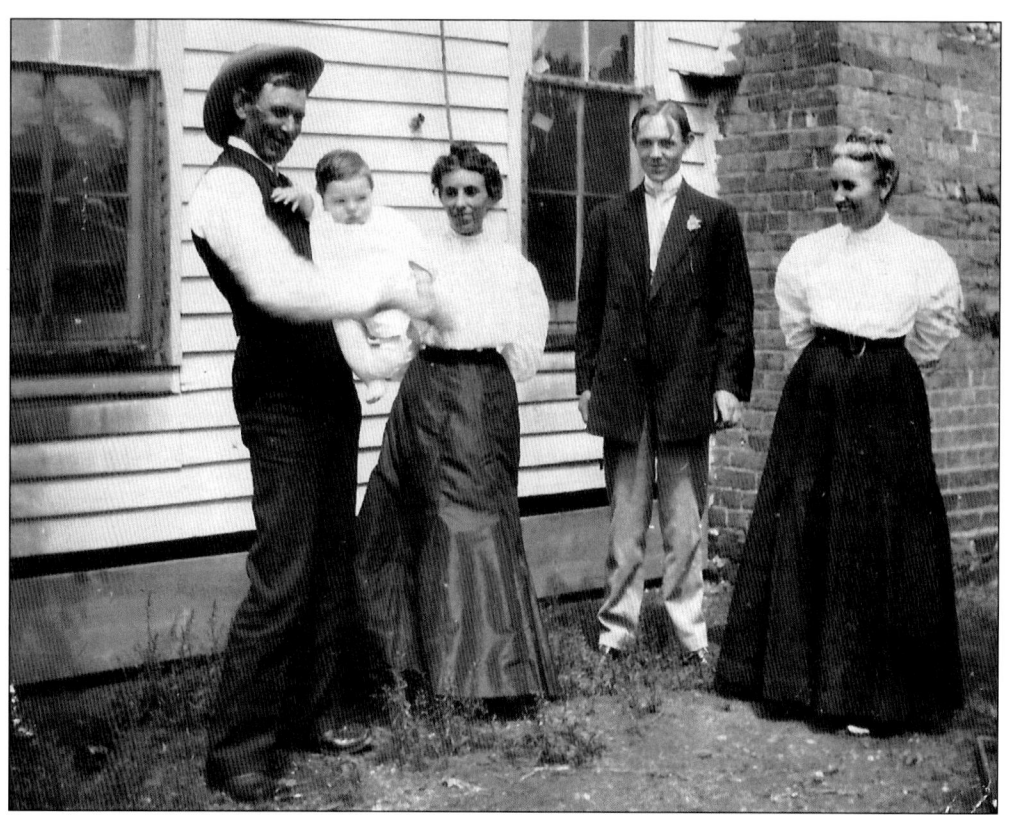

In the outdoor photograph above, pictured are, from left to right, Berry Hood holding grandson Hood Jenkins; daughter Hattie; her husband, Hugh Jenkins; and Caroline "Callie," Berry's wife and Hattie's mother. This photograph was taken adjacent to the Hood home. Berry Hood, a prominent businessman, hired Hugh Jenkins when Jenkins first arrived in Roanoke. Hood mentored the young man, and Jenkins soon married Hood's daughter. The second photograph features, from left to right, Berry Hood, E. D. Farmer, and Caroline Hood. The Hoods and Farmer had adjoining ranches in Aledo. (Both, courtesy of Alberta Lincecum.)

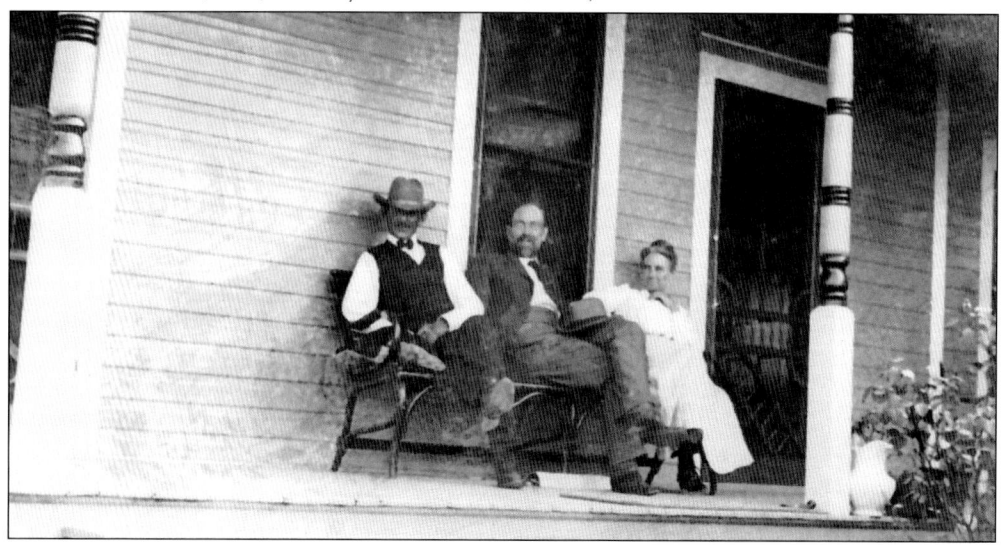

28

In this 1950s photograph, Berry Hood is standing near what is now Grapevine Lake at the old Eli Harris log cabin. Hood was orphaned at age two when his parents died in an epidemic. Harris and his wife, Anna (she was kin to the Hoods), took Berry to live with them. When young Hood was 15, Harris furnished him with a horse and sent him out to work, since he was now a man. Hood became a valued employee of Samuel Reynolds, who appreciated Hood's ability to figure sums in his head even though he lacked a formal education. (Courtesy of Alberta Lincecum.)

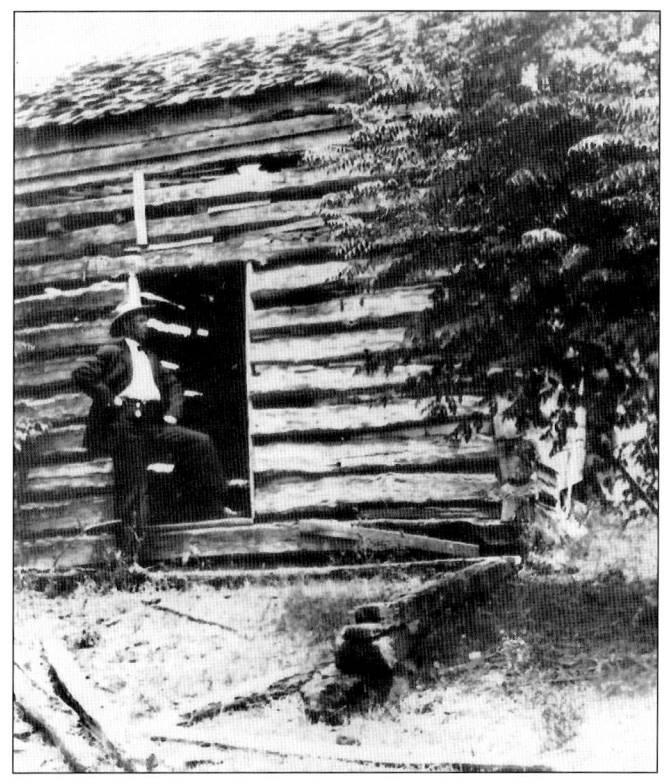

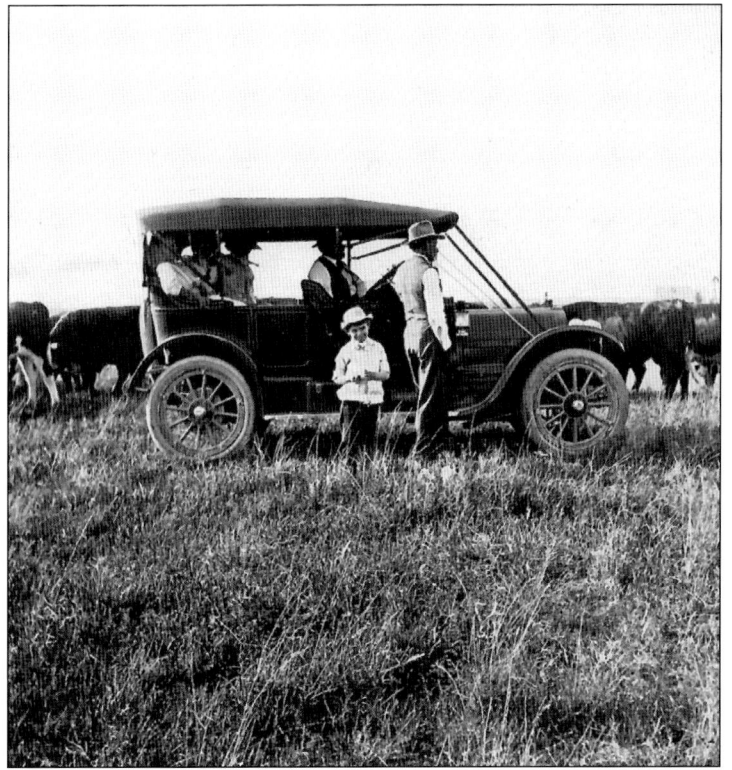

In this c. 1914 photograph, Berry Hood and his namesake grandson, Hood Jenkins, are shown standing next to a vintage automobile. The elder Hood's neighbor in Aledo, E. D. Farmer, is in the front seat of the vehicle; the people in the back seat are unidentified. It appears Hood has taken his grandson and the others to look at his cattle. (Courtesy of Alberta Lincecum.)

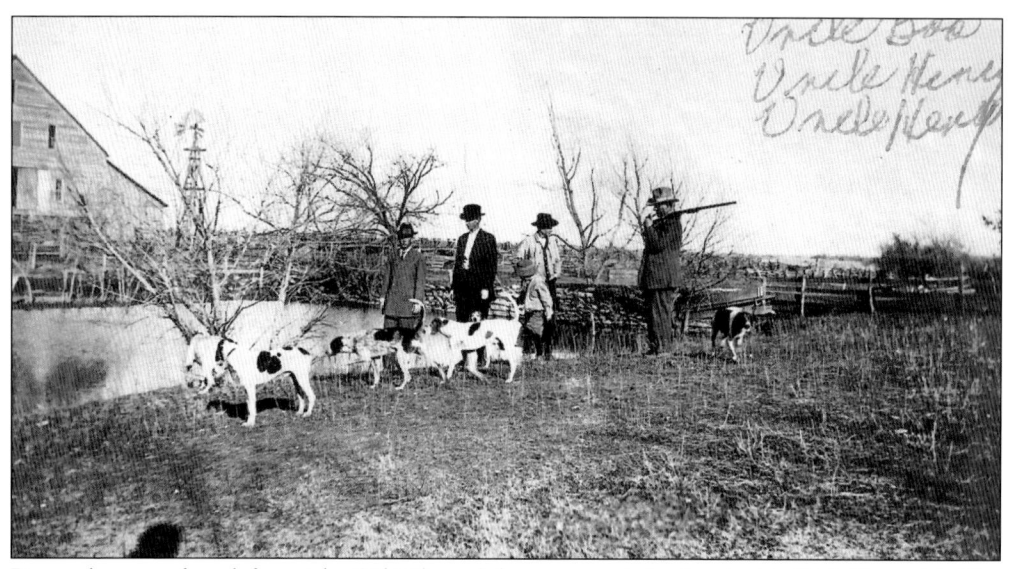

Picture here are, from left to right, Sid Gibson (who was married to Louise Medlin), Henry Medlin, an unidentified man and child, and Bob Carruth. The large structure in the background is the Medlin barn, which was well known in the area. (Courtesy of John Medlin White.)

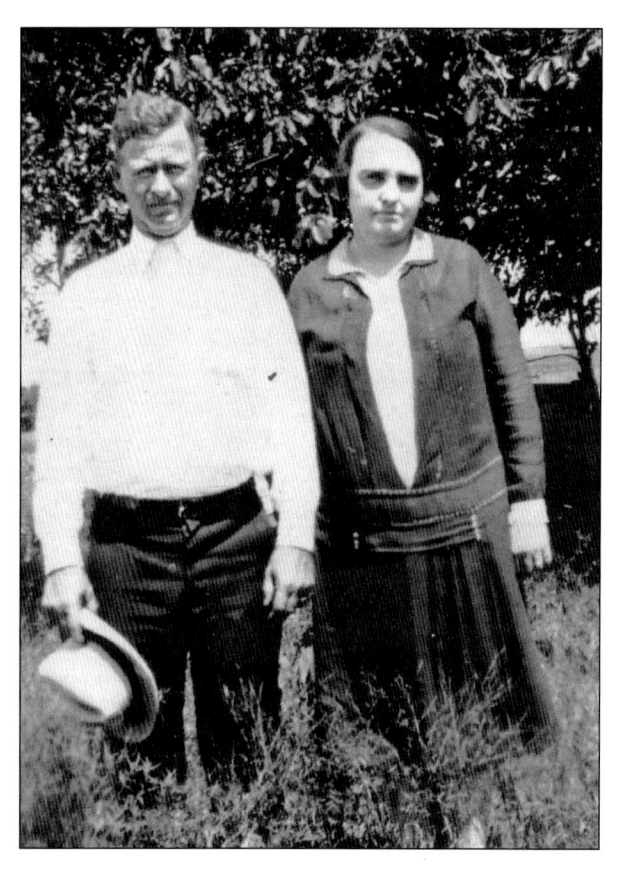

Clent Haynie (June 20, 1892–February 14, 1960) and Mamie Haynie (August 24, 1896–July 16, 1984) were married on October 31, 1928. During World War II, Clent worked for American Manufacturing Company in Fort Worth. At that time, the company was manufacturing ammunition shells. The Haynies were adamant that their children would attend college. Mamie sold butter and milk to provide the funds. Their daughter, Frances, who delivered the milk or butter, was afraid of a large dog one of the customers had, since he was known to bite. When she arrived at the home, the dog attacked her, causing her to drop the milk. She was taken to Dr. Joe Allen in Justin, but she still had scars from the ordeal. (Courtesy of Frances Gay.)

In this c. 1916 photograph, the wagons loaded with lumber are parked on Rusk Street between the old Silver Spur Saloon (left) and Hugh Jenkins's Hardware and Lumber (right). Jenkins built the hardware store and lumberyard in 1916. It appears this photograph dates to shortly after that. (Courtesy of Alberta Lincecum.)

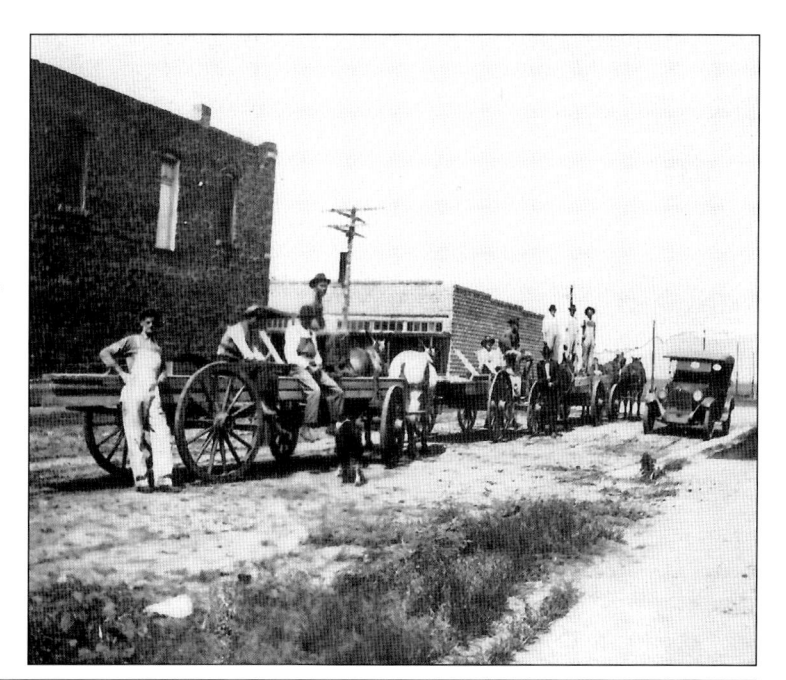

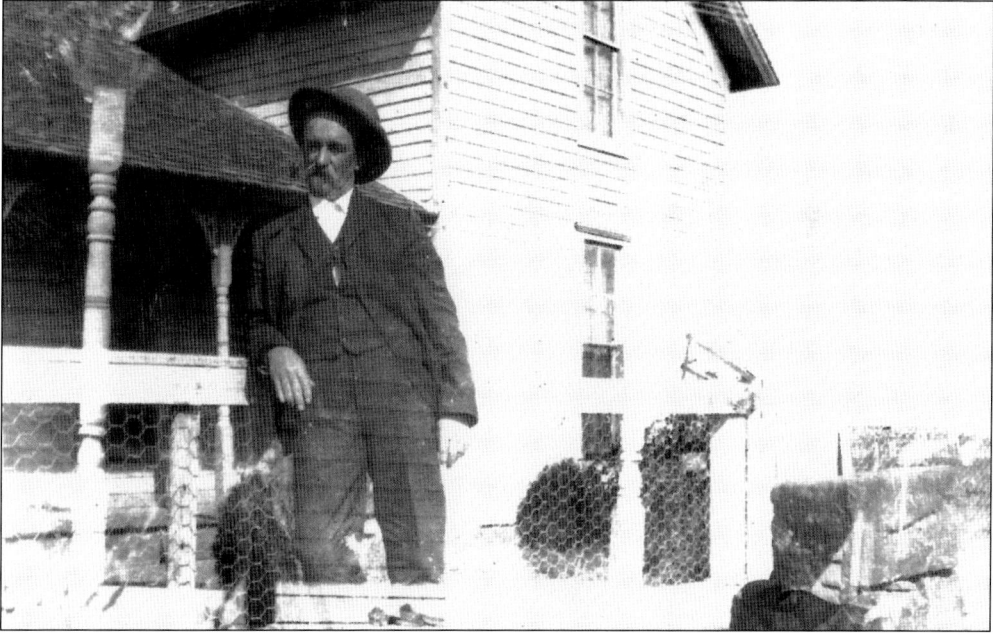

Charles Stone, pictured here, was a well-to-do rancher who arrived in Roanoke from Abington, Virginia. He worked for years at the Continental State Bank on Oak Street. Stone, a widower, donated a stained-glass window in memory of his wife and infant son to the Presbyterian church, one of the buildings he constructed. He lived for a time at the Eureka Hotel, owned by the Brand family, before building a home at the south end of Oak Street. Upon his death, this house was bequeathed to the Presbyterian church for use as a parsonage, and his farmland outside Roanoke was passed on to relatives. Stone was close to the Brand family, as evidenced by the fact that a surviving grandchild of Thomas and Elizabeth Brand refers to him as "Uncle Stone." (Courtesy of Alberta Lincecum.)

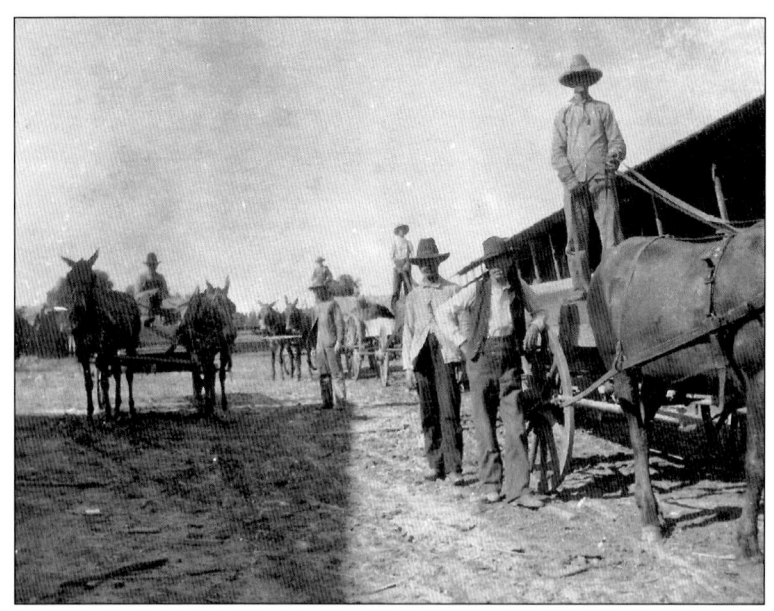

The individuals in this c. 1915 photograph are identified by a label found on the photograph, which listed, from left to right, Hugh Jenkins, Lon Wilkerson, and Jim Reed, unloading lumber for a house shortly after Jenkins bought the lumberyard. The townspeople in the background are unidentified. (Courtesy of Alberta Lincecum.)

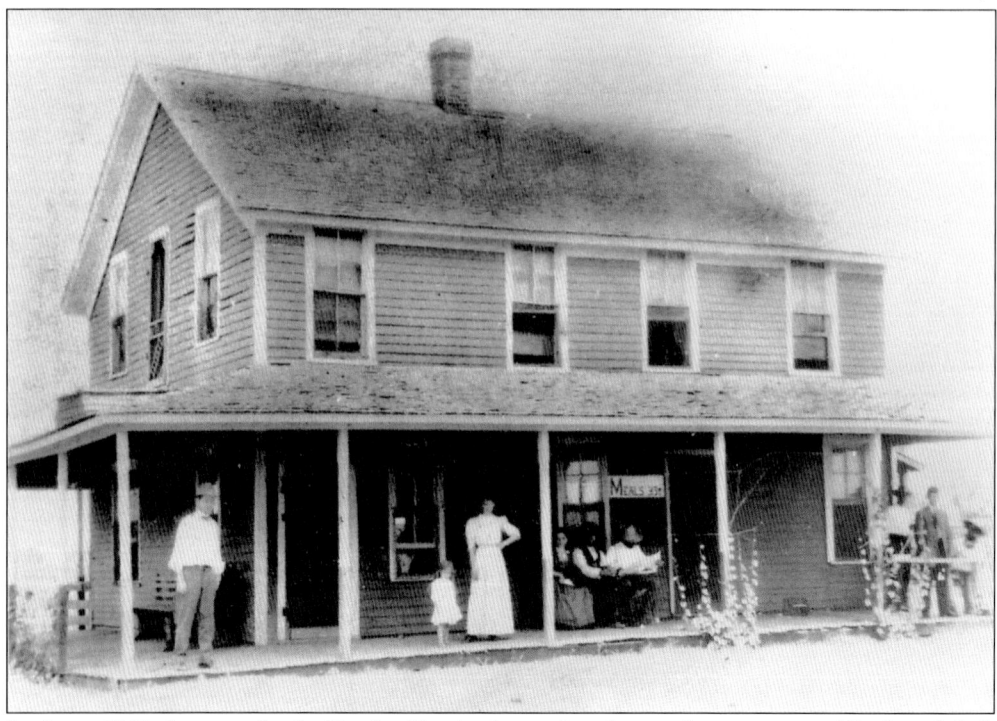

In this c. 1905 photograph, the Eureka Hotel is located at the northeast corner of Rusk and Oak Streets. The hotel was directly across Rusk Street from the Silver Spur Saloon. The Eureka was owned and operated by Thomas and Mary Elizabeth Brand. The woman in the photograph is Elizabeth Brand, and the young girl at her side is probably her daughter, Una. The others pictured are unidentified. After the hotel burned, the property was sold to Hugh Jenkins for his hardware and lumber business, which he built in 1916. The hardware building is still standing at this location; however, patrons now buy a delicious meal there rather than nails or lumber. (Courtesy of Alberta Lincecum.)

John Henry Stickland (1864–1938) and daughter Jimma Belle (1887–1973) are shown sitting on the fence in front of the barn at their home on Pecan Street. Jimma Belle married Baxter Ragsdale (1885–1973). When her mother, Ellen, became ill, Jimma Belle moved into the house to take care of her. Jimma Belle continued to live in the family home after her mother died. (Courtesy of Emily Ragsdale.)

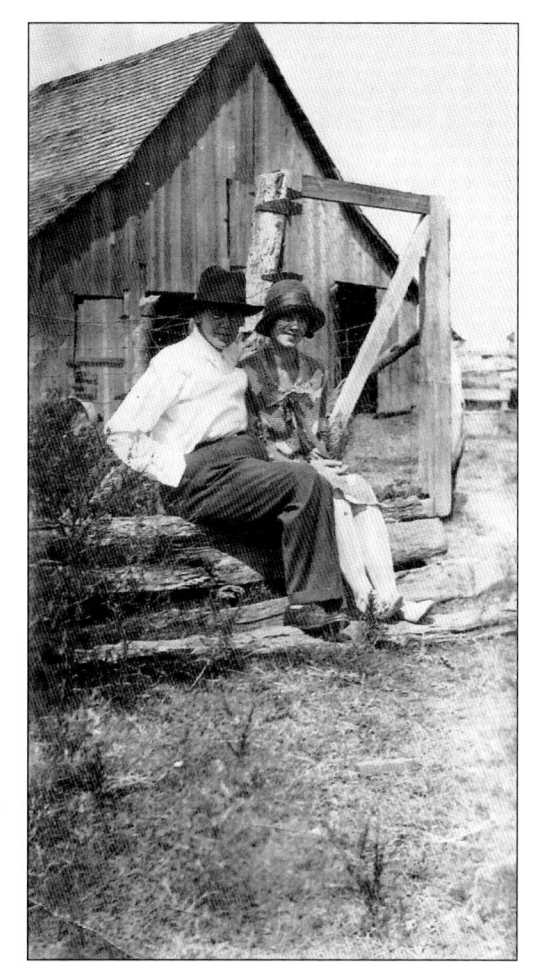

The Roanoke band is posing in front of one of the Seagraves' houses, located on Oak Street. The band members, pictured from left to right, are Henry Pickett, Prof. ? Edwards, Grover Howe, Sam White, E. C. Robinson, Wilson Smith, Tom Peck, Will Taylor, Claud Raibourn, Minnie Cade, unidentified, and C. L. Lane. (Courtesy of HSC.)

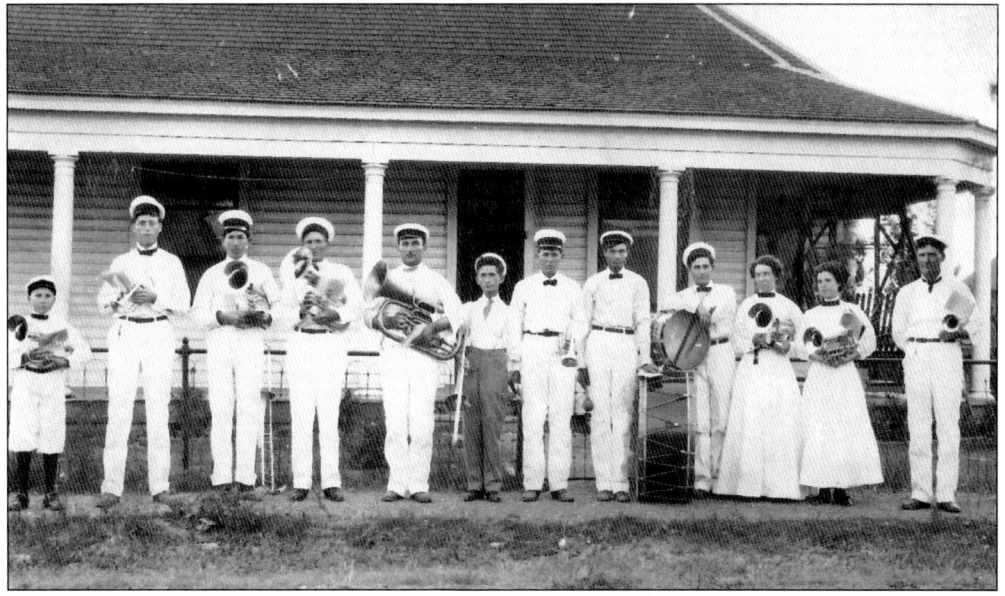

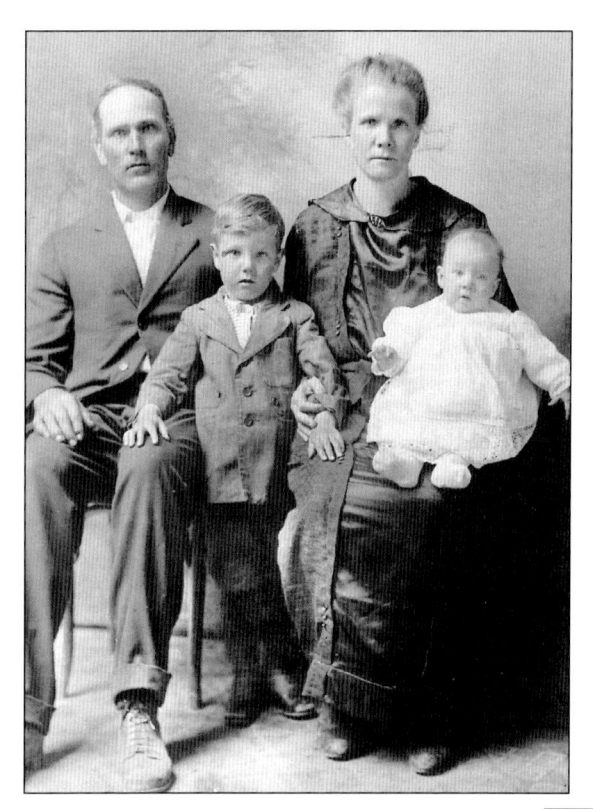

Charles Harvey Bogart is pictured here in 1918 with his wife, Lyda Ada, and two of their children, Manuel and Emily. After the family moved from a farm south of Roanoke, they bought a house across the railroad tracks just west of the depot. Charles had a wagon and team of horses that he used to haul gravel and sand to help with the construction of Highway 377 through Roanoke. (Courtesy of Emily Ragsdale.)

Hood Jenkins is shown with his grandmother Martha Jenkins from Tennessee on the front porch of the home that his maternal grandparents, Berry and Caroline "Callie" Hood, built. The elder Hoods gave the home to Hugh W. Jenkins and their daughter, Hattie, when they married. The Hoods then moved to their farm. Hood Jenkins lived in the house to adulthood and then moved to California. (Courtesy of Alberta Lincecum.)

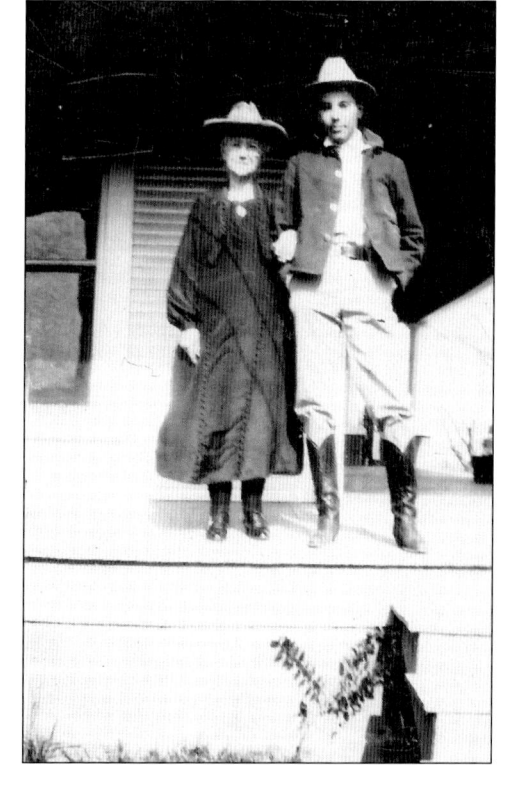

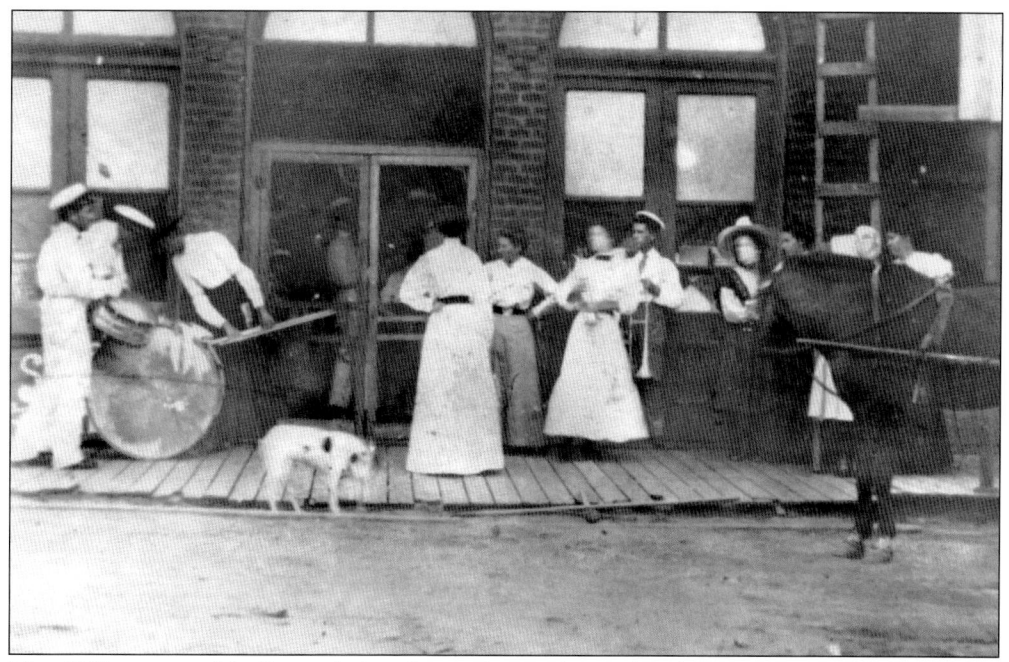

This 1908 picture of the Roanoke band was taken in front of Cade's store on Oak Street. At one point, the store was Welborn and Cade's Dry Goods. Unfortunately, most of the participants here are unidentified. The seventh person from the left appears to be Wilson Smith, the barber and jockey. (Courtesy of HSC.)

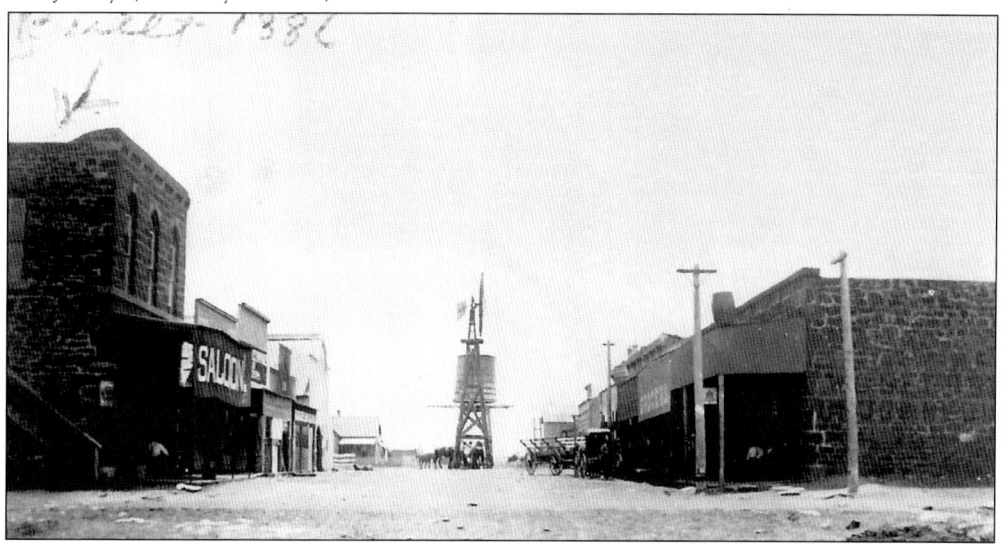

The building near left in this late-1800s photograph is the Silver Spur Saloon, owned by Robert M. and Burrell S. Snead. Byram Seagraves, a doctor in Roanoke, once had his office upstairs in this building. At one time, an agitated man ran into the saloon seeking a doctor. Seagraves, seated at the bar, was pointed out, and the man demanded that Seagraves come with him, as his wife was having a baby. Seagraves told him that he did not want him to come because he was not a real doctor. The man pulled a gun, aimed it at Seagraves, and proclaimed, "You are now." Presumably the delivery of the baby went well since "Doc" Seagraves lived to see another day. (Courtesy of Alberta Lincecum.)

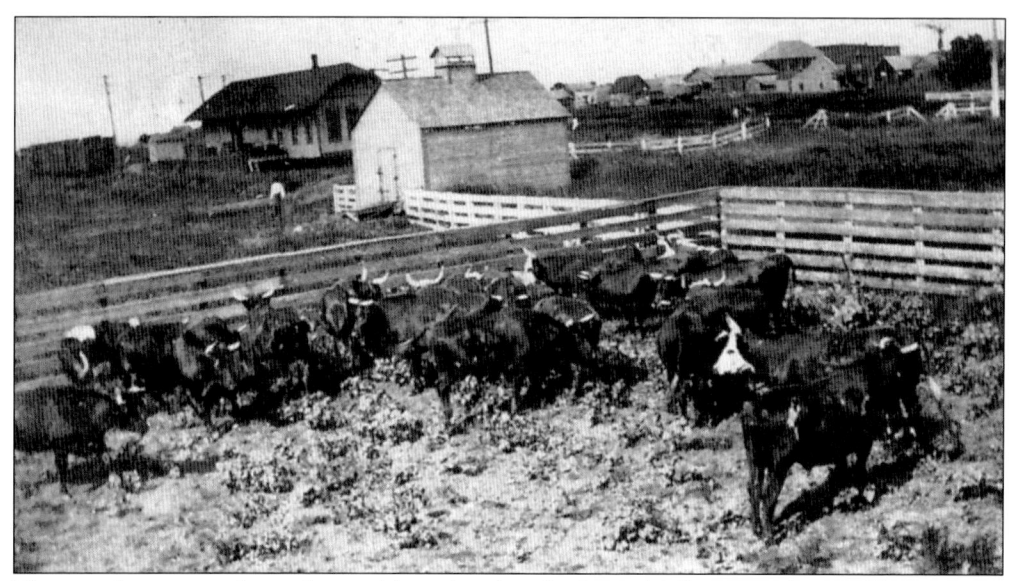

These cattle pens were located west of the railroad tracks. Several different ranchers and businessmen had pens in this location, including Hugh Jenkins. Roanoke was a cattle town in its early days, and the railroad solved the problem of driving a herd of cattle across the country. The railroad station is clearly seen to the left of this picture. The structures to the right are private residences. (Courtesy of Alberta Lincecum.)

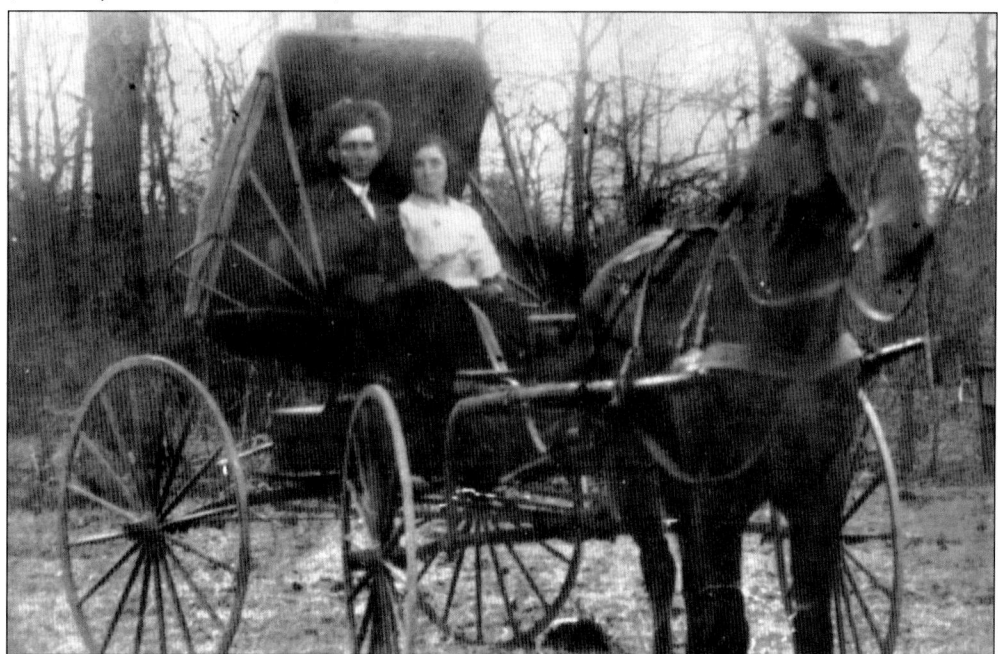

Charles and Emma (Schooling) Blackburn are shown in their buggy on their wedding day. Both family histories date back to the Revolutionary War, in which men from both families fought. The families ended up in Virginia. It is not known when they came to Roanoke; however, this couple lived at the corner of Oak and Houston Streets in a small house, which was later moved near the railroad tracks. They worked at the Armour Star packing plant in Fort Worth and were the parents of four children. (Courtesy of Melvin Walls.)

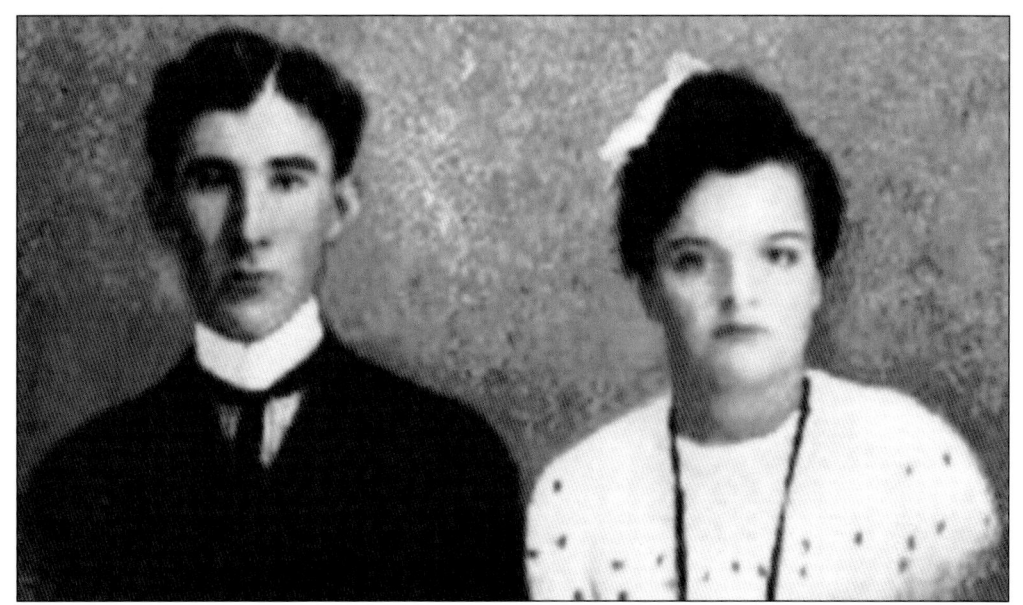

Marvin Newman (born February 2, 1881) and Pearl Newman (born November 16, 1888) both came from large families. Marvin had eight siblings, and Pearl had 12 siblings. They lived on several acres near what is now Reed Street. He worked as a carpenter, and she was a homemaker. Hartwell, one of their sons, owned several service stations in Roanoke. (Courtesy of Loye Steen)

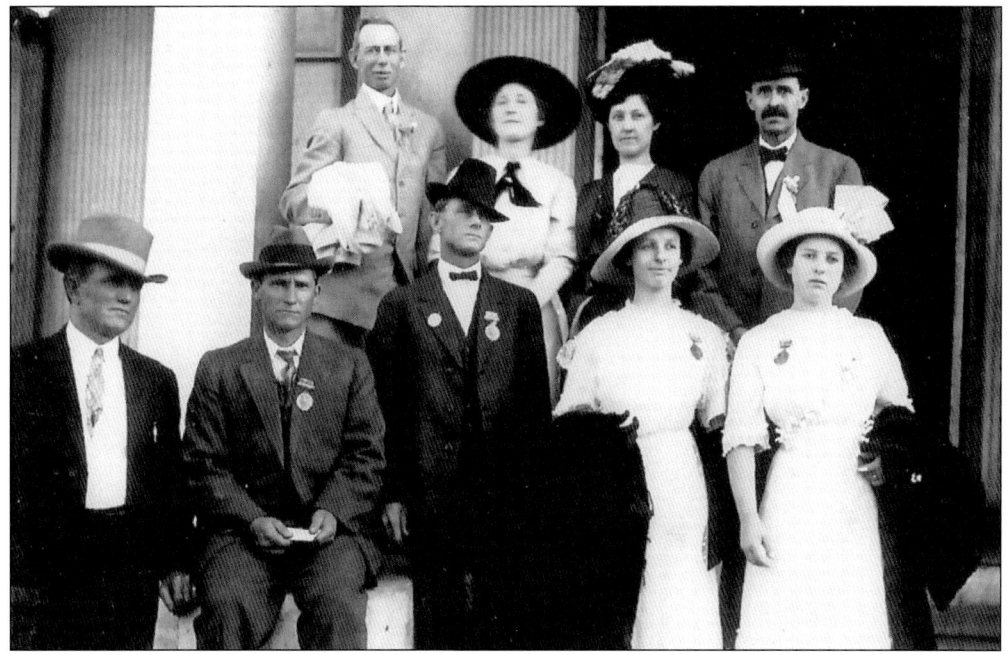

In this c. 1910 photograph, the convention attendees are unidentified except for the three men on the front left. They are, from left to right, Perry Davis, Hugh Jenkins, and ? Baldridge. Jenkins became the mayor and a leading citizen of Roanoke. He is credited with many innovations for the city, including the water system and introducing the first automobile to the town. As more people bought automobiles, Jenkins imported gasoline, brought by train, to sell at 8¢ a gallon. (Courtesy of Alberta Lincecum.)

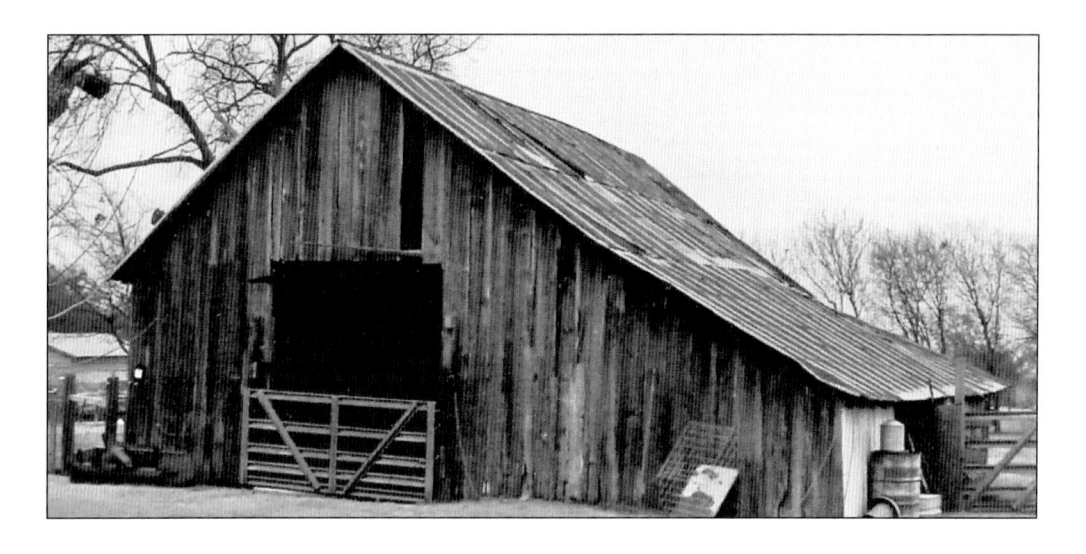

In the above photograph, the barn (constructed around 1915) is one of the out buildings on the property. It was constructed by Ben Turk Hambright for his family. Hambright was well known in the community, as he worked at the Continental State Bank and also served as the stationmaster for the railroad. Hambright was a member of the International Order of Odd Fellows No. 42 in Roanoke. He had three daughters, Jane, Polly, and Sue, with his wife, Nora Hambright. The second family to own this property was Monroe Noah and later his son, James, who also owned a grocery for years on Oak Street. The family home is the second picture on this page. The bottom of a drawer in the kitchen has a poignant passage written by Vallee, Monroe Noah's wife, professing her loneliness after her husband's death six months before. (Above, courtesy of Ann and Bobby Tidwell; below, courtesy of Wanda Smith.)

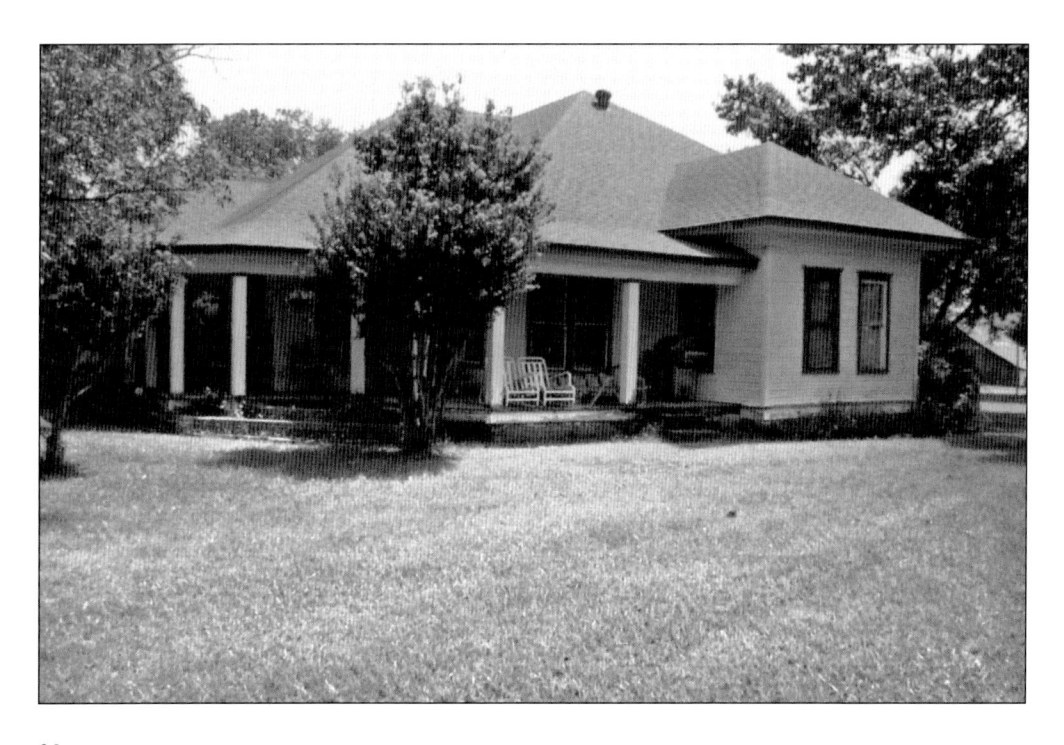

There is little information to identify the people pictured at right; however, the man in the white shirt standing on the train is Ben Turk Hambright, and the young girl is probably one of his three daughters. In the picture below, Ben Turk Hambright and Lenora Sells Hambright are shown in a studio portrait. They were a prominent couple in Roanoke. Their house on Walnut Street is still standing and is an imposing sight with the large front lawn covered in oak trees. (Both, courtesy of Cathy Phipps Noble.)

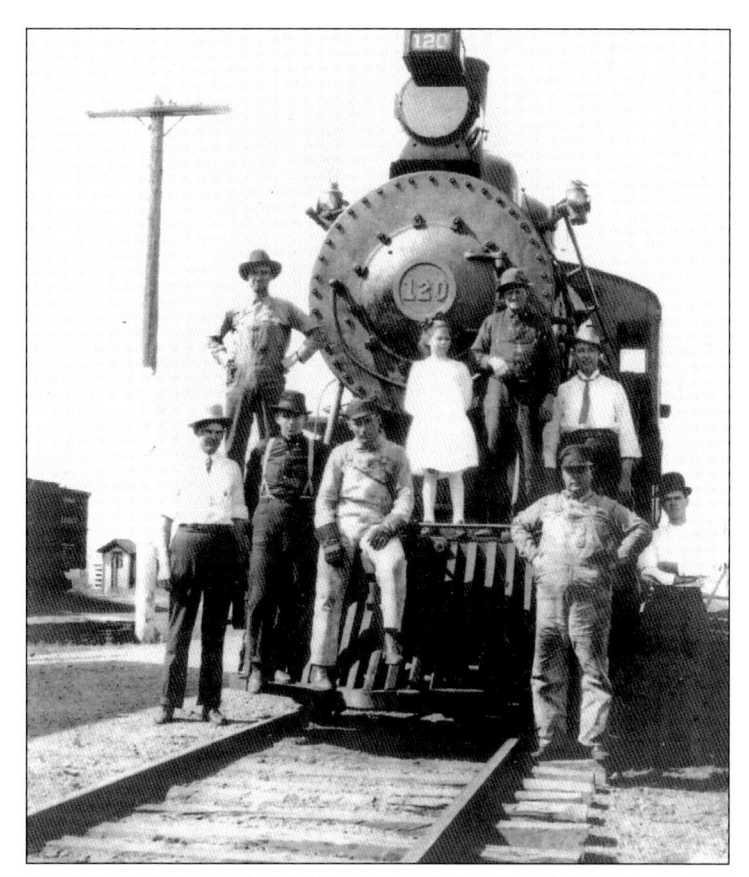

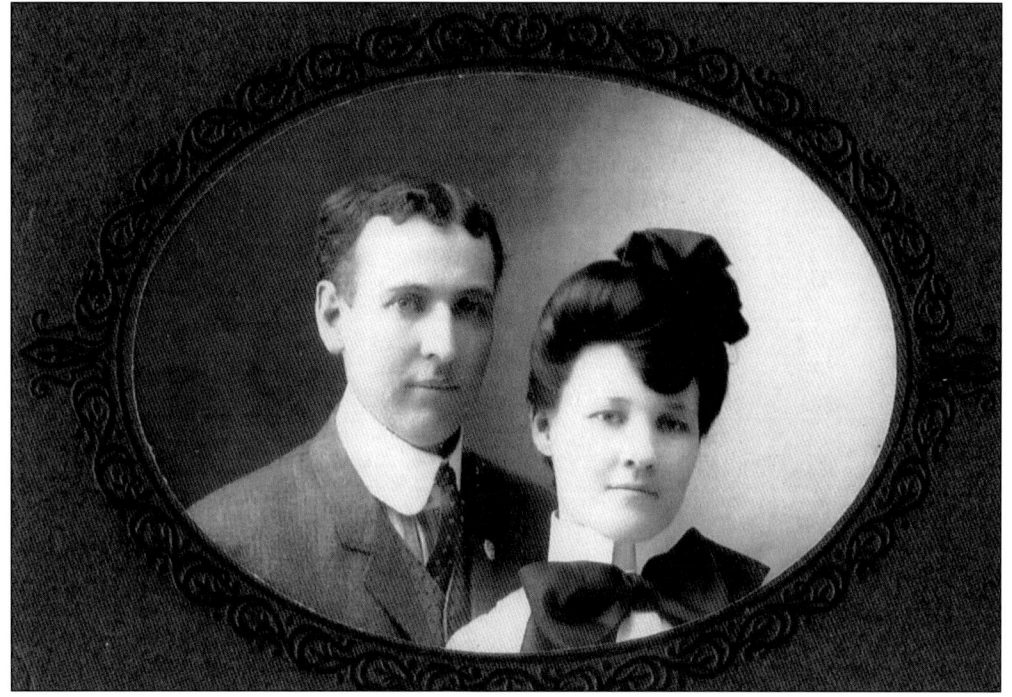

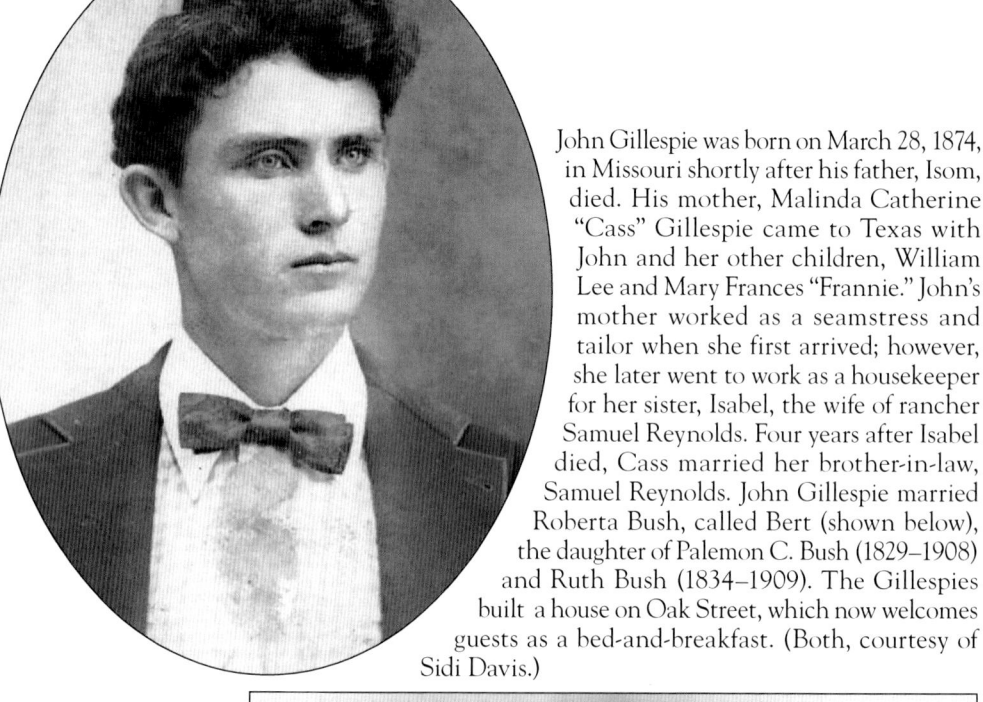

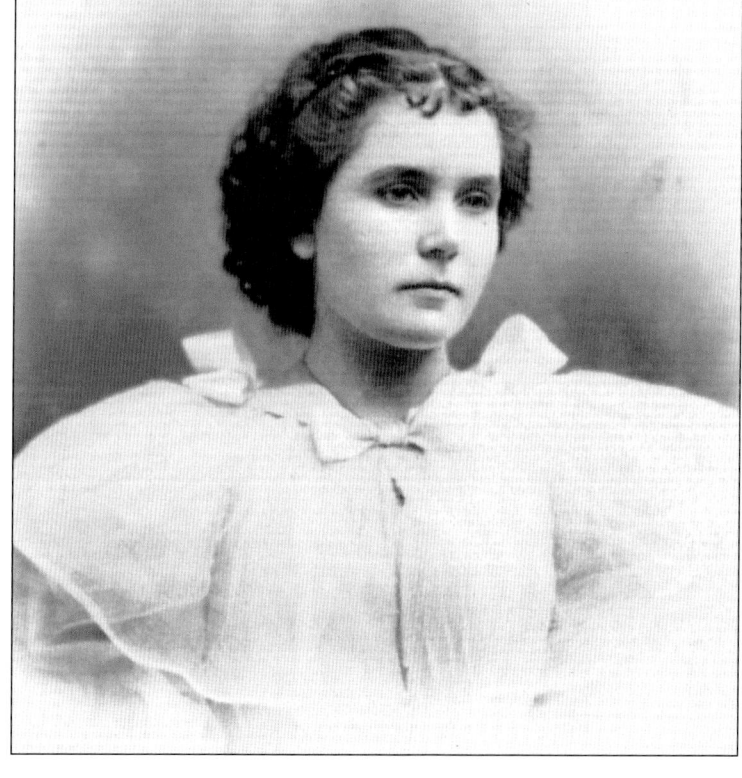

John Gillespie was born on March 28, 1874, in Missouri shortly after his father, Isom, died. His mother, Malinda Catherine "Cass" Gillespie came to Texas with John and her other children, William Lee and Mary Frances "Frannie." John's mother worked as a seamstress and tailor when she first arrived; however, she later went to work as a housekeeper for her sister, Isabel, the wife of rancher Samuel Reynolds. Four years after Isabel died, Cass married her brother-in-law, Samuel Reynolds. John Gillespie married Roberta Bush, called Bert (shown below), the daughter of Palemon C. Bush (1829–1908) and Ruth Bush (1834–1909). The Gillespies built a house on Oak Street, which now welcomes guests as a bed-and-breakfast. (Both, courtesy of Sidi Davis.)

Ellen Marshall Love married John Henry Strickland in 1887, and they moved to Roanoke. They had two daughters, Jimma Belle and Katherine, and three sons, Robert Paul, John Henry, and Julius Merrill. Roanoke was a farming and ranching town, but John Henry was a landowner. He owned 100 acres west of the railroad tracks and also several houses and lots in Roanoke. (Courtesy of Emily Ragsdale.)

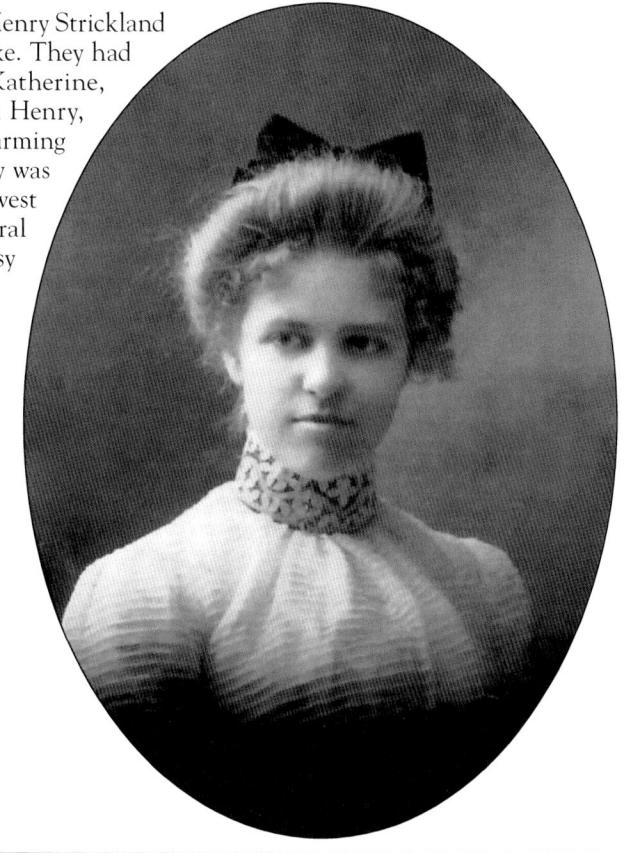

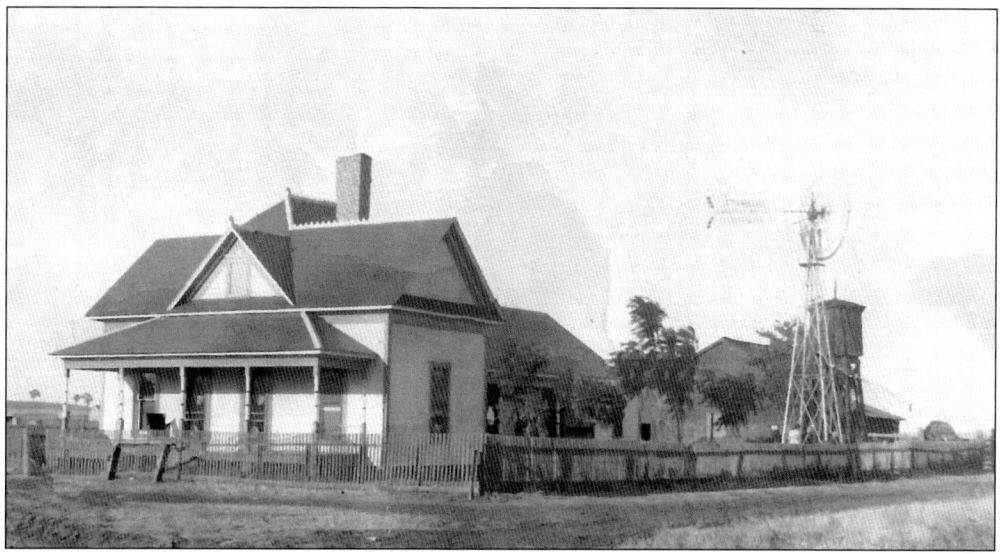

This photograph is of one of the houses that John Henry Strickland owned on Pecan Street. This house burned down in 1947, and John Henry moved another house he owned on Bowie Street to this location. After his death, John Henry's daughter Jimma Belle inherited the property. At her death, her granddaughter bought the property. There have now been five generations of Stricklands living on the property. (Courtesy of Emily Ragsdale.)

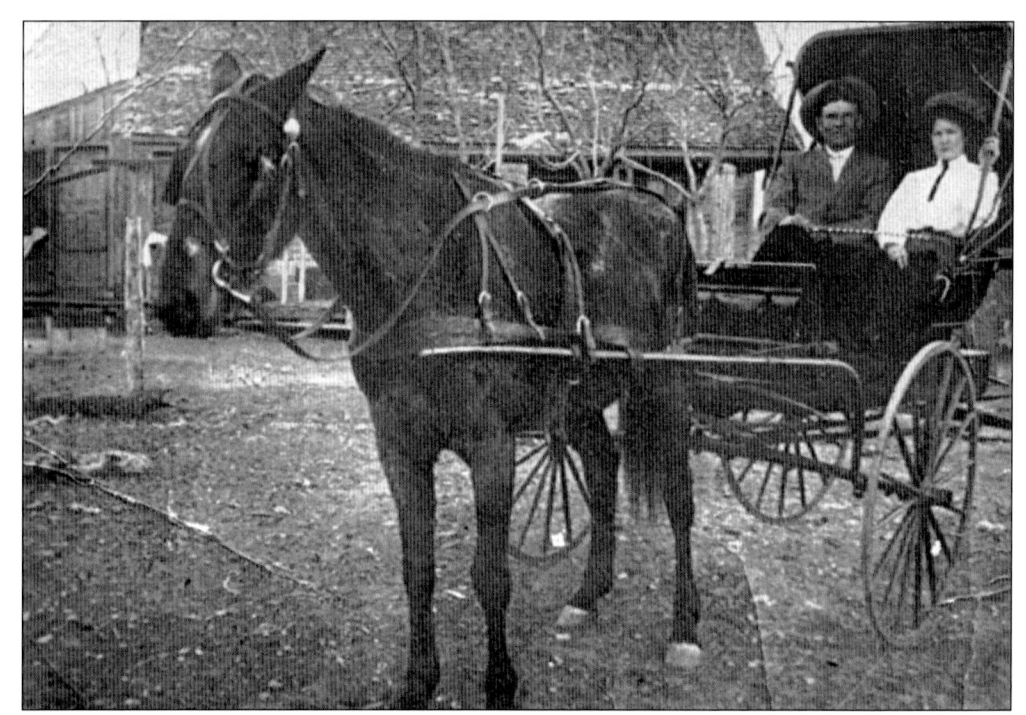

Carl and Addie Peterson are shown out for a buggy ride. Carl was the son of Frederick Peterson, the first of the large Peterson family to migrate to the Roanoke area from Sweden. Like his father and most of the Peterson men, Carl was a farmer. Addie Peterson worked for golfer Byron Nelson, and she was known as an excellent cook and down-to-earth woman. Relatives say she was a big hit with Nelson's famous friends. (Courtesy of Cozette Harris.)

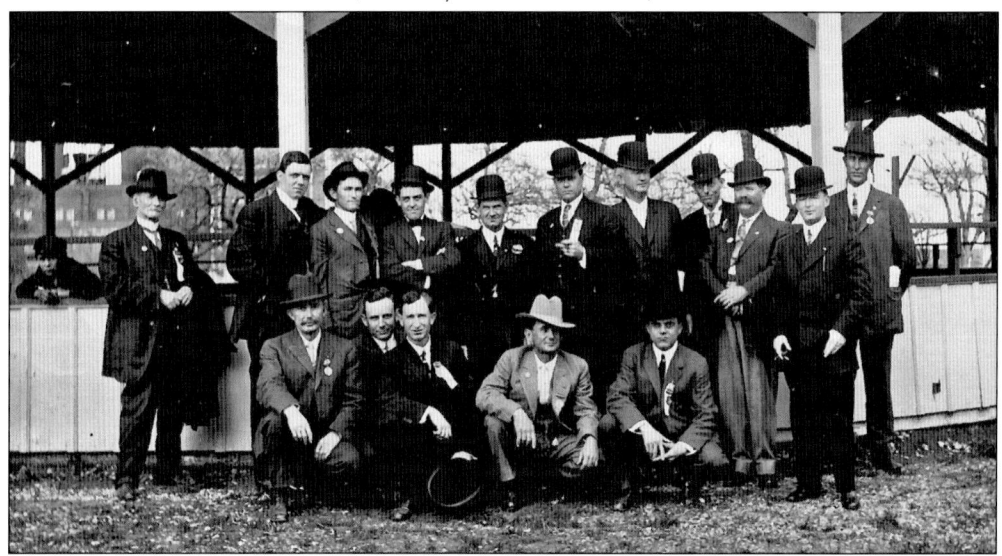

It is unknown whether this was the racetrack in Roanoke or in Denton, and none of the race attendees in this c. 1915 photograph are identified. One Roanoke racetrack was west of the railroad tracks, and another was near the Circle T Ranch, though they were not in operation during the same time period. Roanoke's only known jockey was Wilson Smith. The Medlins also raised race horses at their farm, west of Roanoke. (Courtesy of Alberta Lincecum.)

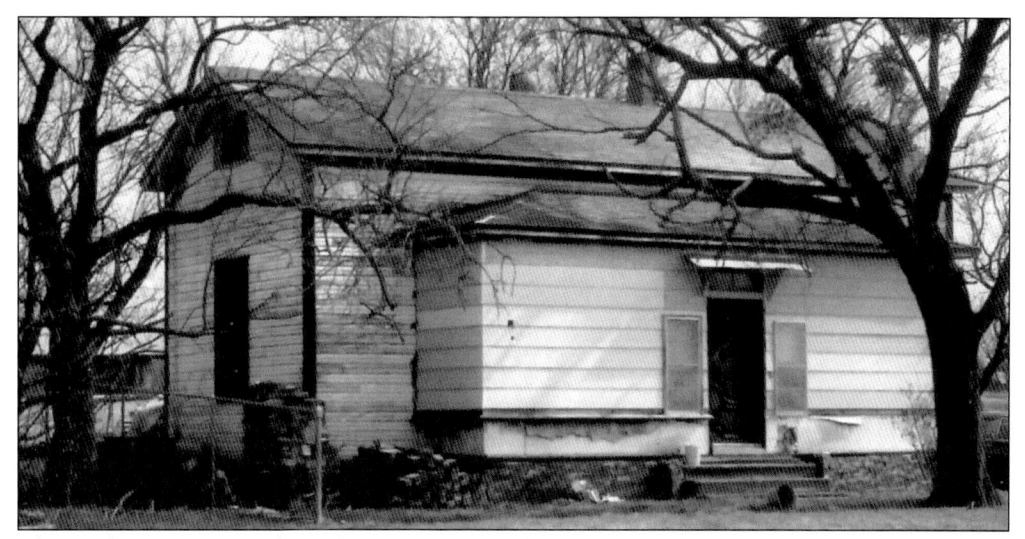

This modest structure is the only existing section house built by the railroad. The home is located on Highway 377 in Roanoke, which is one of the main thoroughfares through the city. One of the last railroad families to occupy this house was Simon Garcia. Garcia was so grateful to his children's teacher for teaching them English that he often brought her homemade tamales to express his thanks. (Courtesy of Wanda Smith.)

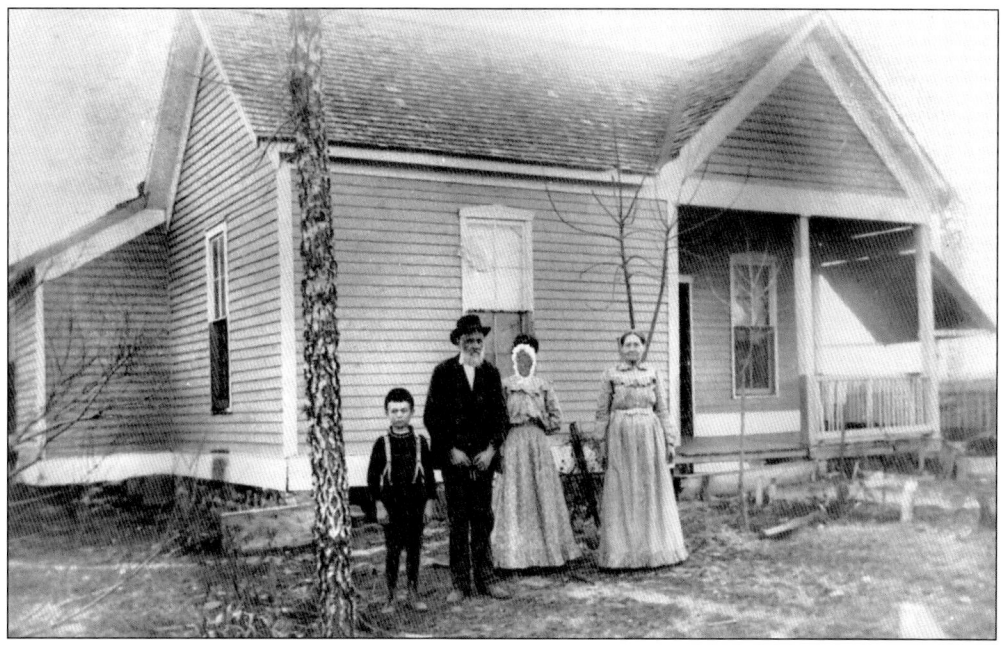

Pictured here are, from left to right, Claude Fanning as a young boy; William Cowan; his daughter, Ida Cowan; and Sarah Grayson Cowan, William's wife. The Cowans married in Tennessee and embarked from the town of Jasper, Tennessee, for Texas in 1878. They moved to Roanoke in 1898. In 1898, William was postmaster in Roanoke, having been appointed by Pres. William McKinley, and was succeeded by his daughter, Ida, who was appointed postmistress for life by Theodore Roosevelt. William died in November 1910. The Cowans had five children—Ida, Sam (an attorney for the Cattle Raisers' Association), Clint (a rural mail carrier), Hickson (a railroad engineer), and Alice Lewis, who moved in with Ida after her husband died. (Courtesy of HSC.)

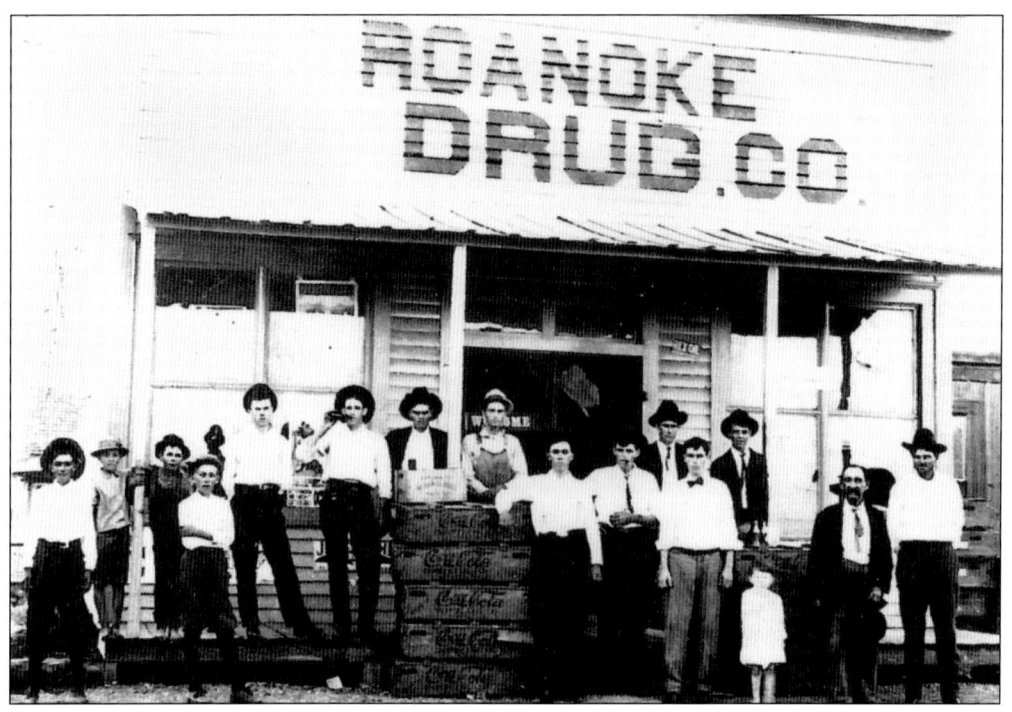

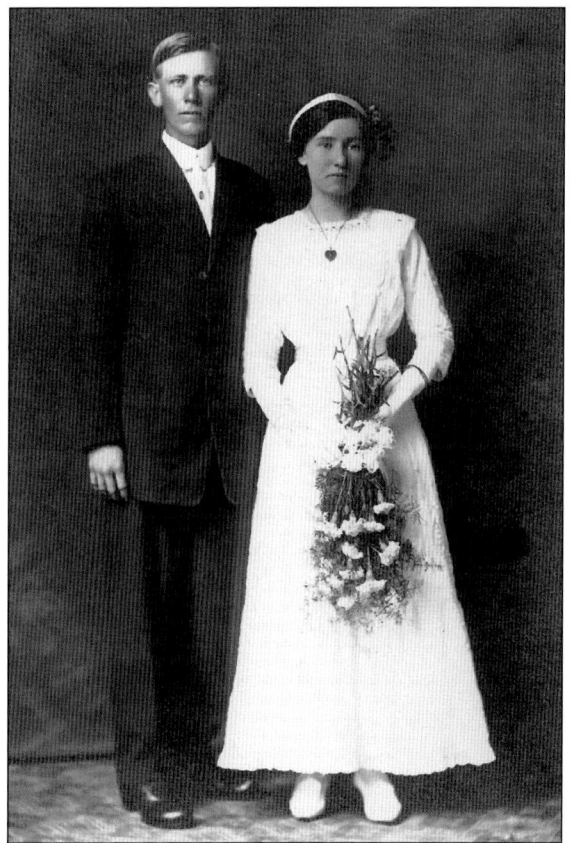

The Roanoke Drug Company, featured here, was obviously one of the early buildings in Roanoke, based on the mode of dress for the people shown. One of the men in the photograph bears an uncanny resemblance to the grandson of Ben Warder Yancey, who came to Roanoke in the mid-1800s. (Courtesy of HSC.)

Margaret Franscisco and Omas Peterson were married on June 2, 1912, on the front porch of her aunt's house, west of Roanoke. Their oldest son, Howard, took great delight in telling everyone his parents married on June 2, and he was born on June 4. He neglected to tell his listeners that he was born on June 4, 1913, a year after their marriage. His parents quickly set people straight about the dates. (Courtesy of Calvin Peterson.)

Two
People and Places

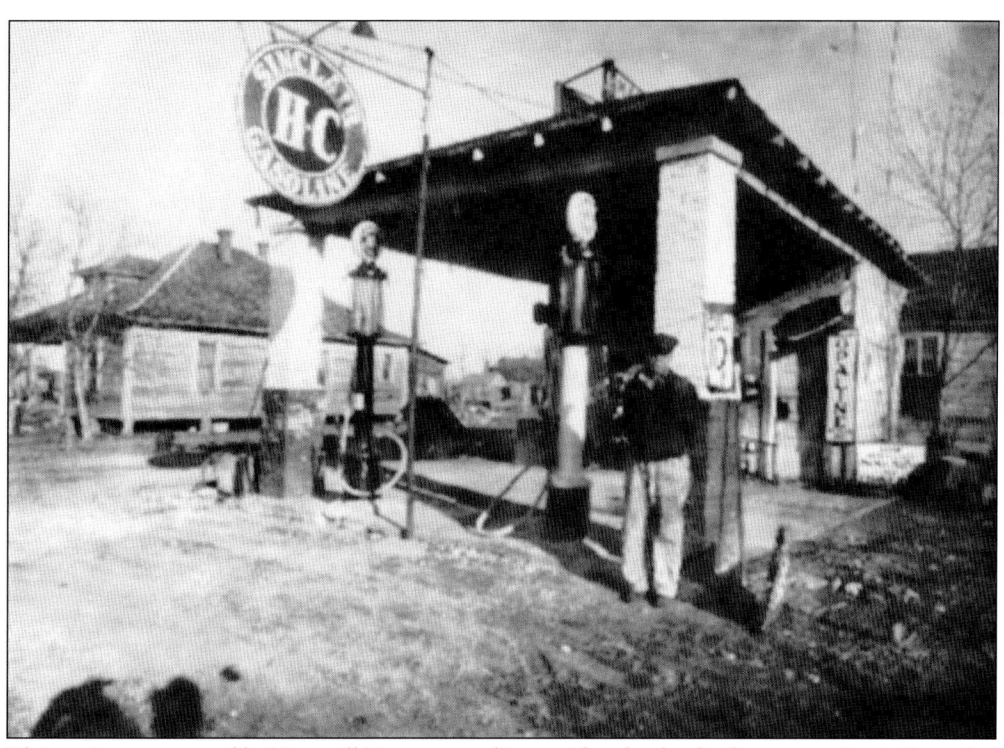

This station was owned by Hartwell Newman and is considered to be the first gas station in Roanoke. Hugh Jenkins sold gas from barrels at his hardware store; however, he did not have a station. Later Newman moved to a new station on Highway 377 in Roanoke. (Courtesy of Loye Steen.)

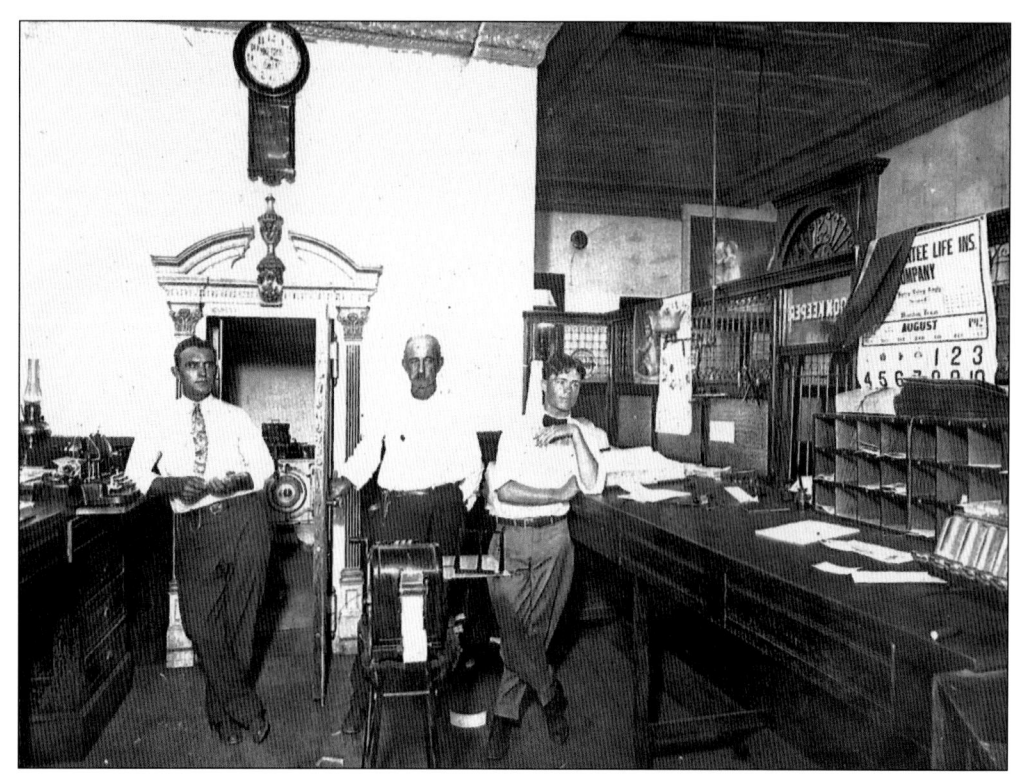

The interior of the Continental State Bank of Roanoke is shown in these two 1900s views, which were obviously taken at different times. The above photograph features, from left to right, Ben Hambright, Charles Stone, and Clint Yancey. Notice the kerosene lamp in the back left corner of the picture. The view below of the bank shows, from left to right, Charles Stone, Clint Yancey, and an unidentified man; however, the bare bulb hanging in the foreground at left heralds the arrival of dependable electricity. The kerosene lamp is no longer visible, but it may have still been available for emergencies. (Both, courtesy of Ann Clark.)

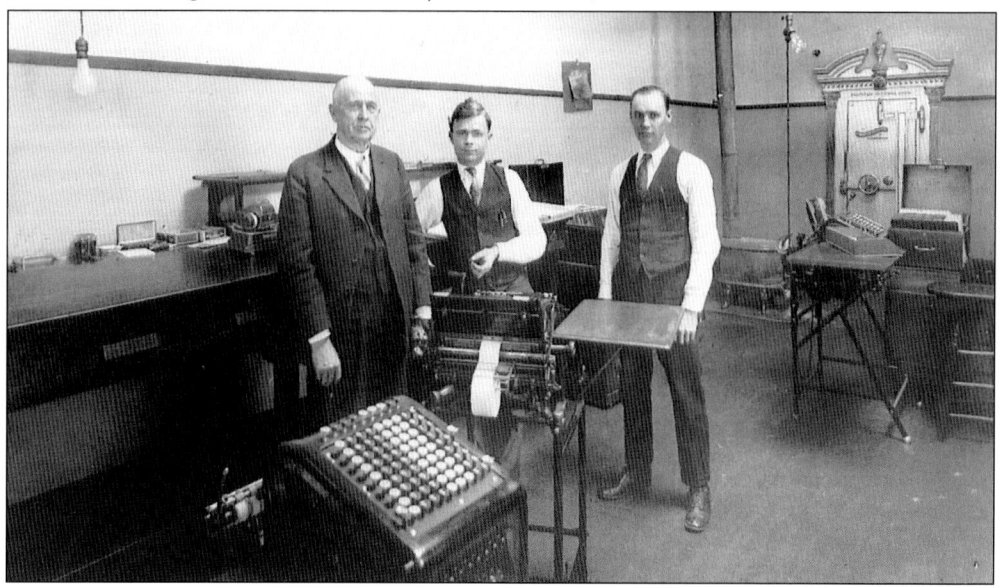

Both pictures shown on this page feature the Silver Spur Saloon. In the photograph at right, the two young boys enjoying their treats are the first thing to capture one's attention. They are Donald Paddock (right) and Melvin Paddock, the sons of Lola and Sterling Paddock of Roanoke. In the background is the saloon, built in 1886 for Robert (R. M.) and Burrell (B. S.) Snead. They were sons of Mary Counsel Medlin and John Snead. Ross Brown, whose truck is shown in the picture, had a grocery here at one time. The photograph below shows the saloon building in need of considerable restoration, which it had in 2007. (Right, courtesy of Melvin Paddock; below, courtesy of HSC.)

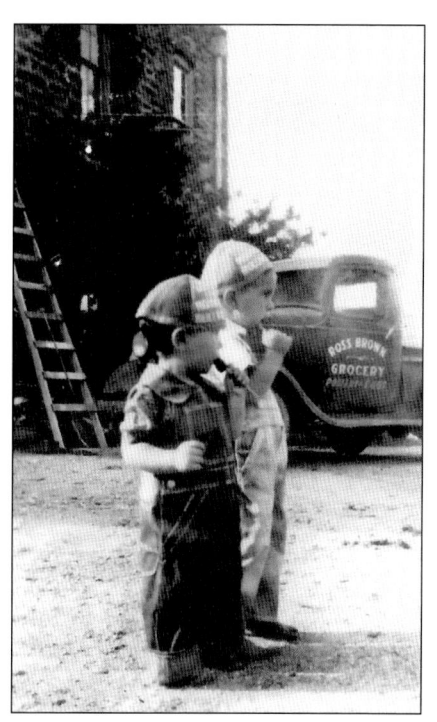

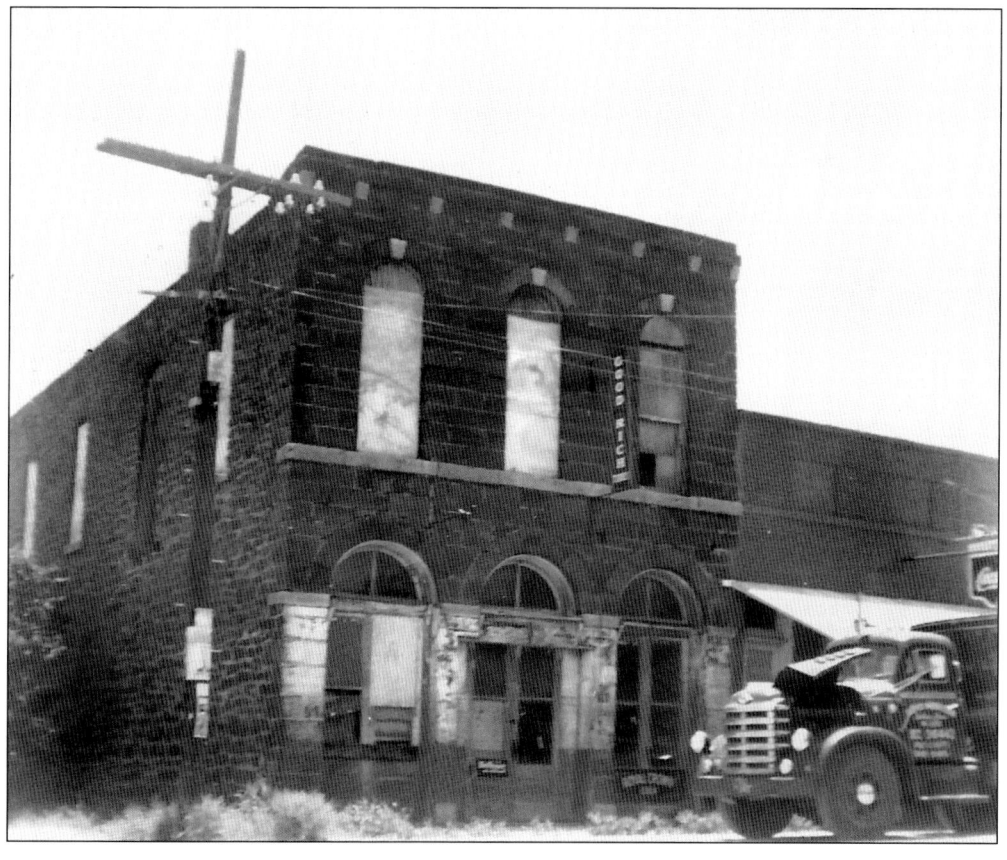

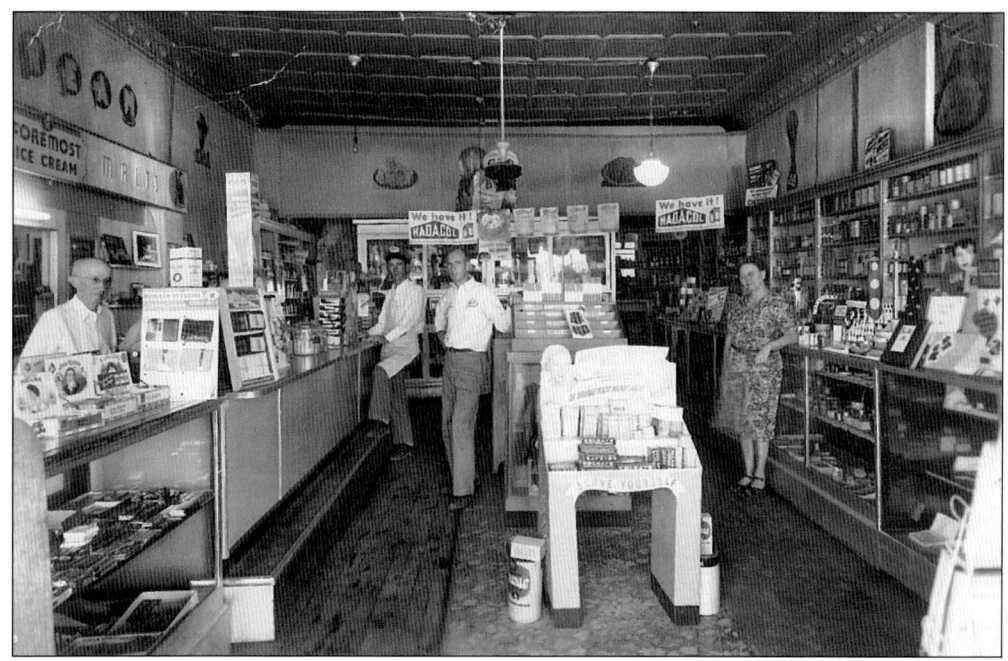

A drugstore owned by Joseph Stewart (left) is featured in this late-1940s picture, and the woman on the far right is Lula Barron, one of the store's employees. The two men in the center of the store are unidentified. Stewart was born in January 1890 and was a widower when he married Nell Carmen Hamblett in 1947. The couple moved to Roanoke in August 1947 after seeing a newspaper advertisement of a drugstore for sale there. They bought the store and relocated from Texarkana, Texas. They had two children, Jo Nell and Peggy. Stewart died in February 1953, only six years after his second marriage. (Courtesy of Peggy Way.)

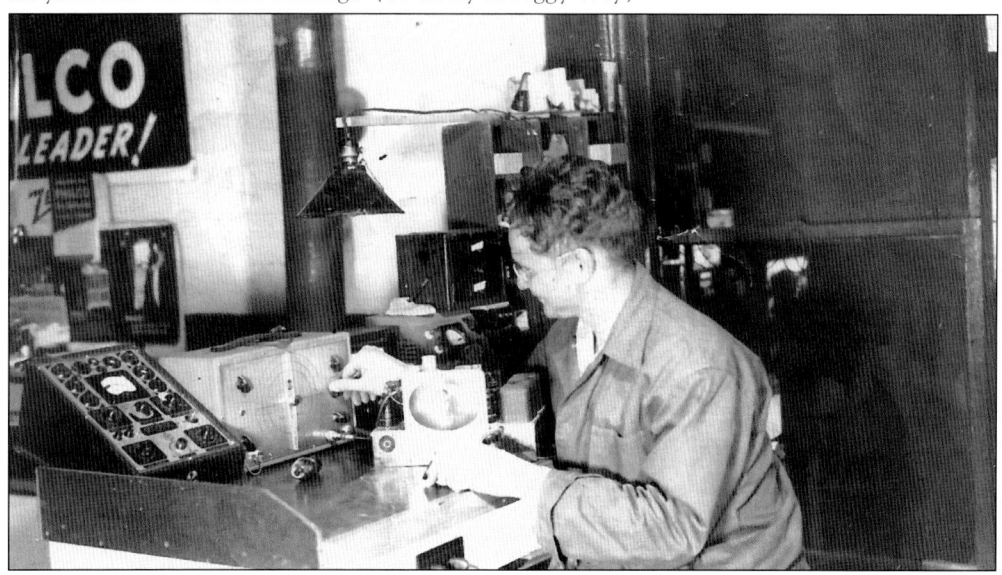

Walter Dunn was a genius at repairing radios for the residents of Roanoke. Dunn was a familiar sight around town, as he often rode a bicycle down Oak Street. If Dunn was stumped by something, other than electronics, he went straight to the Northwest Bank to get the information. It did not matter if it had nothing to do with the bank's regular services. (Courtesy of James Redwine.)

Hood Jenkins was the only child of Hattie and Hugh Jenkins. He was named for his paternal grandfather, Berry Hood, who was an early settler and with whom he had an extremely close relationship. Hood was born in the house pictured below on June 10, 1906. The house was previously the home of his grandparents Berry and Rachel Caroline "Callie" Hood, who bestowed it as a wedding gift to their daughter, Hattie and her husband, Hugh Jenkins, in 1905. The elder Jenkins lived out the rest of his life here as one of the leading citizens of Roanoke, respected as the first mayor and a successful business man. (Right, courtesy of Alberta Lincecum; below, courtesy of Wanda Smith.)

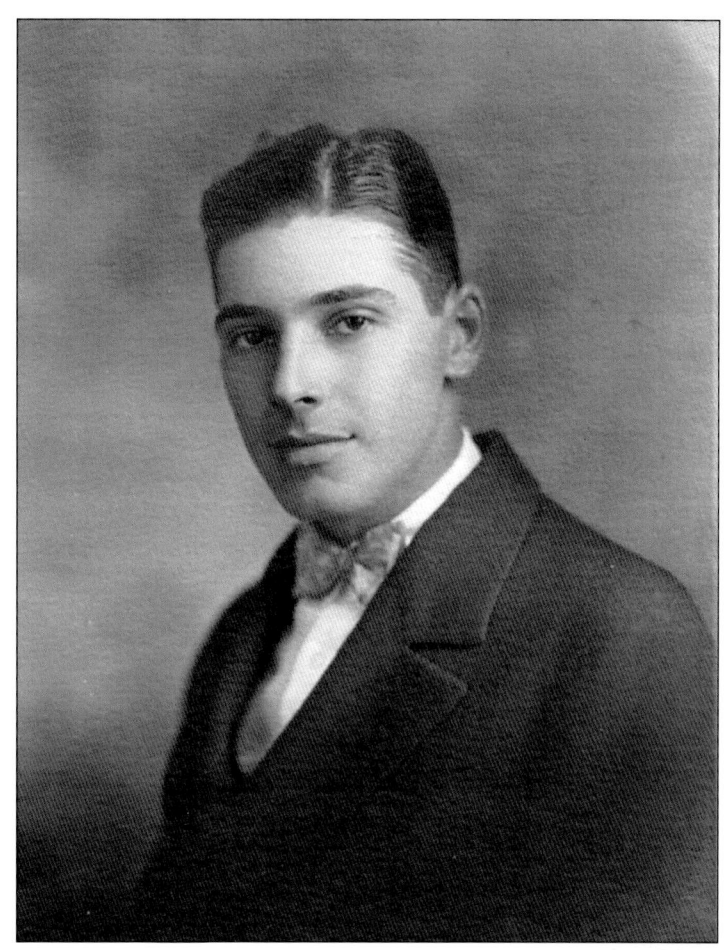

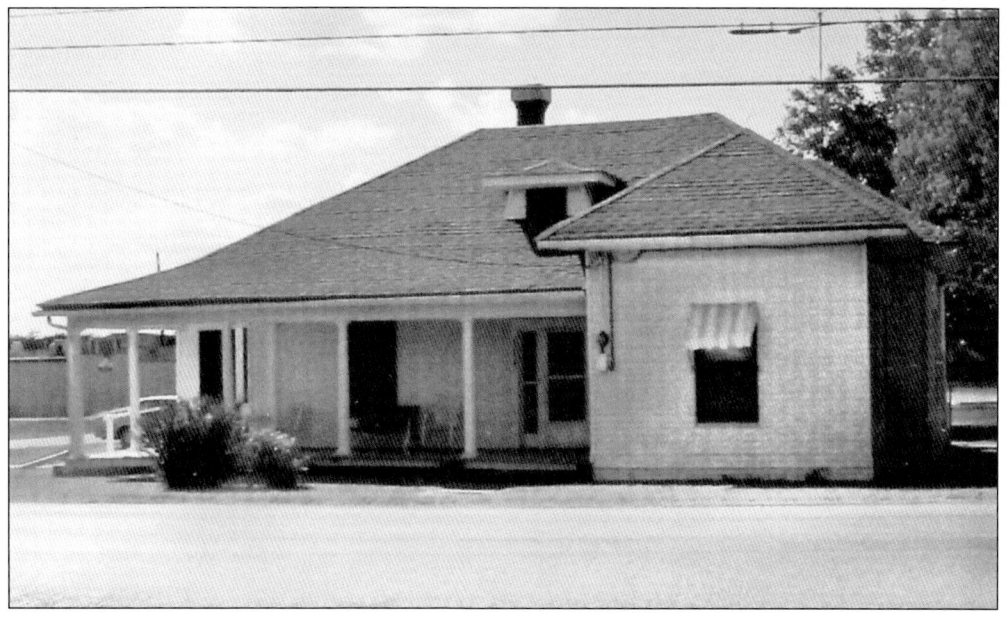

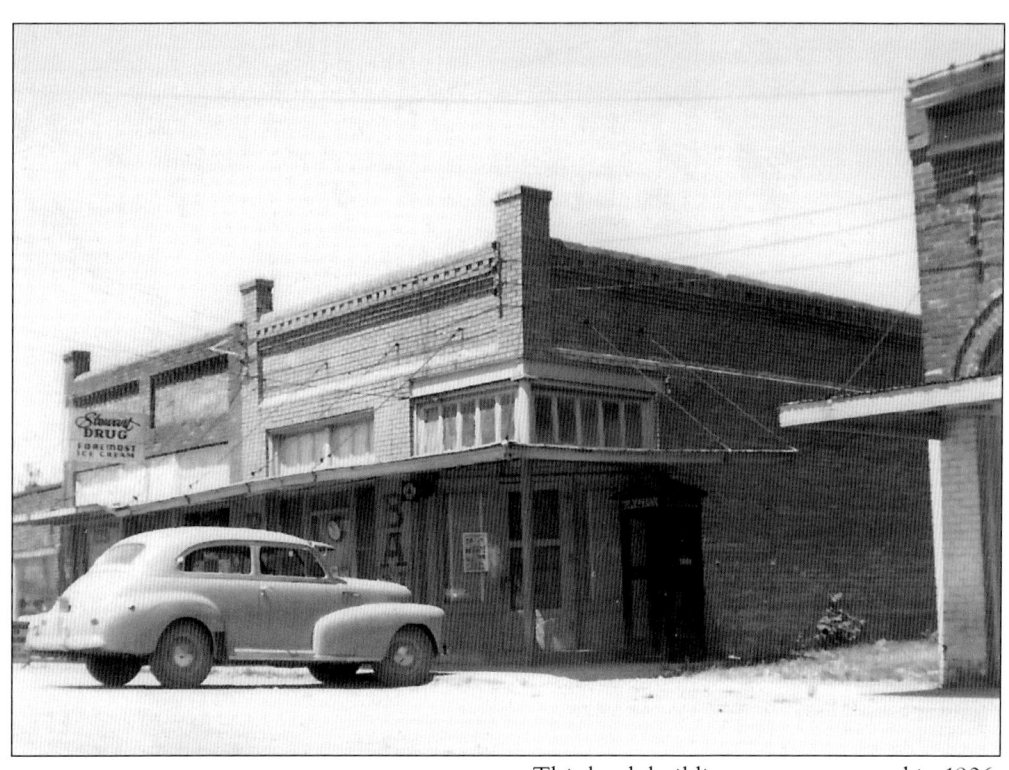

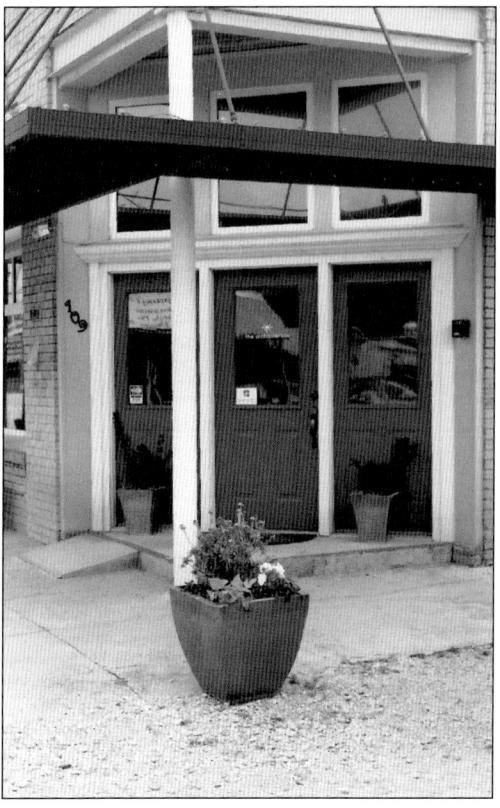

This bank building was constructed in 1906, with Eliaphet Brand as president. It served as a bank until it closed. In 1936, Claude "Buster" Fanning opened it again as a credit union. Townspeople referred to the structure as "Buster's Bank." The interior houses a built-in safe that is more than 100 years old. The yellow-brick building boasts 1-foot-wide masonry walls. The structure is currently owned by Leon Fanning, a son of "Buster" and Nell Fanning. (Above, courtesy of HSC; left, courtesy of Ann Clark.)

The adorable child pictured in the 1918 photograph at right is six-month-old Emily Lavada Bogart. A grown-up Emily is shown with the rest of her family in the photograph below. Pictured from left to right are (first row) Charles Harvey Bogart and his wife, Ada; (second row) Emily, Manuel, and Minnie Bogart. In this picture, the family is standing near their home, which was on the west side of the railroad tracks. In the background is the Roanoke depot. They formerly lived on the Cartwright farm. (Both, courtesy of Emily Ragsdale.)

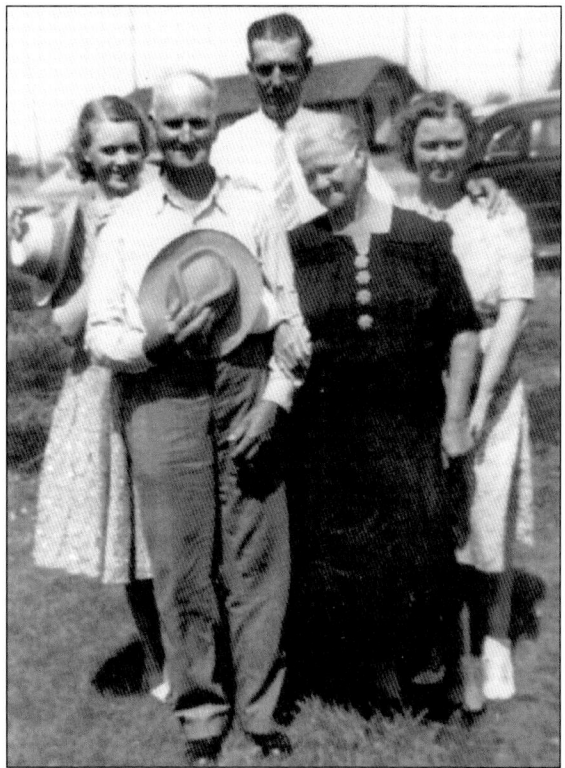

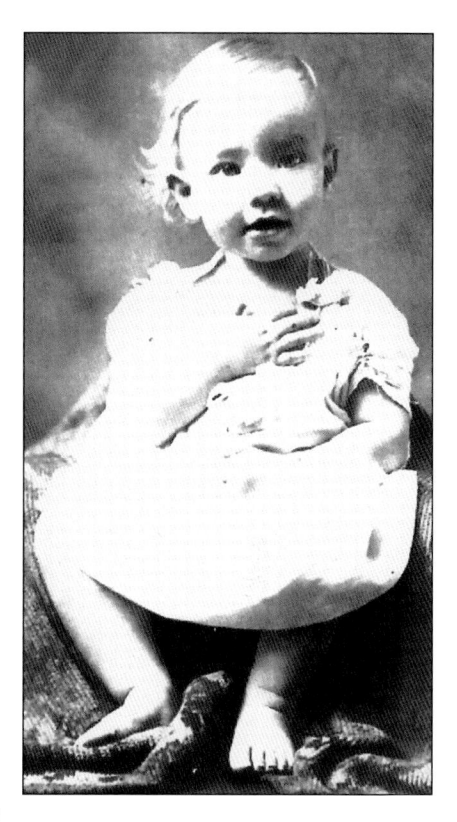

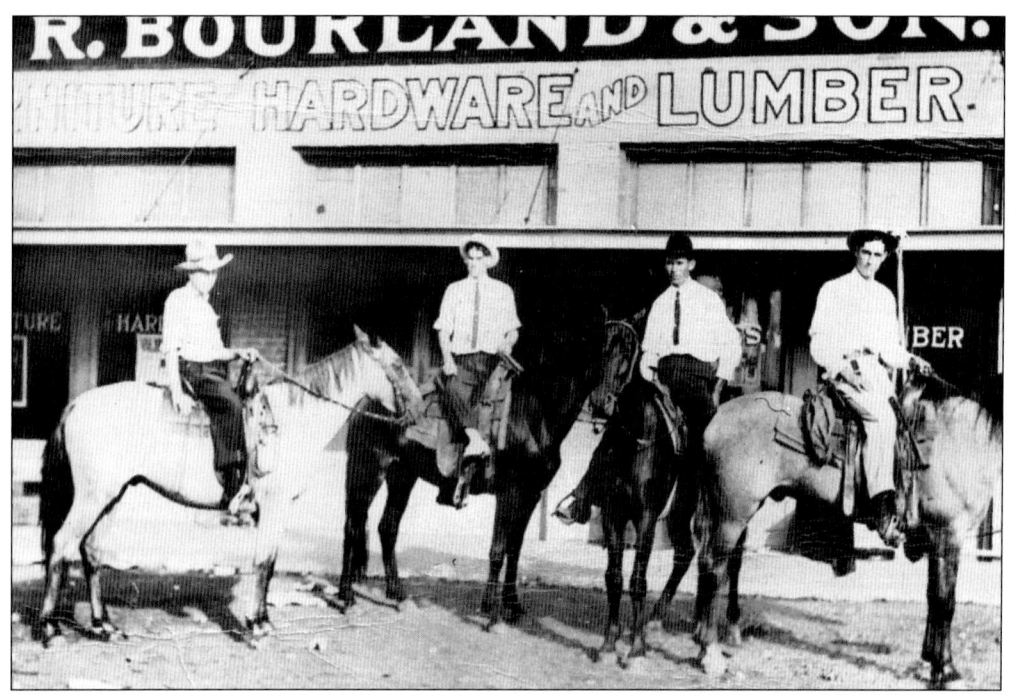

The building shown in these 1913 photographs is depicted during different time periods. The first photograph was taken in front of J. R. Bourland and Sons Furniture, Hardware, and Lumber Company on September 1, 1913. The men on horseback are, from left to right, Charles Pickett, Jesse Jones, Merl Strickland, and Foy Barrow. The c. 1970 photograph below shows the building when it was used as the Arnold Welding Service, though the Noah's Grocery sign is clearly visible. James Monroe Noah owned the grocery. Upon his death, his son, James, became the proprietor. He was aided by his wife, Corrine, who worked with him in the store. The building was originally constructed as a furniture store for Thomas Brand. (Both, courtesy of HSC.)

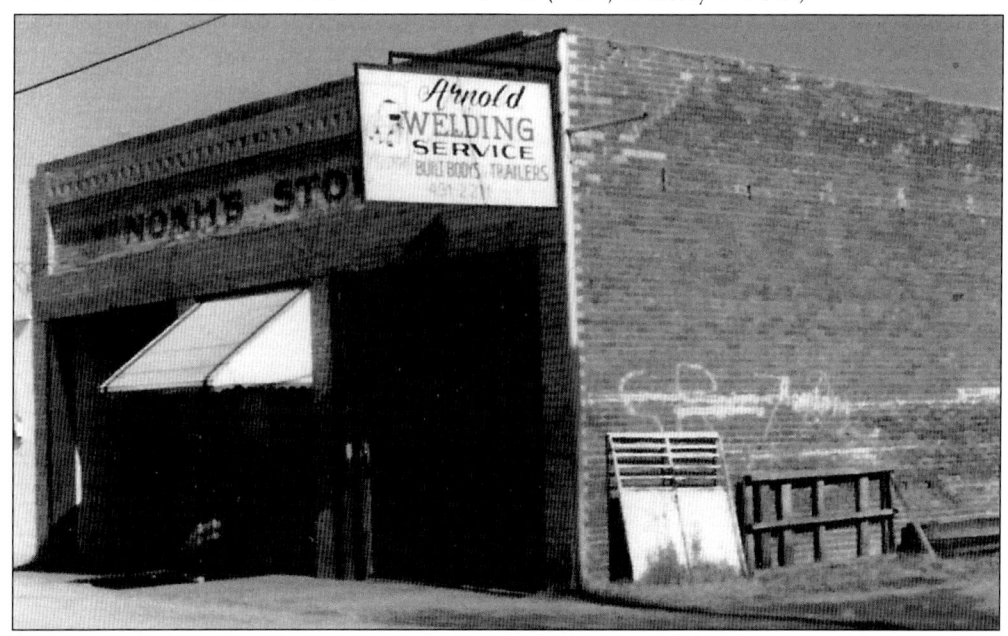

Pauline and John Henry Ragsdale were both born in Roanoke and went through school there. John Henry worked for his father at his mechanic shop on Oak Street and also did farm work while still in school. Pauline married Jack Brittain, and they lived in the rock saloon building on the upper floor. Jack had a mechanic shop on the bottom floor. Pauline had a cafe on the west side of Oak Street between the post office and the drugstore. (Courtesy of Emily Ragsdale.)

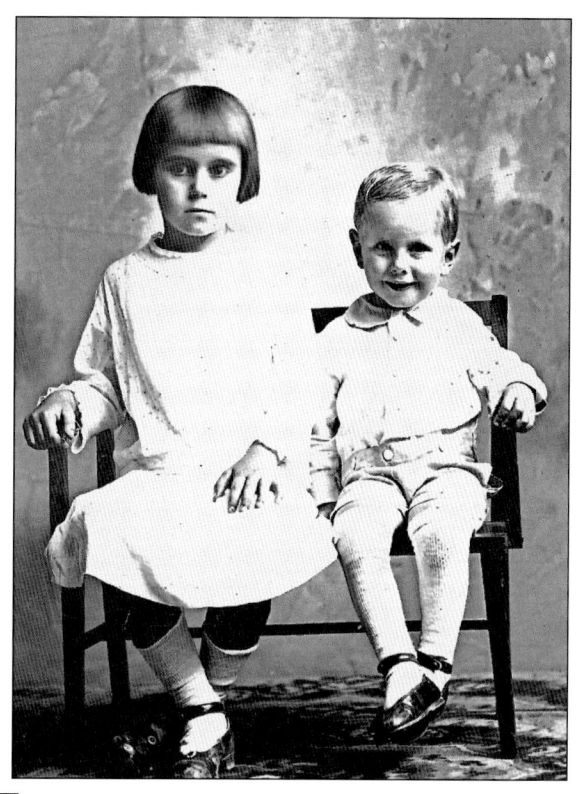

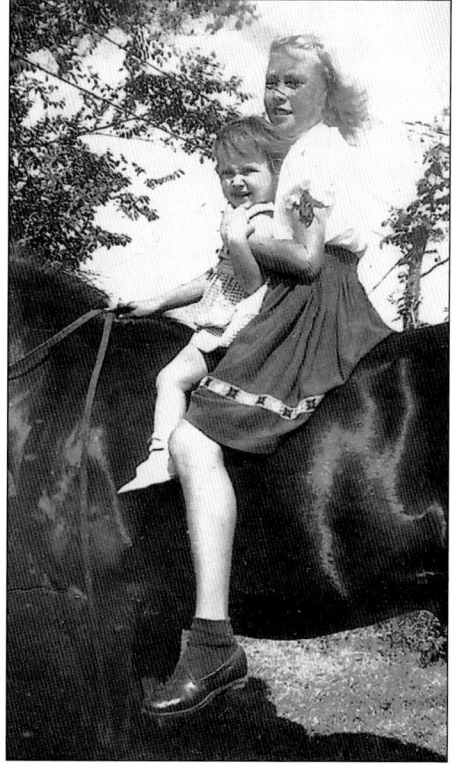

These young girls on horseback are, from left to right, Eileen Tidwell, the daughter of Rosetta and John Tidwell, and Cozette Pinion, the daughter of Nellie Ann and Emmitt Pinion. Almost every child in Roanoke grew up riding horses. The children had the run of the town, visiting each other's homes and riding alone to any of the businesses. (Courtesy of Cozette Harris.)

53

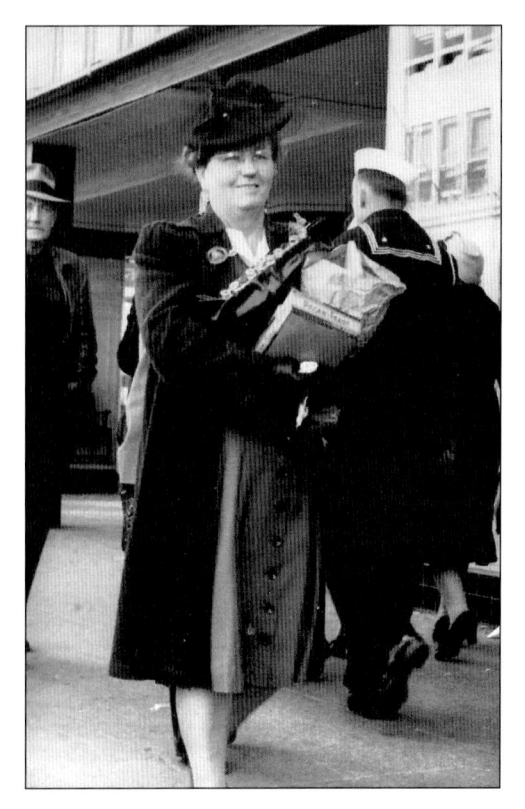

In this 1940s photograph, Mineola "Ola" Wheeler is shown loaded down with parcels while shopping during World War II in Fort Worth. Men in uniform were a common sight in communities across the United States during this time period, as evidenced in this picture. Mineola was named in honor of Mineola, Texas, her birthplace. The photograph below is of Obie "Dub" Wheeler, the son of Mineola and Ora Wheeler. Obie served in World War II, when he was stationed at Okinawa as a mechanic, charged with keeping the tanks running. Obie, or "Dub" as he is known, hosts a musical venue at the Roanoke Senior Center, which has boasted as many as 23 musicians at one time, playing guitars, fiddles, or harmonicas. (Both, courtesy of Obie "Dub" Wheeler.)

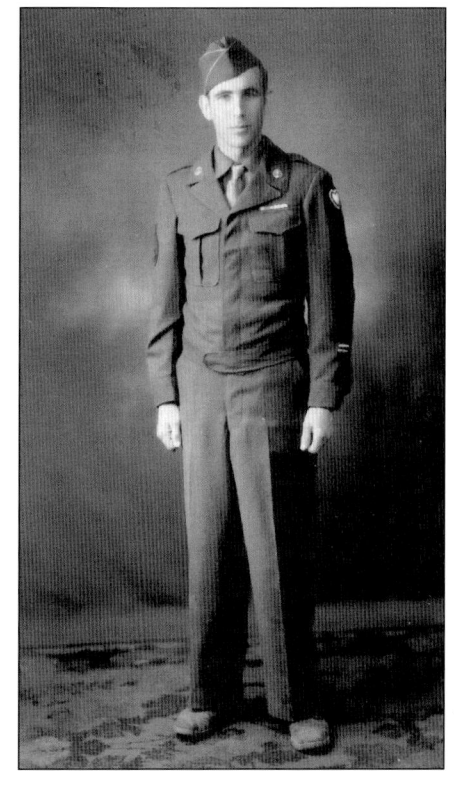

Mary "Mollie" Craig and Jesse Brock (at right) were the grandparents of Vertalee Brock, shown in the photograph below with her family. The Coleman family pictured below are, from left to right, (first row) Dale, the youngest son; (second row) Estelle, John Alan, John, and Vertalee. The family is standing in front of a former home, located on Dallas Drive. The Colemans and the Brocks, Vertalee's parents, were longtime residents of Roanoke. (Both, courtesy of Vertalee and John Coleman.)

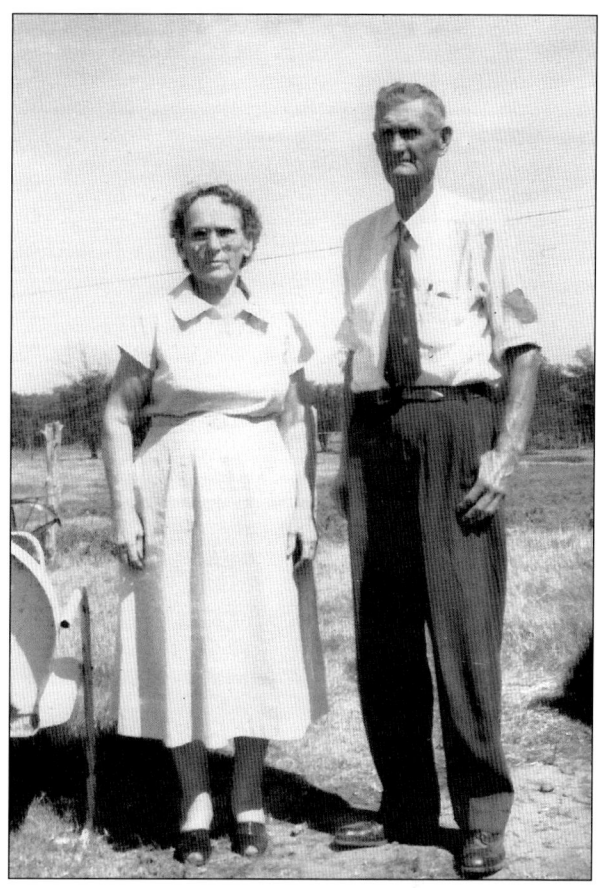

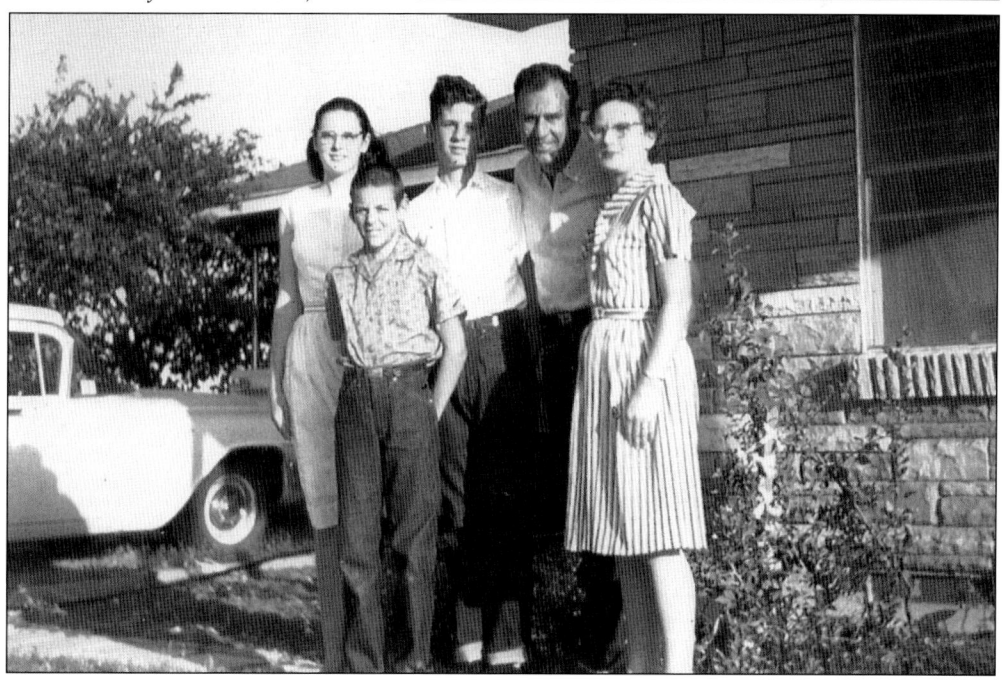

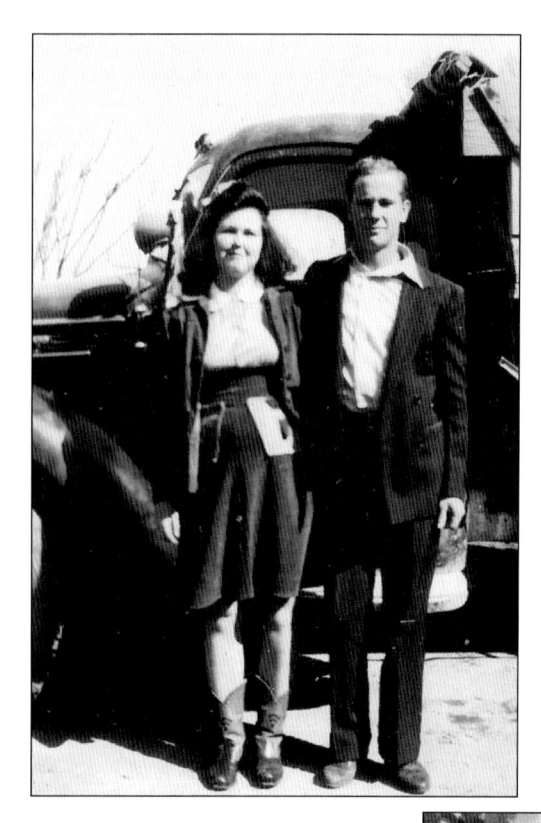

Bernice and Ray Wheeler are pictured in front of the truck Ray used to haul gravel and sand for his father's business. Bernice is ready for anything in her cowboy boots. Ray grew up in the Roanoke area, because his dad, Ora Wheeler, had a garage called the Green Valley Garage north of Roanoke on what was then Highway 10, the road to Denton. (Courtesy of Obie "Dub" Wheeler.)

In 1976, Eugie Thomas proudly displays a quilt she made and sold for a mere $100. Eugie, born on September 22, 1885, was one of 10 children of John Dolford "Bob" Jones and his wife, Almeady Chisum. In this photograph, Eugie is 90 years old. The members of the Jones family had a stellar reputation in the area. Eugie died in 1985. (Courtesy of Molly Cummins.)

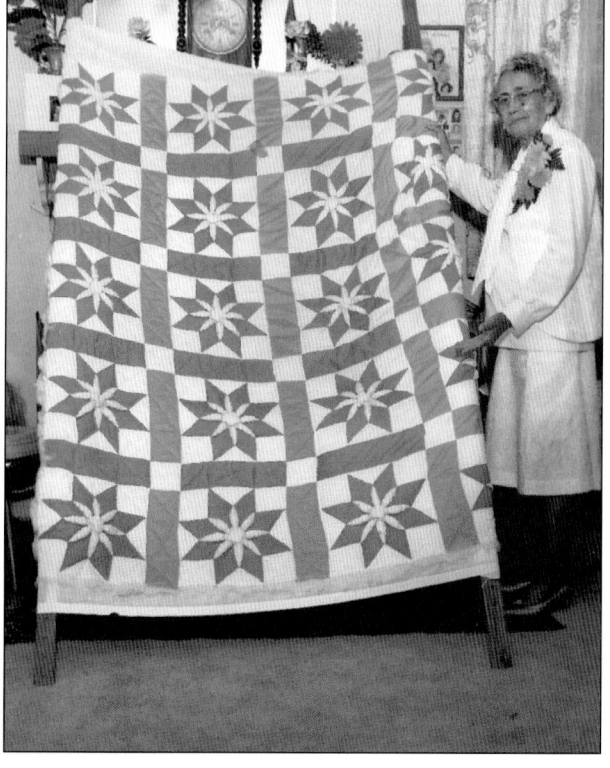

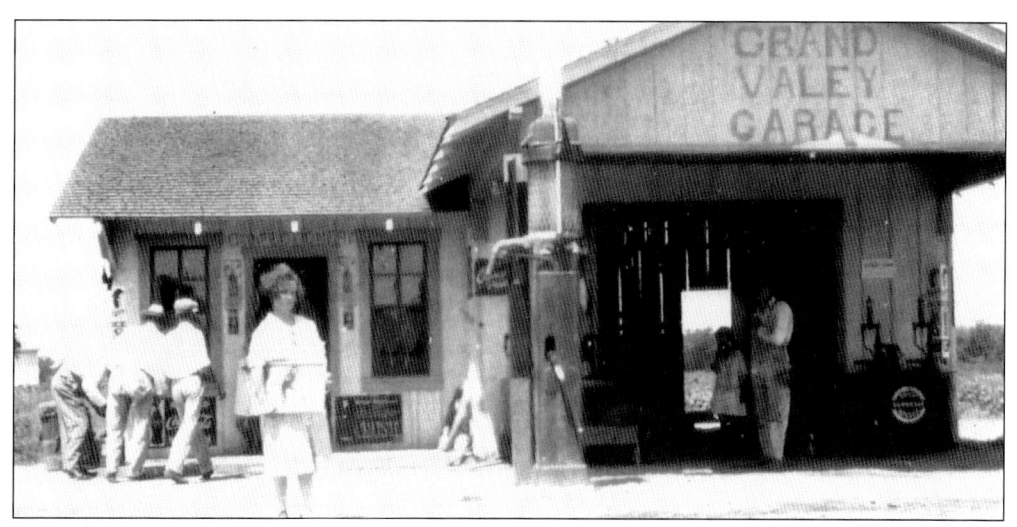

Ora Wheeler operated a garage in Lake Dallas prior to opening the Grand Valley Garage. Mineola Wheeler (pictured above), Ora's wife, is seen in the foreground of this 1940s photograph. Ora and daughter Evelyn are in the shadows of the garage at left. The men on the left are unidentified. Pictured below are, from left to right, (first row) Obie "Dub" and Frank; (second row) Clara, Evelyn, and Clarence. Missing from this group is the youngest child, Racine "Ray." The garage was often converted into a music and dance hall venue when brothers Tal and Lynn Tidwell arrived with their fiddle and guitar. Wood chips were scattered on the garage floor to accommodate the dancers. In 1934, Bonnie Parker and Clyde Barrow stopped here for gas. They were frequent visitors to the area, as a granddaughter of James Medlin remembered her father pulling the outlaws' car out of the mud near his ranch. Later they shot and killed a lawman on Highway 114, west of Roanoke. (Both, courtesy of Obie "Dub" Wheeler.)

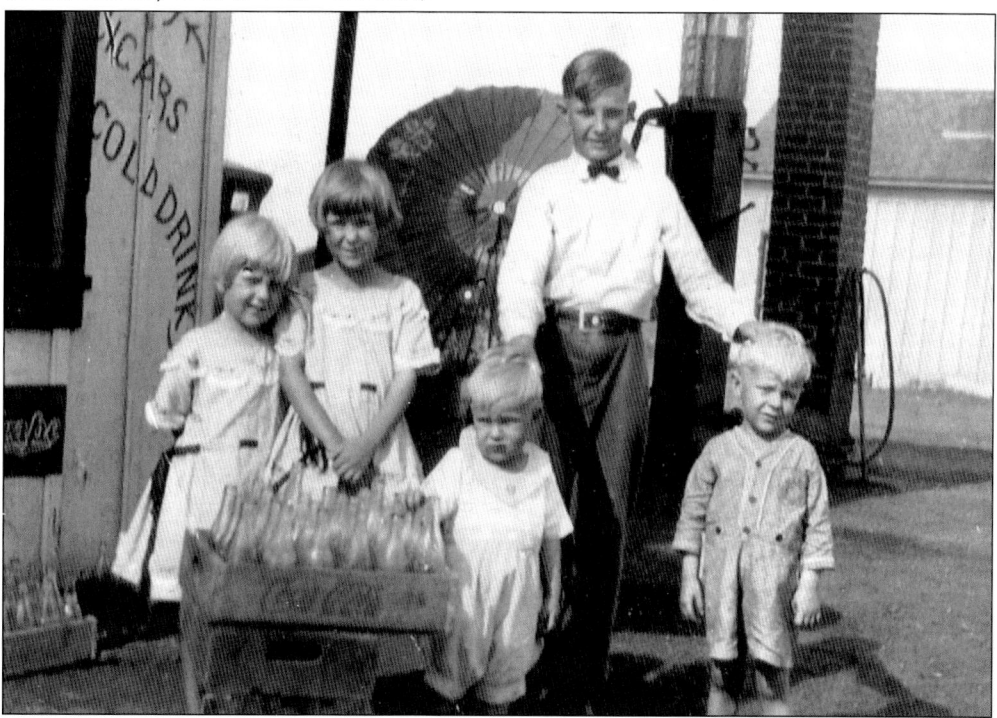

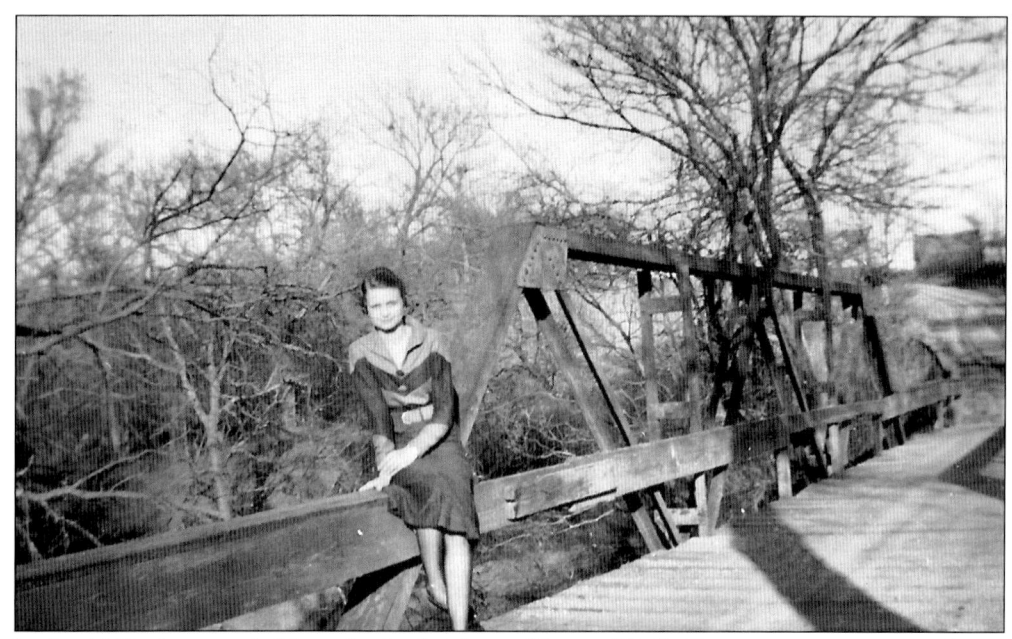

In this 1940s photograph, Hannah, the daughter of Ben and Della Yancey, is seen posing on Litsey Bridge, which was slightly west of Roanoke. In the early 2000s, the bridge was deemed unsafe by Denton County; however, the City of Roanoke plans to relocate the bridge to one of the city parks to be preserved and used as a foot bridge. (Courtesy of Ann Clark.)

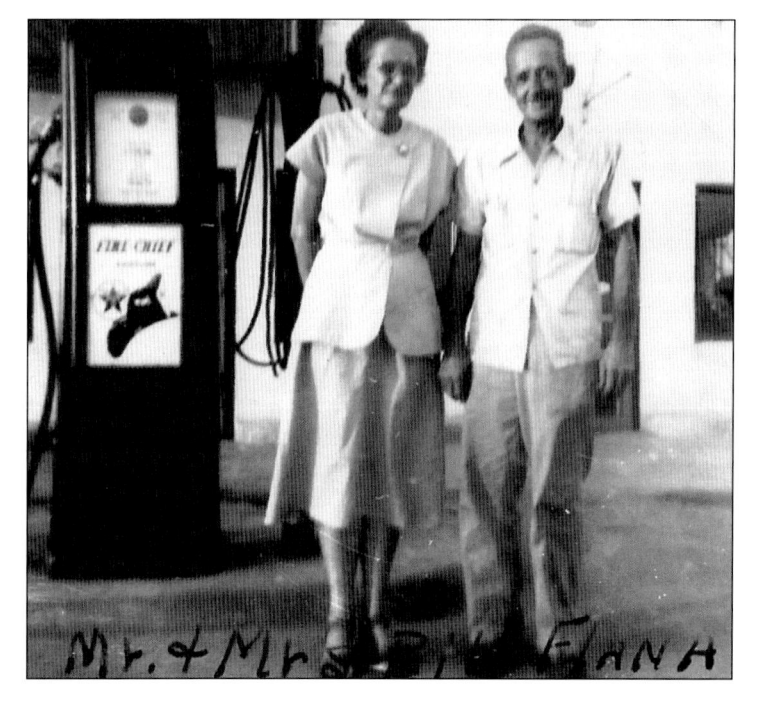

Lillian and William "Bill" Flanagan both worked at the crossroads at a combination service station and café that William helped Henry "Mc" Howe build. Lillian operated the café with her husband's assistance. The Flanagans were loyal basketball fans, following the high school basketball careers of their sons William Jr. and Wallace Ray "Rooster," who excelled at the sport. (Courtesy of James Redwine.)

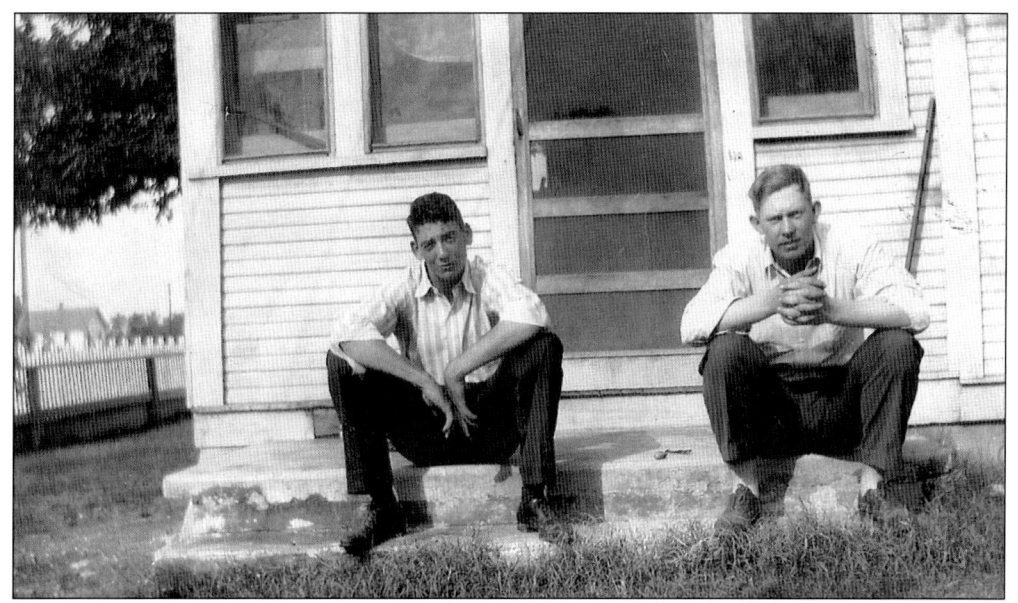

In this 1940s photograph, Henry "Mc" Howe (left) and Conway Peterson, longtime friends and classmates, are languishing on the back steps. These two collaborated on many of the aerial photographs taken of Roanoke. Henry "Mc" flew the airplane, and Conway took the pictures. Henry's middle name was McAffee, the maiden name of a grandmother. He was called Henry "Mc" to distinguish him from his father. (Courtesy of Conway and Calvin Peterson.)

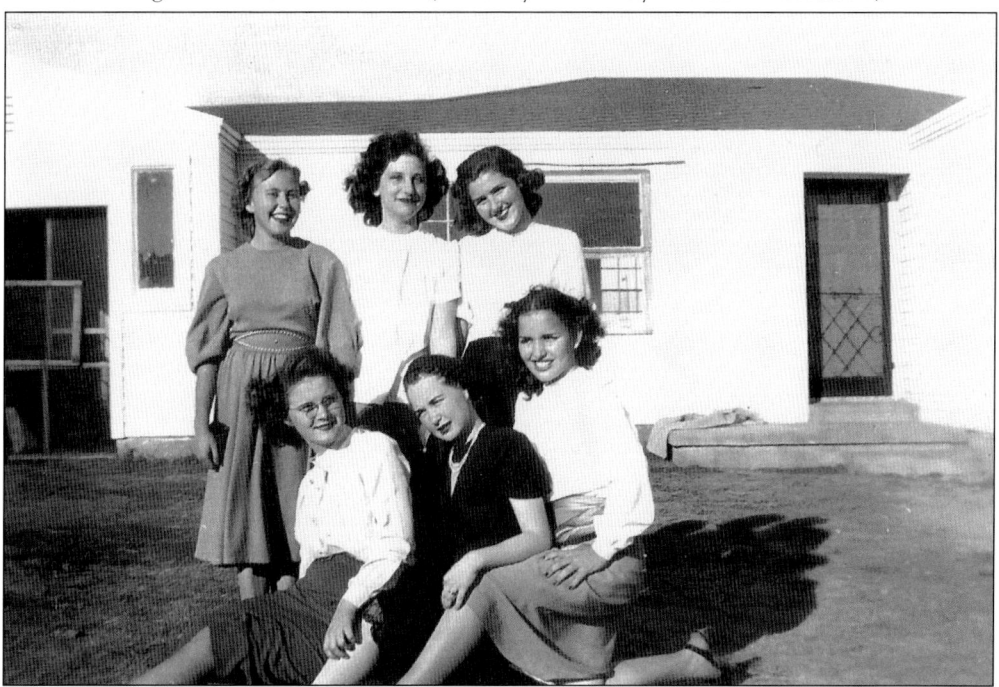

These young women were great friends throughout their school years and beyond. They are, from left to right, (first row) Mary Lou Harris, Frances Haynie, and Patsy Luttrell; (second row) Cozette Pinion, Edna Mae Moreman, and Doris Woodruff. Several of these women still live in the Roanoke area. (Courtesy of Cozette Harris.)

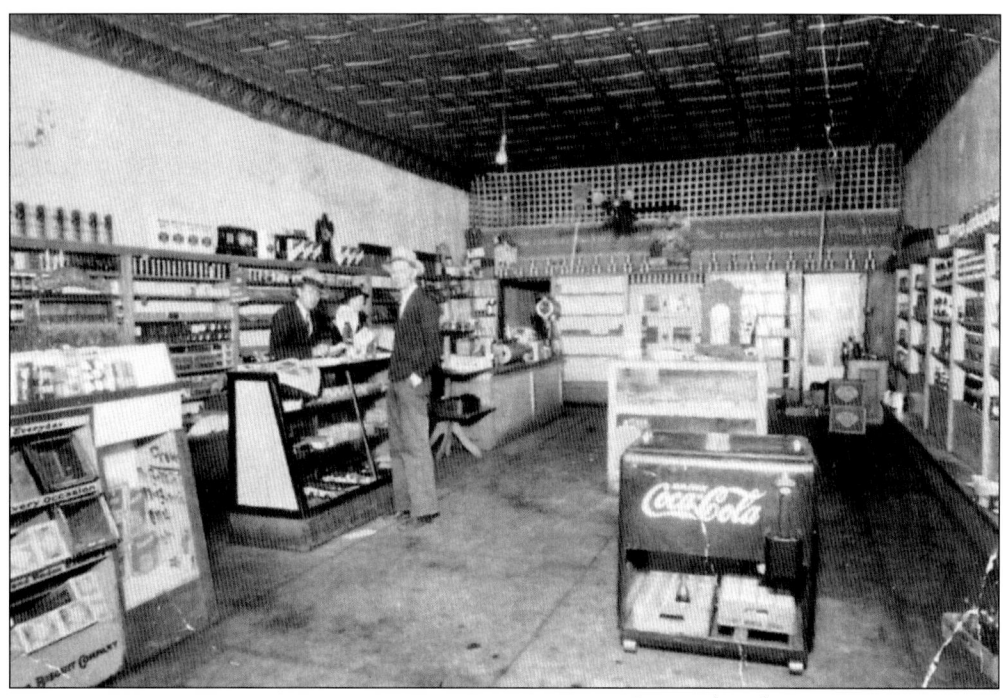

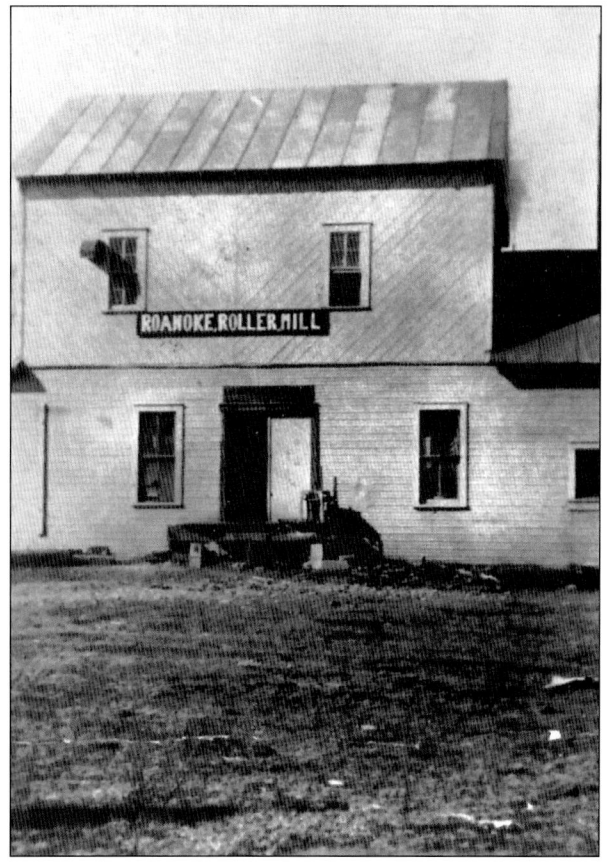

Pictured in the Manire Grocery on Oak Street are, from left to right, Ernest Manire, the proprietor; Idelle Love, the first-grade teacher; and another customer, Anson Cannon. Manire and his family lived on Rusk Street, about a block and a half from the grocery store. Local produce was sold here—for example, the Wheeler family brought corn they grew to the store and Manire ground it, returning half of the now-ground corn to the Wheeler family and selling the rest. Others sold eggs and butter to the store. (Courtesy of Inez and Henry "Mc" Howe.)

The Roanoke Roller Mill, operated by Pete Lassen until it burned in 1925, is shown in this 1920s photograph. The mill, which was located west of the railroad tracks, distributed flour from this location to other cities, most notably Fort Worth. There were a number of service buildings in this area, including gins and the railroad depot. (Courtesy of HSC.)

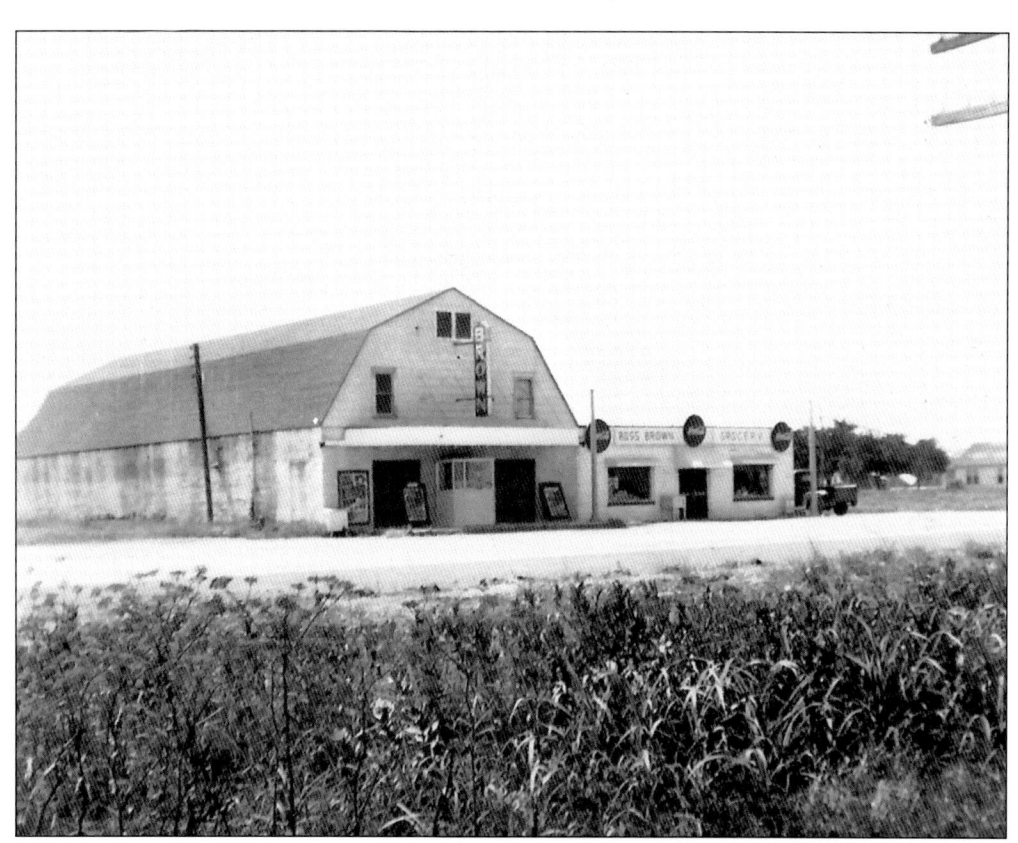

Ross Brown and his wife, Pearl, owned this theater and grocery store combination (pictured above around 1955), which was located on the east side of Highway 377 in Roanoke. Pearl was the daughter of John Henry Jones, who was called "Farmer" Jones by the townspeople. Friends Elaine Peterson (left) and Barbara Medlin are shown in front of the box office of the theater. Brown had a grocery at one time on Oak Street across the street from the grocery store owned by John and Mary Jones, Pearl Brown's parents. (Above, courtesy of HSC; right, courtesy of Barbara Medlin Langston.)

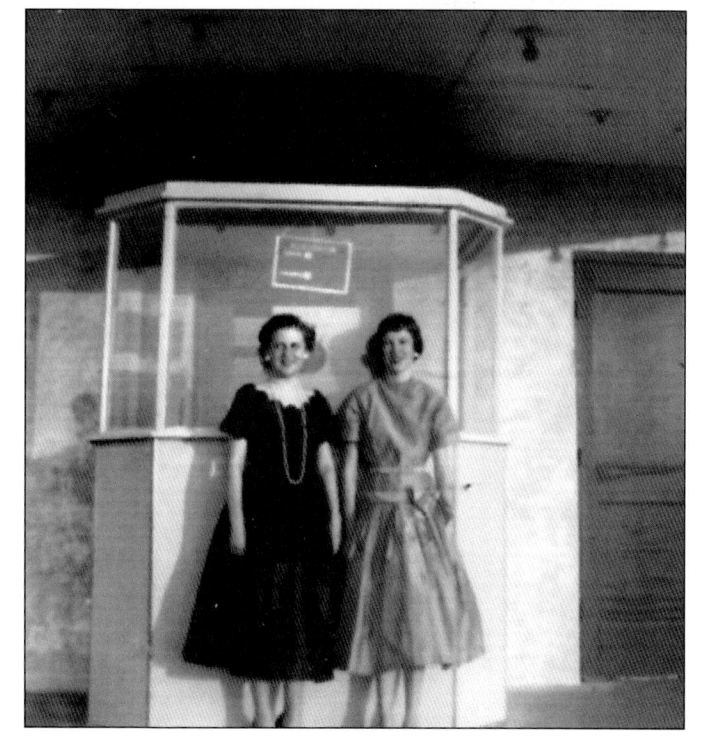

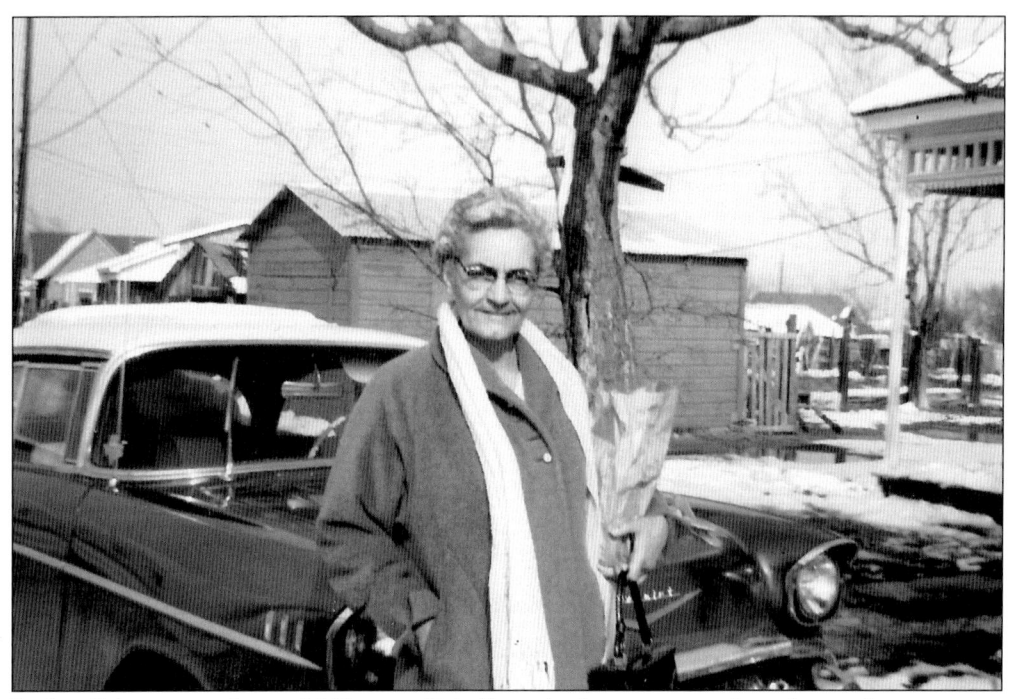

Pauline Fisher operated several different cafés in Roanoke, but no matter where she was, her customers always said she made the best cobbler they had ever eaten. Her first cafe was in a building that had previously been a saloon. In the photograph below, Harmon Fisher, Pauline's husband, is shown in deep conversation with grandson Marty Wren. (Both, courtesy of Toya Fisher Wren.)

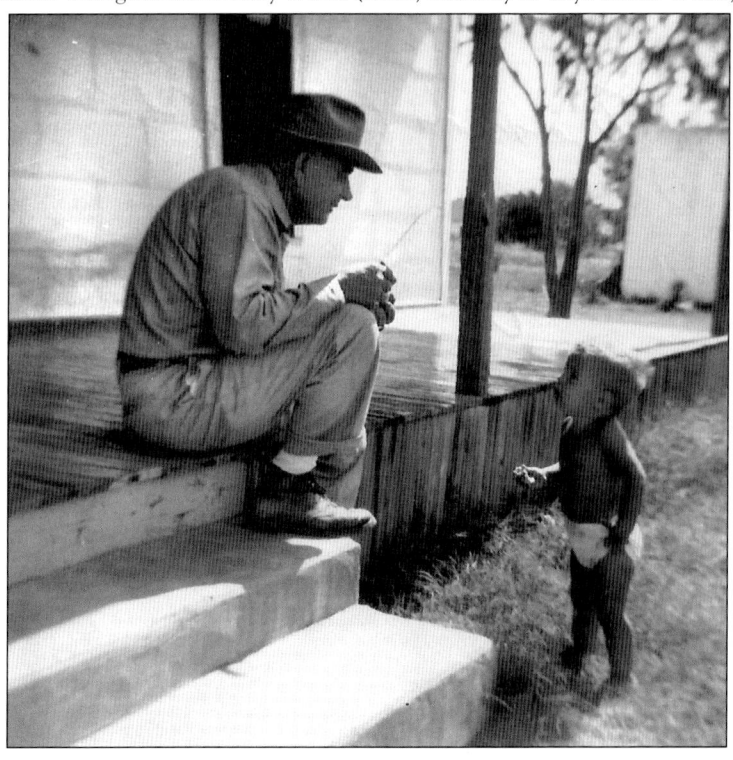

From left to right, Bobby Joe Peterson, Cozette Pinion, and Bill Peterson are sitting in front of the home of Cozette's parents, Emmett "Gabe" and Nellie Pinion. Pinion was nicknamed "Gabe" because he always headed for home when newsman Gabriel Heater was on the radio. During World War II, Heater would start a broadcast by saying, "There's good news tonight." The Peterson boys were two of the sons of Carl and Addie Peterson. All of the children loved their adult neighbor, Alma Mason, because she allowed them to play her pipe organ. (Courtesy of Cozette Harris.)

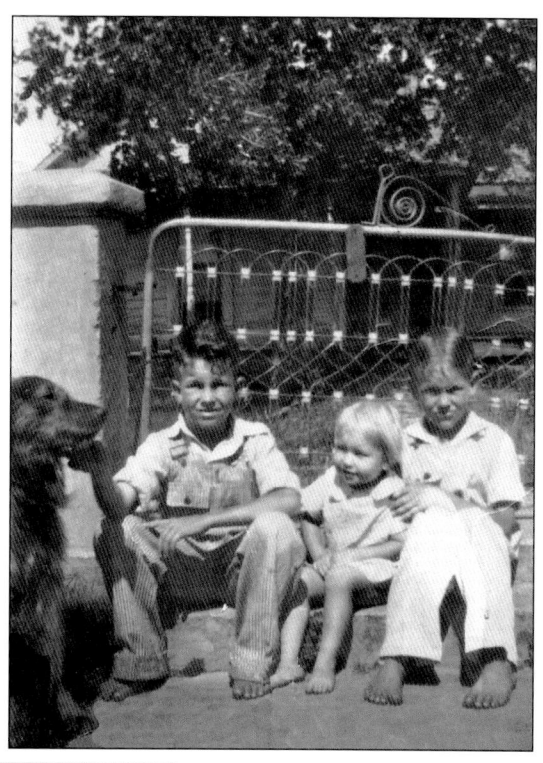

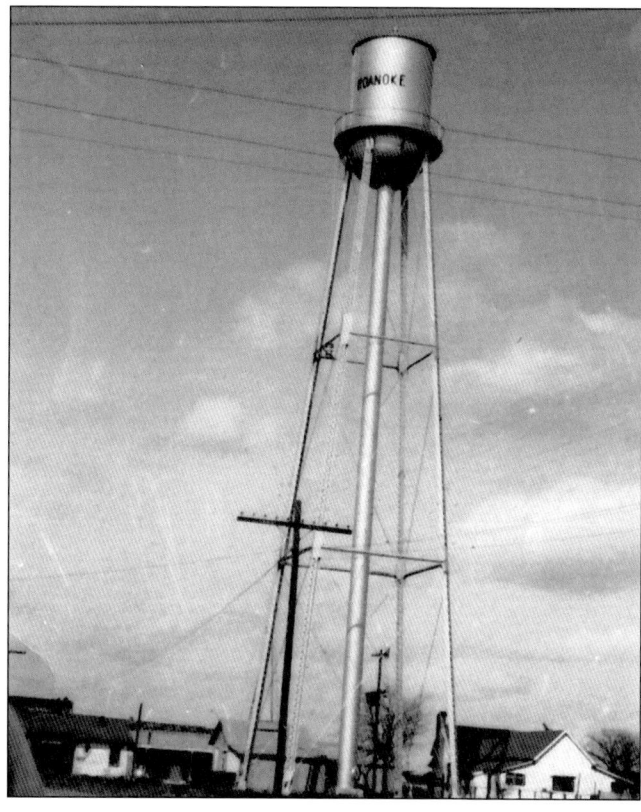

Hise Seagraves Jr., a local historian, took this 1950s picture of the water tower, which was built in the 1930s to take the place of a smaller, wooden tank. This tower, though no longer in use, still stands at the northeast corner of Oak and Main Streets. There were many photographs made from the top of this tower. The younger crowd had a good time climbing the tower, much to the chagrin of their parents. (Courtesy of HSC.)

63

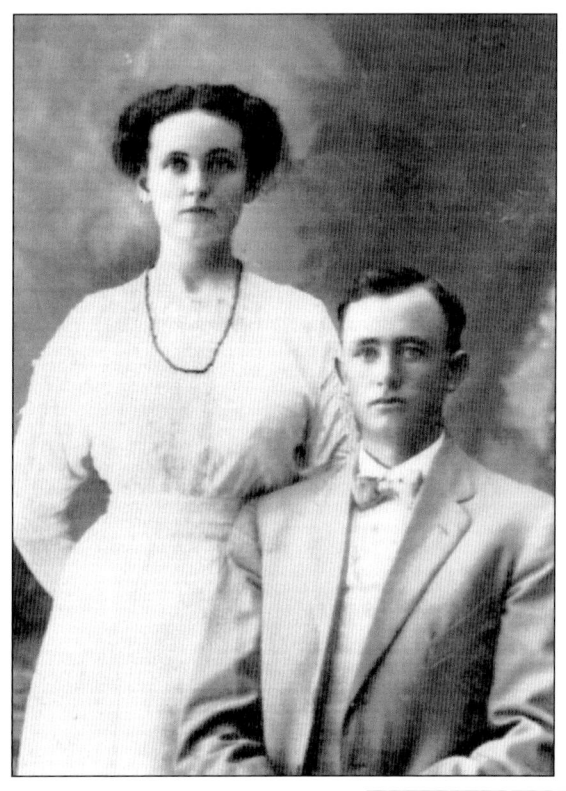

Zera Ballew and Ernest Manire are shown on their wedding day, July 11, 1907. The Manires owned a grocery on Oak Street. They were the parents of seven children, who all graduated from college. Learning was important, as evidenced by the fact that five Manire children were connected to education. Nancy, Lois, Phillip, and William were all educators, and their sister Katherine was a school nurse (Courtesy of William Manire.)

Obie "Dub" Wheeler, shown in front of his 1938 International dump truck, was the son of Ora "Buck" and Mineola Wheeler. Obie was one of six children who grew up on the outskirts of Roanoke. Obie had two additional siblings; however, they died as infants. The family lived on Highway 10, which was once the main road from Fort Worth to Denton. The younger Wheeler served in the army in World War II and remembers that troops celebrated the end of the war by firing their guns in the air. The gunshots caused inadvertent injuries, so as a prudent man, Wheeler departed to his tent when the celebration became too boisterous. (Courtesy of Obie "Dub" Wheeler.)

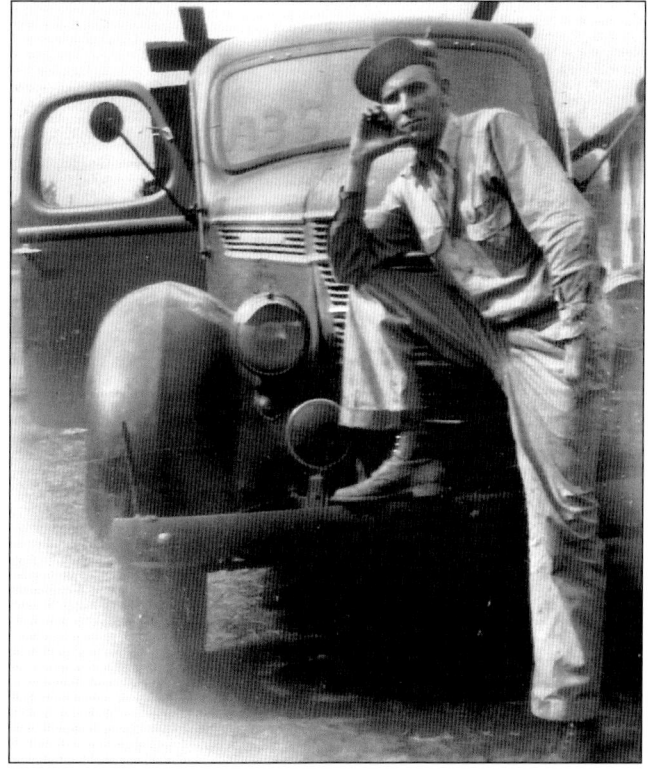

Juanna Jean Pinion and Bobby Ross Smith both worked in Washington, D.C.; Juanna for the treasury department and Bobby for the Federal Bureau of Investigation. Juanna and Bobby married and moved to Roanoke. Bobby served as mayor, and Juanna Jean worked at the post office for 20 years. (Courtesy of Cozette Harris.)

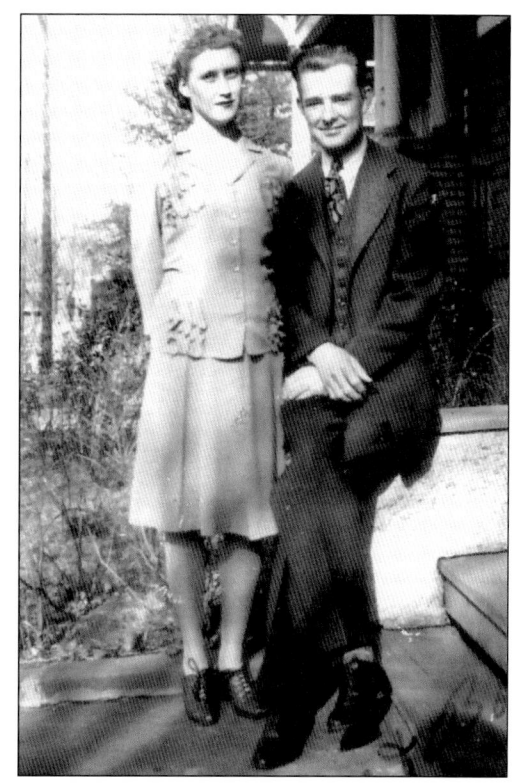

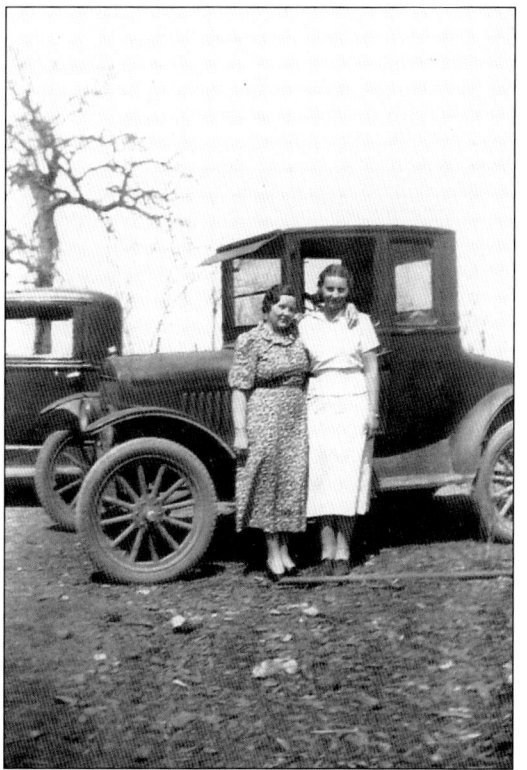

Madge Luttrell (left) and Mary Luttrell Carpenter are shown here posing in front of a vintage car. Mary was a talented athlete as a young woman and a well-known historian, particularly with the Medlin Cemetery. Mary's mother was Mittie Ann Medlin, and her grandfather was James Medlin, who established the cemetery. Madge was married to Marvin Luttrell, Mary's brother, who was in charge of maintenance at Northwest High School and was also a longtime school bus driver. Northwest students honored Marvin by having a yearbook dedicated to him. (Courtesy of the Mary Carpenter Estate.)

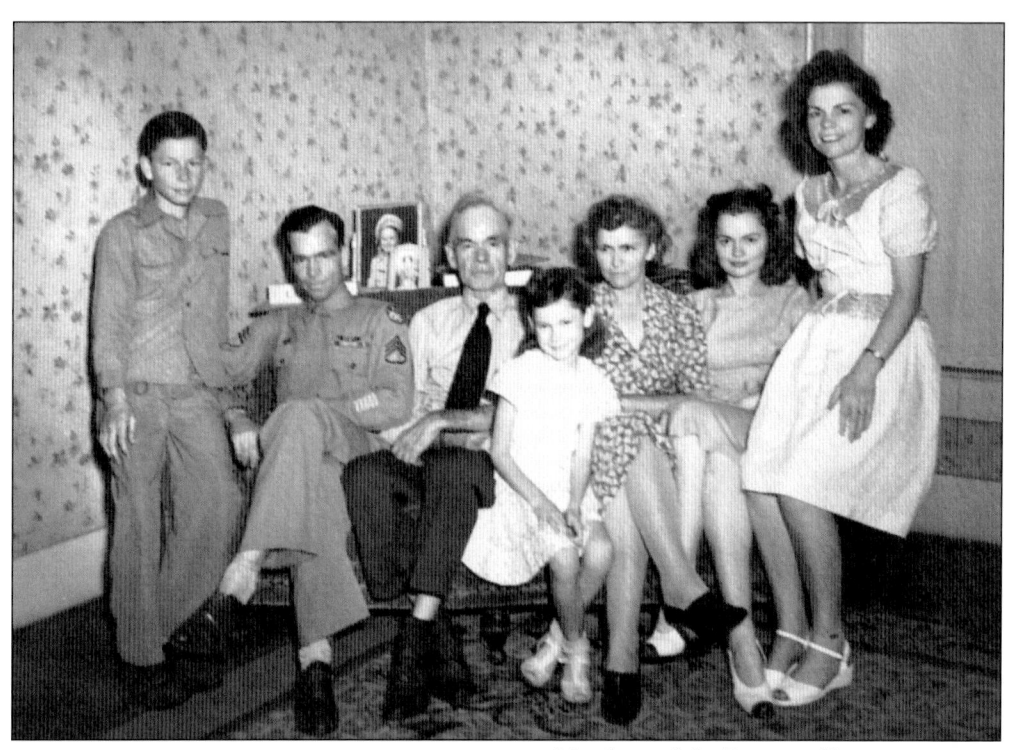

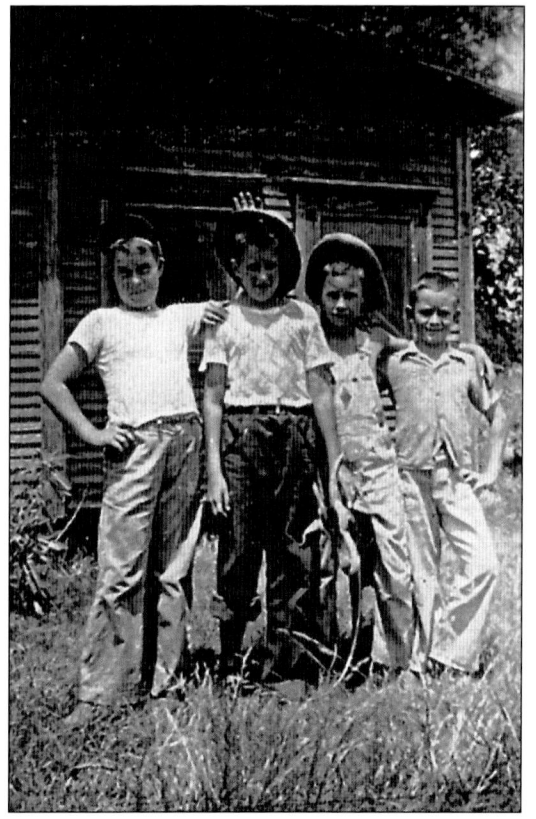

Members of the Raymond Lewis Clark family are shown in this 1940s photograph. From left to right are John Henry, Ben Warder, Raymond, Mary Frank, Bessie, Peggy Louise, and Lucy Clark. This picture was taken at the home of Bessie's mother, Della Sandifer Yancey, who lived in Denton. The Yancey family migrated from Kentucky in the mid-1800s, and the Yancey children were all born in Roanoke, as were the Clark youngsters. (Courtesy of Ann Clark.)

In this c. 1942 photograph, the carefree boys of summer are, from left to right, Bob Haynie, David Vanderpool, Richard Graham, and James E. Sheaner. David Vanderpool became a doctor and has recently been involved with ensuring that medical equipment that is replaced in the United States but still in good condition can be sent to underdeveloped countries. (Courtesy of RVCM.)

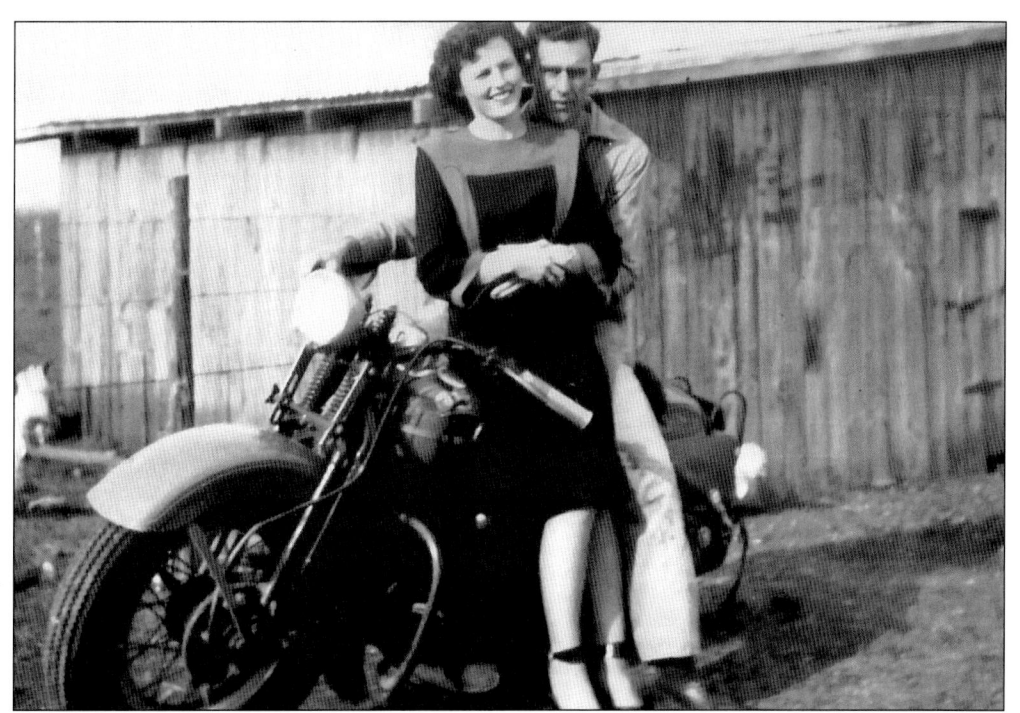

Vertalee Brock and John Coleman are shown sitting on John's motorcycle. These two were classmates who married shortly after World War II. The picture below shows Vertalee and John Coleman on his newer Honda motorcycle. The Colemans have not slowed down much from their early days, as both are active volunteers in the church and community, and they still hit the open road, though in these days it is in the comfort of a fifth-wheel trailer. Both Colemans have been stalwarts of the community, as were their parents before them. Vertalee worked as a teacher in the Northwest School district, and John worked for the Chicago Rock Island and Pacific Railroad as an engineer. (Both, courtesy of Vertalee and John Coleman.)

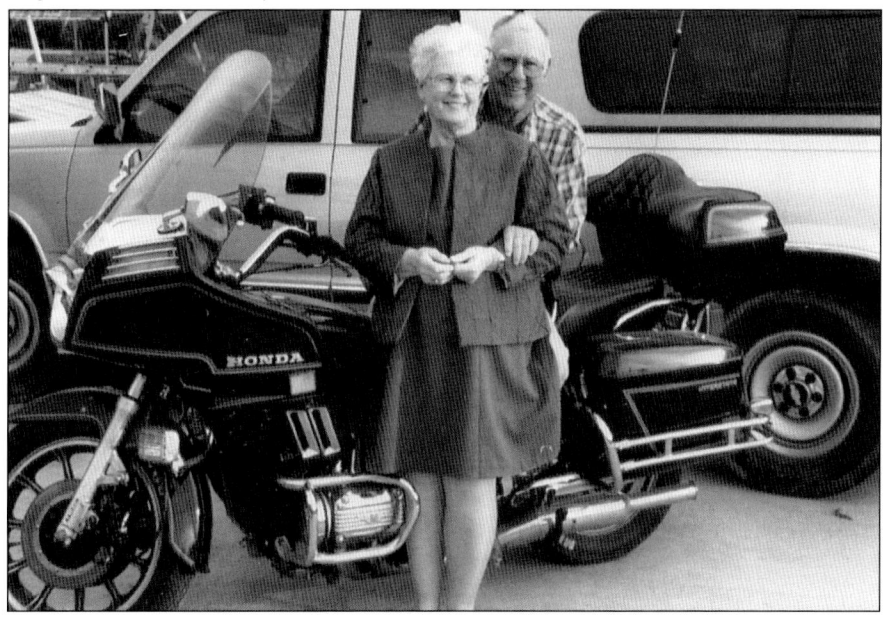

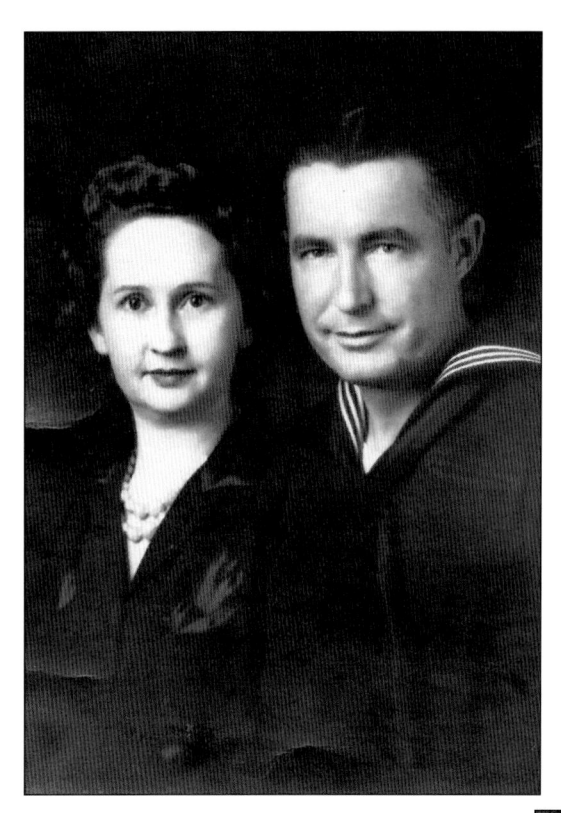

Norma and Charles Redwine lived on Rusk Street in the area originally platted as the town of Roanoke. Charles was serving in World War II when he met Norma Taylor on a Continental Trailways bus as he was coming home. They later married, and their son James was born in August 1946. (Courtesy of James Redwine.)

Sisters-in-law Ina Knowles (left), holding baby Roxie, and Mary Wheeler holding Doris, are pictured on an outing to Fort Worth. The shoppers in the background are unidentified. Fort Worth was a popular destination for the citizens of Roanoke. In fact, many residents commuted there to work, and it was a favorite place for shopping and entertainment. (Courtesy of Obie "Dub" Wheeler.)

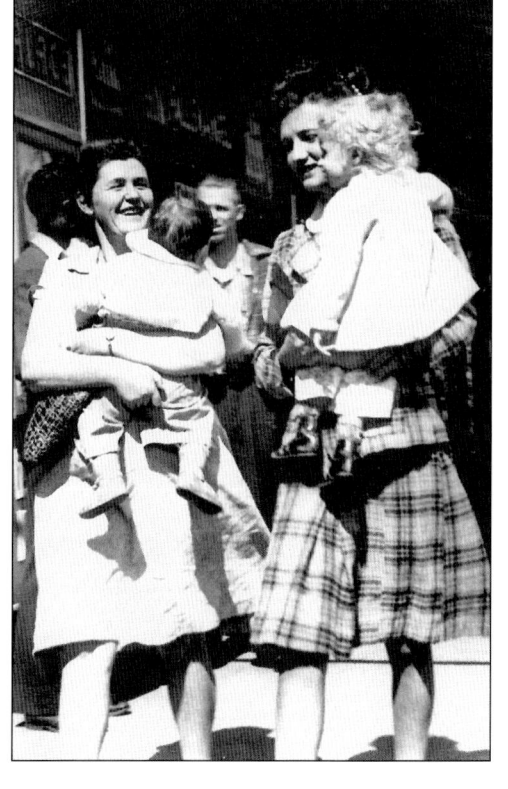

Brothers Gilbert L. Parish (left) and Joe Parish are shown standing in front of a vintage vehicle, owned by their family. Their parents were Thomas and Edith Parish, who moved to Roanoke in 1931. Gilbert joined the navy prior to the move, but Joe lived on the Parish farm and continued to work there even after his graduation in Roanoke. Gilbert, who never married, was killed in a logging accident in Oregon in 1948. (Courtesy of Bonnie Parish McKee.)

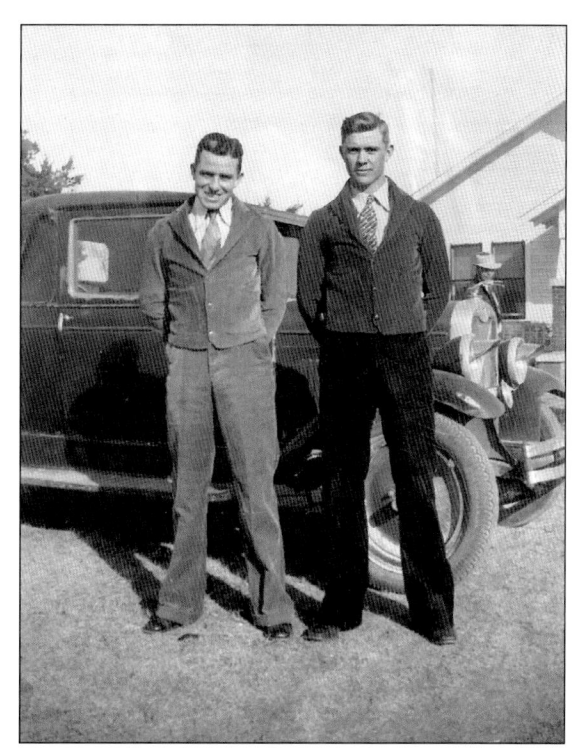

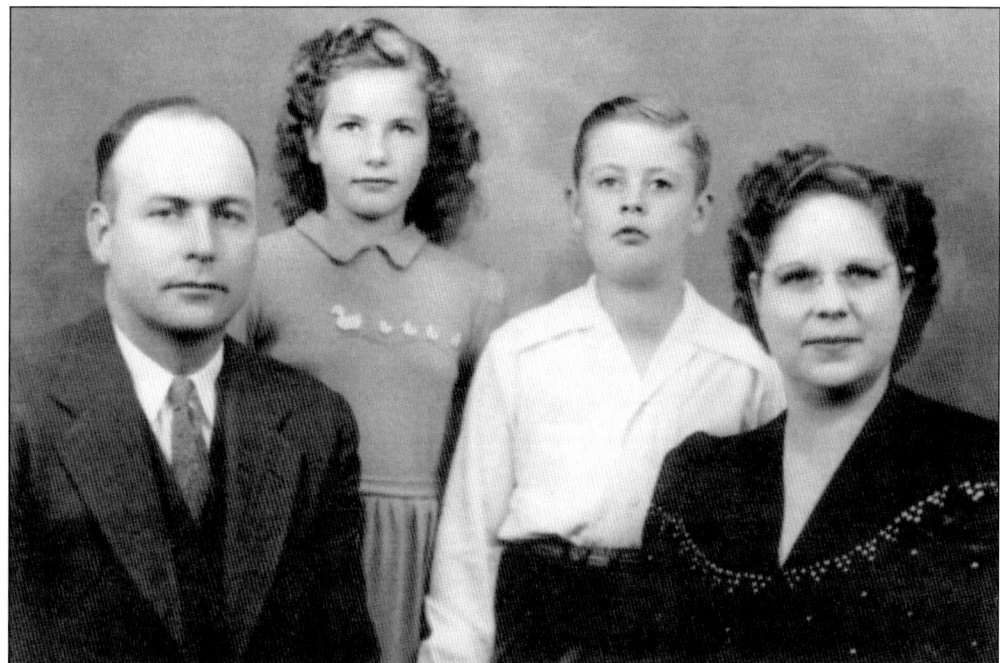

Pictured in this c. 1948 photograph are, from left to right, Terrell (T. W.) King Jr., daughter Genelia, son Terrell III, and his wife, Carrie Lee. Terrell Jr. owned a plumbing business in the building now housing the Prairie House Restaurant in Roanoke, as well as an insurance agency in Denton. The elder King was honored by having a road named for him, which is east of Trophy Club. Terrell III is a well-known businessman in Denton. (Courtesy of Terrell W. King III.)

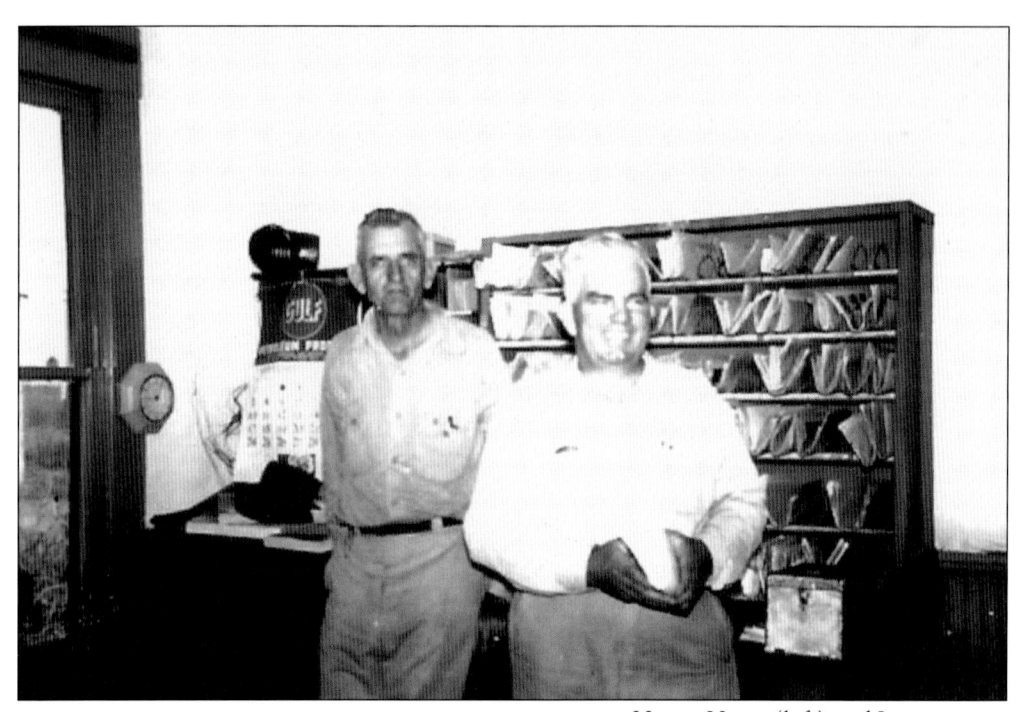

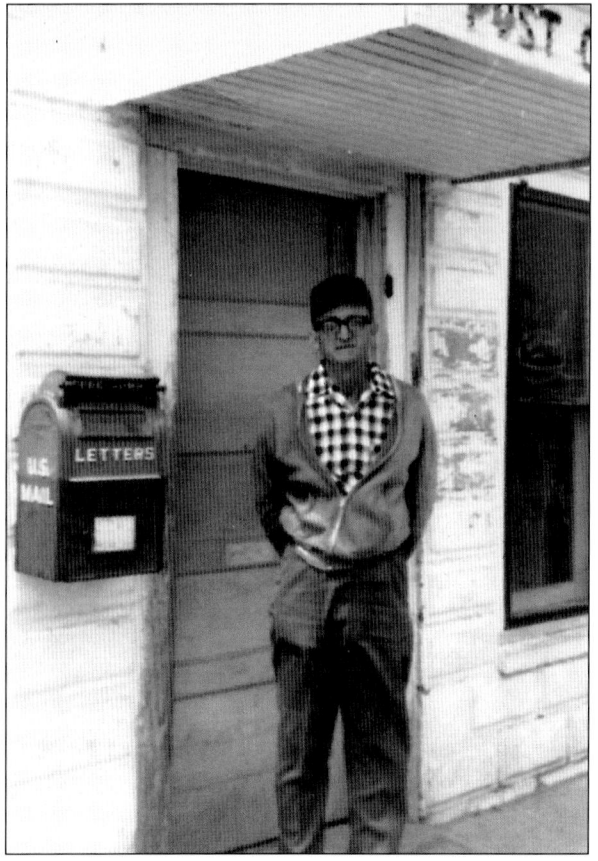

Henry Howe (left) and Lynn Turner, shown above inside the old Oak Street Post Office, were rural mail carriers for the Roanoke area. George Jones, pictured at left in front of the post office, built in 1910, became postmaster and succeeded Ida Cowan, who had been appointed for life by Theodore Roosevelt. Cowan, speaking to a group gathered to celebrate her retirement, said that she got tired of robberies and no parking, so she built a new post office, which is the building shown. The interior of this building is shown in the above photograph. (Above, courtesy of Henry "Mc" Howe; left, courtesy of HSC.)

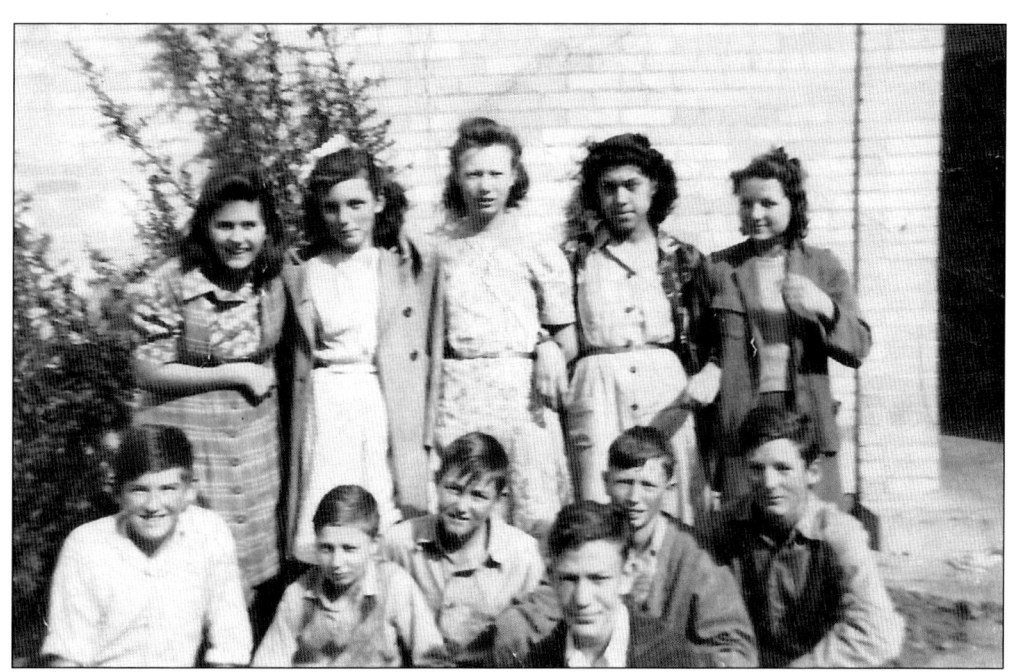

These youngsters are gathered outside of their school. They are, from left to right, (first row) Bob Brigman, Al Steele, Bob Blackburn, Walter Howell, and two unidentified; (second row) Alma Wright, Caroline Turner, Ruby Nell Roberts, ? Garcia, and Stella Faye Brock. (Courtesy of Marjorie Sturdivant Thomas.)

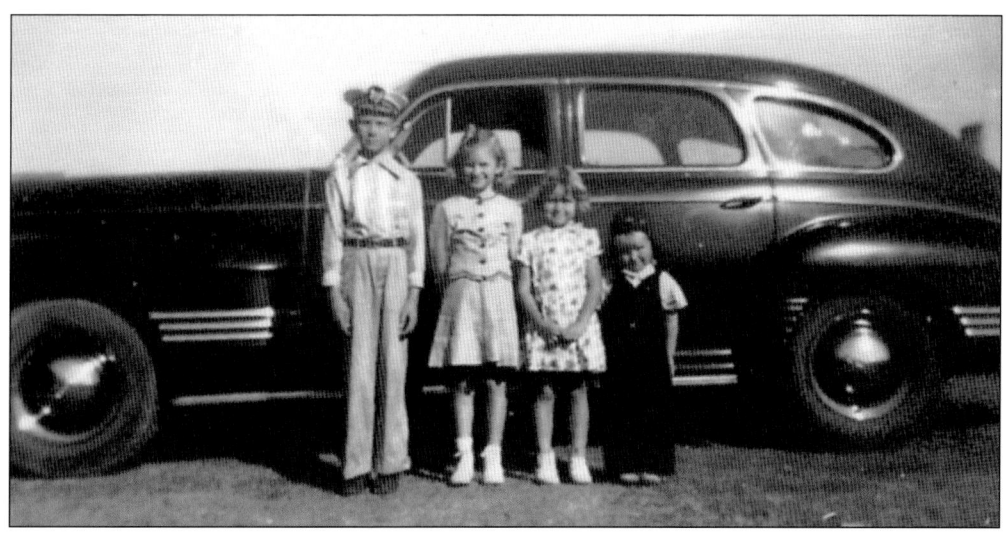

These youngsters are, from left to right, Gene, Elaine, Vondal, and Hugh Brown, the children of Dorothy and Hugh Brown. The elder Browns came to Roanoke in 1938. Dorothy Brown was a rural mail carrier for the post office. Hugh Sr. worked in Fort Worth. All of the children attended school and grew to adulthood in the community. Dorothy and her son, Gene, with his wife, Anita, still own homes in the area. (Courtesy of Dorothy Brown.)

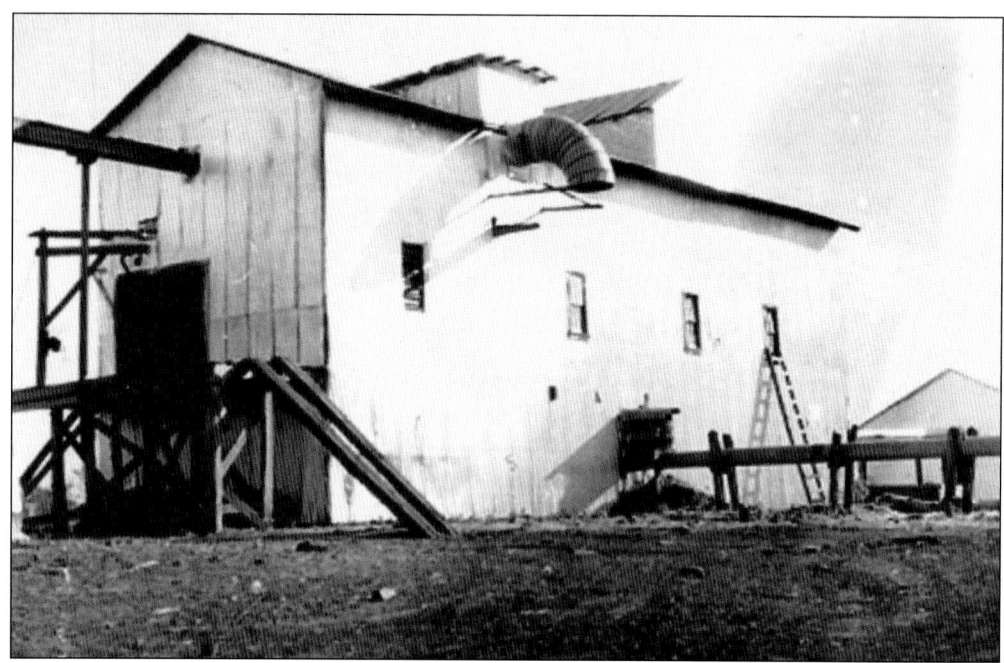

The grain elevator, pictured in this c. 1953 photograph, was built in the early 1900s and was one of the businesses located west of the railroad tracks around what is now Highway 377. It was constructed for Bewley Mills and was still in operation in the 1950s, with Al Mason and his son, Leroy, in charge of operations. (Courtesy of HSC.)

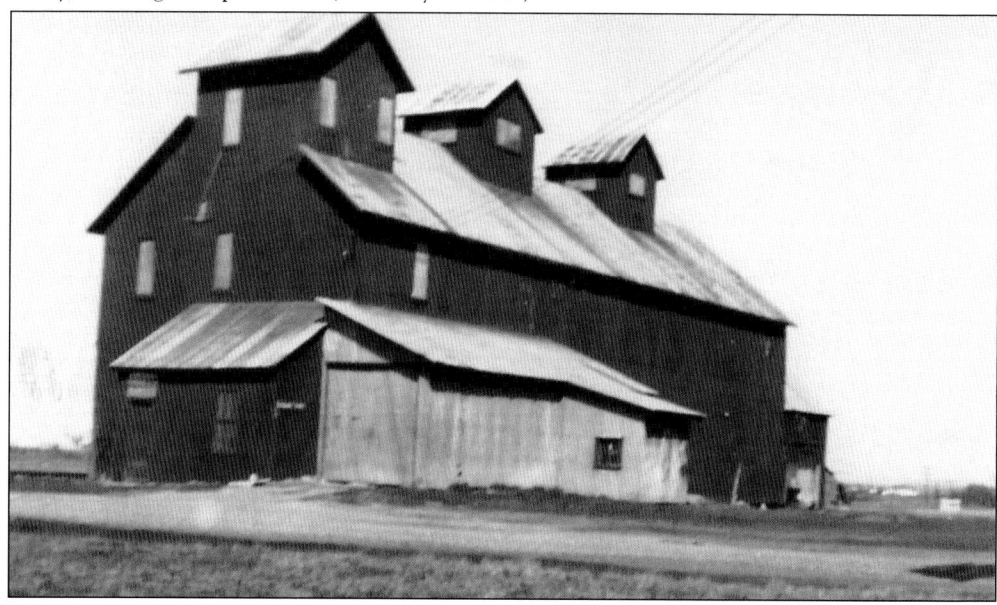

There were several gins in Roanoke. The first one was located approximately a quarter of a mile east of Roanoke. This first gin burned, and several more were then located west of the railroad. Bob Carruth and Jess Medlin owned these gins until Carruth closed his down. The Medlin gin exploded when the boiler went dry. Once the workers realized it was dry, they added water to it, which caused an explosion that killed Sam Seagraves, Clint Merritt, and Charles Cleveland. There were several other men injured, including Dave Ottinger, who lost his arm. (Courtesy of HSC.)

Three
OUT AND ABOUT

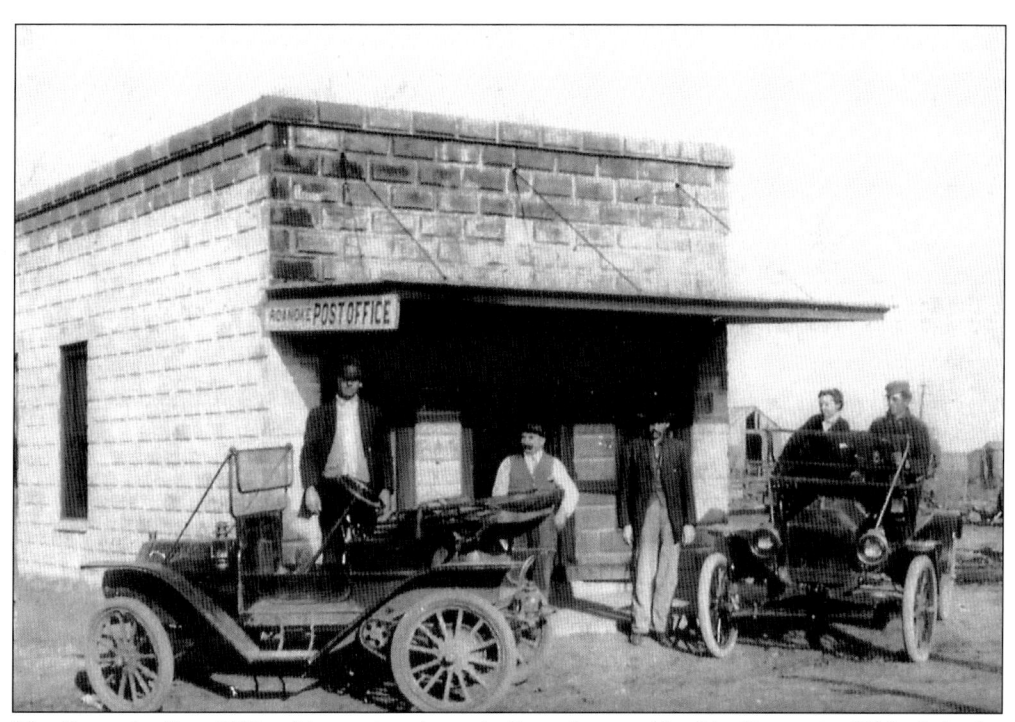

The Roanoke Post Office (shown here) was built and owned by Ida Cowan in 1910 while she was the postmistress. She succeeded her father, William, in the job. The people shown here are, from left to right, Clint Cowan (a rural mail carrier) with his Studebaker, James Seagraves (a cobbler), Charles Fanning (a Route 3 driver, who delivered the mail by horse and buggy), and Ida Cowan and Henry Howe in a Ford Model T, which he bought in 1912. The post office building is still standing; however, having a second story added has significantly altered it. (Courtesy of Inez and Henry "Mc" Howe.)

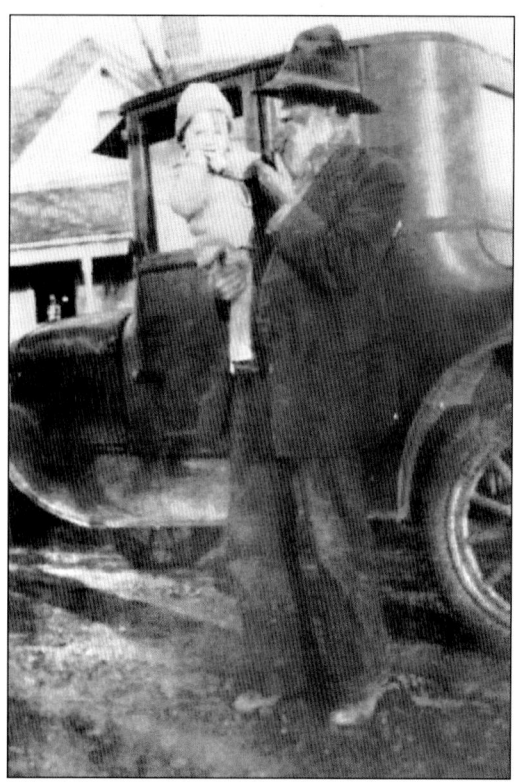

John Henry Strickland is shown holding his grandson Jack Crouch, who was the son of Margie and Robert Crouch. John Henry always wore a long beard, much to the delight of the young boys in Roanoke who would tease him by saying, "billy goat, billy goat baaa," which resulted in John Henry pretending to chase them. John Henry lived on Rusk Street next to the Union Church. His grandson John Henry Ragsdale was named after him. He now has great grandchildren, great-great grandchildren, and great-great-great grandchildren living in Roanoke. (Courtesy of Emily Ragsdale.)

These young girls seem to have overloaded their trusty steed. Pictured from left to right are Clara Coleman, Mary Reynolds, Una Brand, Ruth Reynolds, Illene Harris, and Nellie Strickland. Later in life, Una Brand married Hugh Jenkins, who was one of the most influential citizens in Roanoke. No information is known about the patient animal. (Courtesy of Alberta Lincecum.)

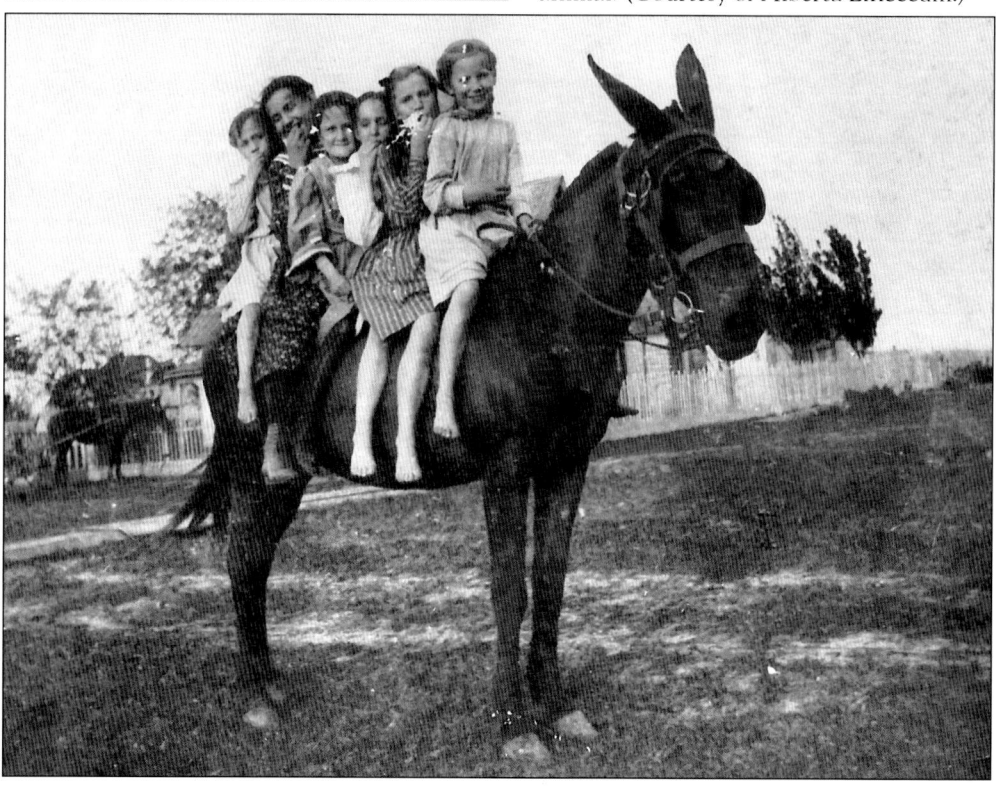

These unidentified boys are ready to participate in a sack race, one of the perennial events at Trade Days in Roanoke. They are lined up across Oak Street not far from the building that was the Silver Spur Saloon. The building in the background, at the left of the two-story saloon, is Hugh Jenkins's Hardware, which was built in 1916. (Courtesy of Alberta Lincecum.)

Pictured in the 1940s, these men were the rural mail carriers. Clint Cowan (left) stands in front of his 1930s Chevrolet, and Henry Howe is in front of his 1944 V8 Ford, which had unusual door openings to the front, nicknamed "suicide doors." At one time, Cowan was the city judge, and Howe was the city secretary. The building on the right behind the men is the post office on Oak Street, and the building in the background at left is the Lassen blacksmith shop, which is still standing and is in its original condition. Eric Lassen later operated a garage in this same building. (Courtesy of Inez and Henry "Mc" Howe.)

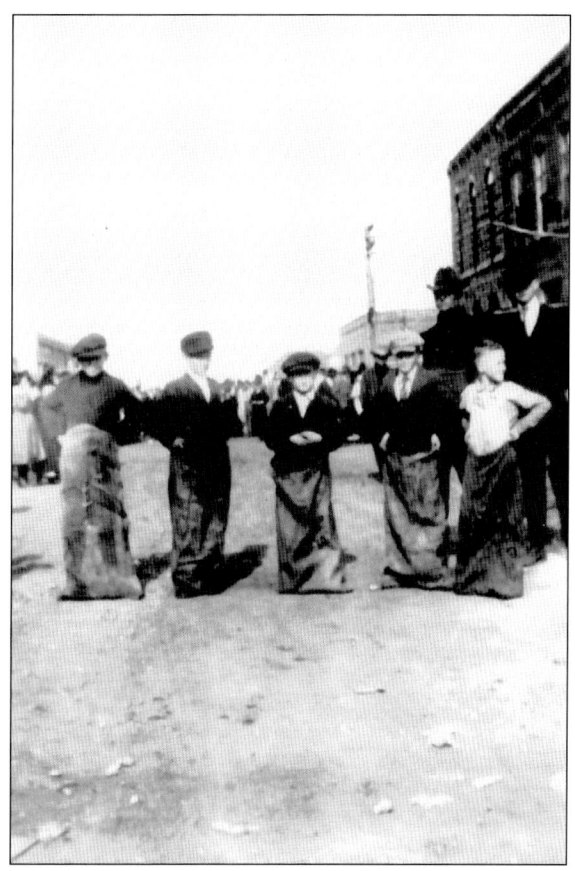

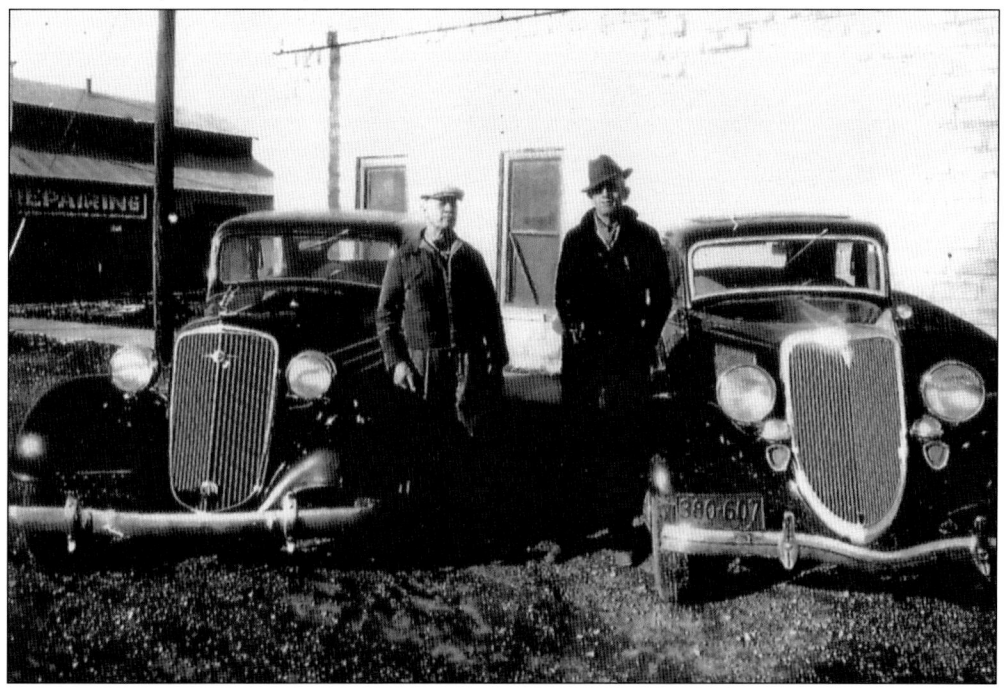

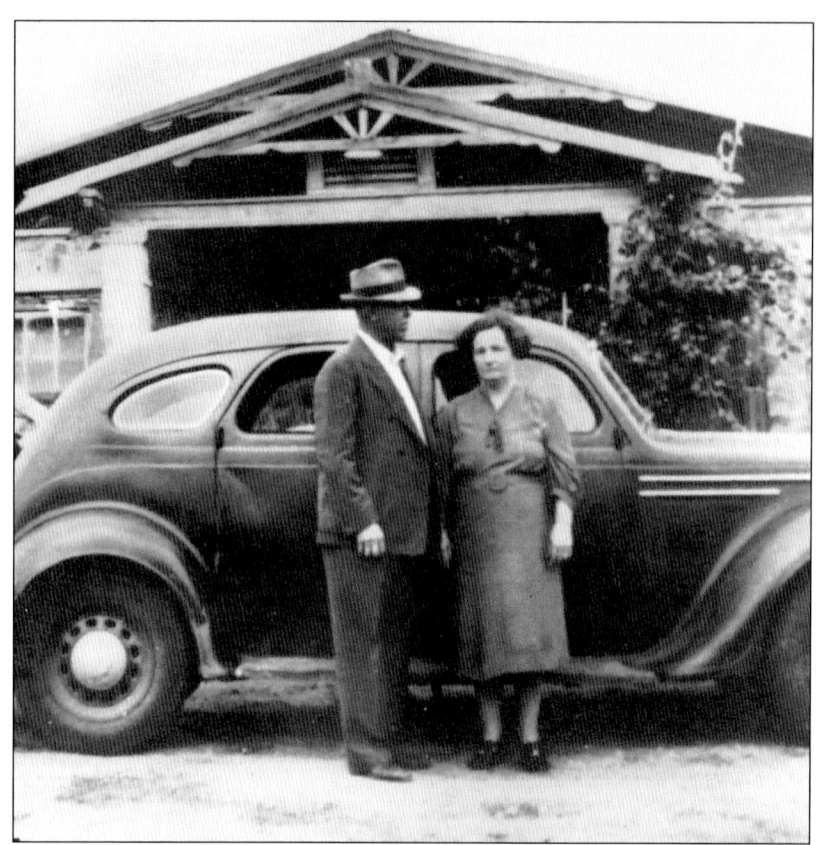

Shown here are Ora (left) and Mineola Wheeler in front of the home they fashioned from the open-air tabernacle where religious services were once held. The Wheelers owned a garage on Highway 10. (Courtesy of Obie "Dub" Wheeler.)

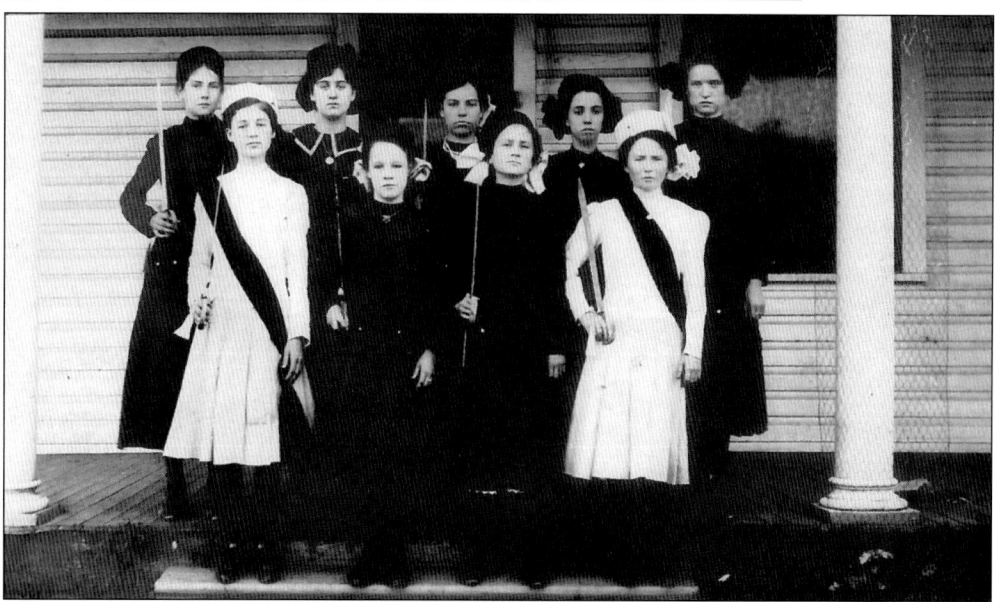

According to the daughter of Una Brand, shown in this picture, these young women may have been part of a drill team or the band. The members are, from left to right, (first row) Ruby Fanning, Lena Norton, Una Brand, and Avis Horton; (second row) Frances Howe, Babe Stump, Johanna Lassen, Nina Cade, and Gladys Melton. (Courtesy of Alberta Lincecum.)

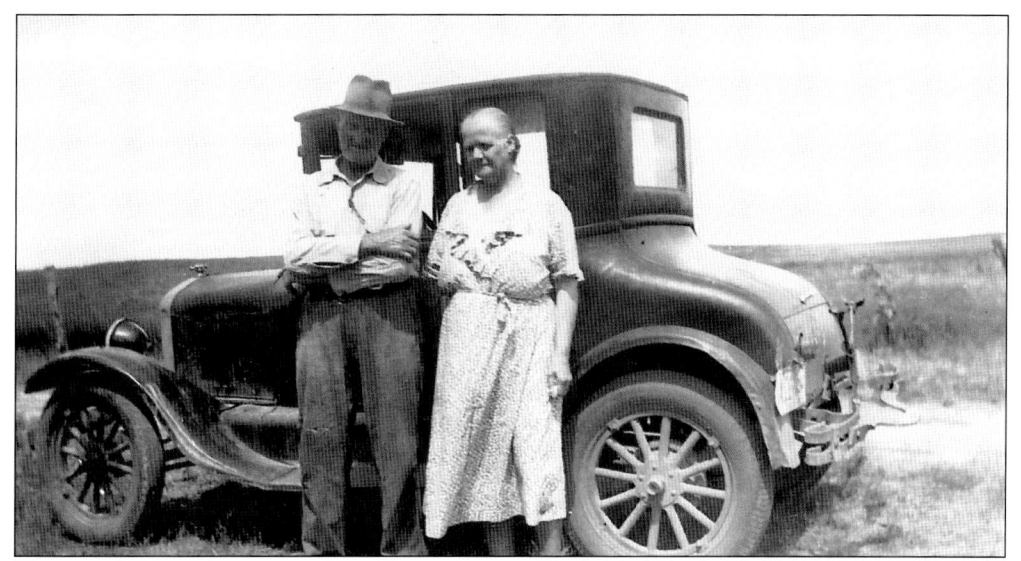

Charles Harvey and his wife, Lyda Ada Bogart, are shown standing in front of their automobile in this c. 1940 photograph. Charles came to Roanoke in 1910 in a covered wagon from Missouri. After his first wife, Elizabeth "Bettie" Susan, died, he sent for Lyda Ada to become his wife. They lived on the Cartwright farm 1 mile south of Roanoke, and he sharecropped 100 acres. He raised cotton, corn, and wheat—some for the animals, some for seed for the next year, and some to sell. He had a well on the property to ensure water was available for the animals and crops, but he had a horse and wagon with a wooden water tank that he would drive into Roanoke to get drinking water from a well behind the Oak Street saloon building. (Courtesy of Emily Ragsdale.)

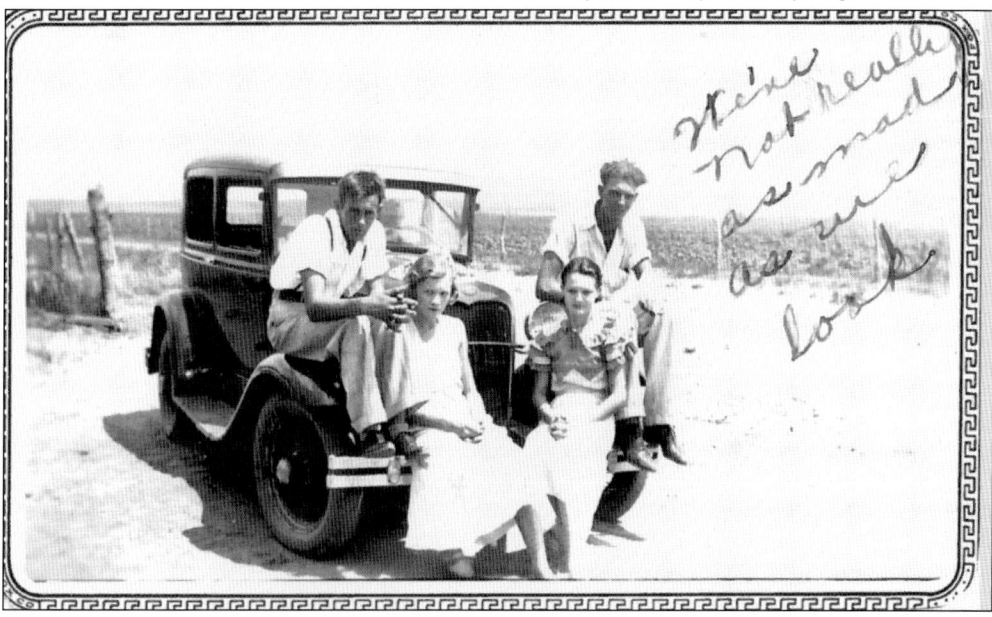

Outlaws Bonnie and Clyde were visitors to the Roanoke area; however, these look-alike couples are John Henry and Emily Ragsdale on the left fender and Emily's brother, Manuel, and his wife, Dora, on the right. Emily and Manuel were the children of Charles and Lyda Ada Bogart. Emily and John Henry were both born in Roanoke and were high school sweethearts, who were married for 52 years before his death. (Courtesy of Emily Ragsdale.)

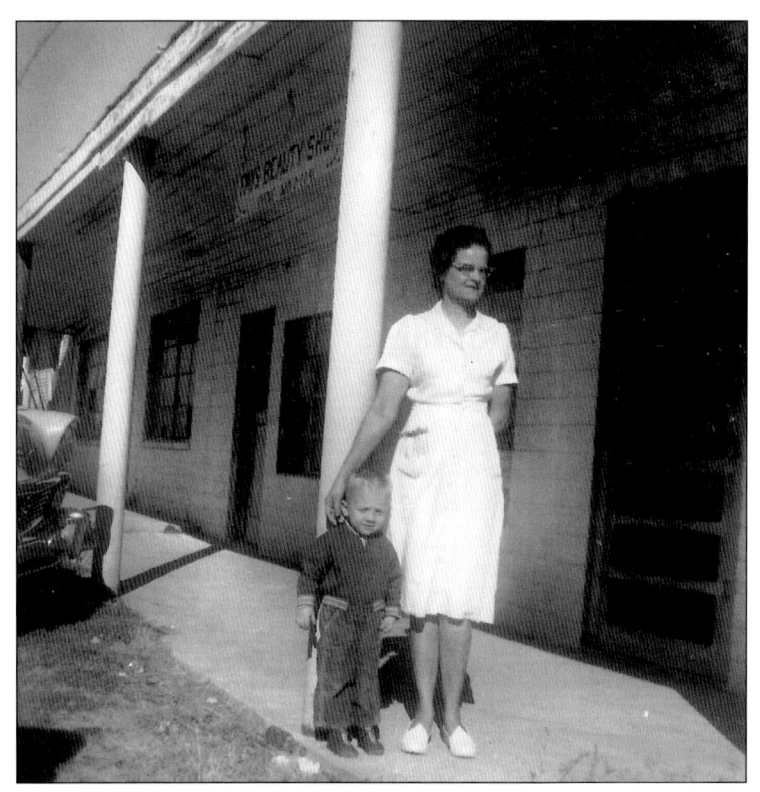

Faye McPherson has a protective hand on Hise Seagraves Jr. in front of the beauty shop McPherson ran on Main Street in Roanoke. Hise Jr. had a coin business inside his father's dry-goods store in later years. Faye was married to Watt McPherson and was an active member of the community. When he was older, Hise Jr. also had a keen interest in the history of Roanoke; many of his photographs are reproduced in this book. (Courtesy of HSC.)

James and Louise Oldham came to Roanoke in 1954. James worked in Keller at a machine shop, and Louise worked in the Keller school. Later she went to work at Steele's Country Market and then at Burrus Grocery. She was also a seamstress who did sewing and alterations for many women in Roanoke. They lived in their Travis Street home in Roanoke for 54 years. Louise died in 2009 at the age of 95. (Courtesy of Windel Oldham.)

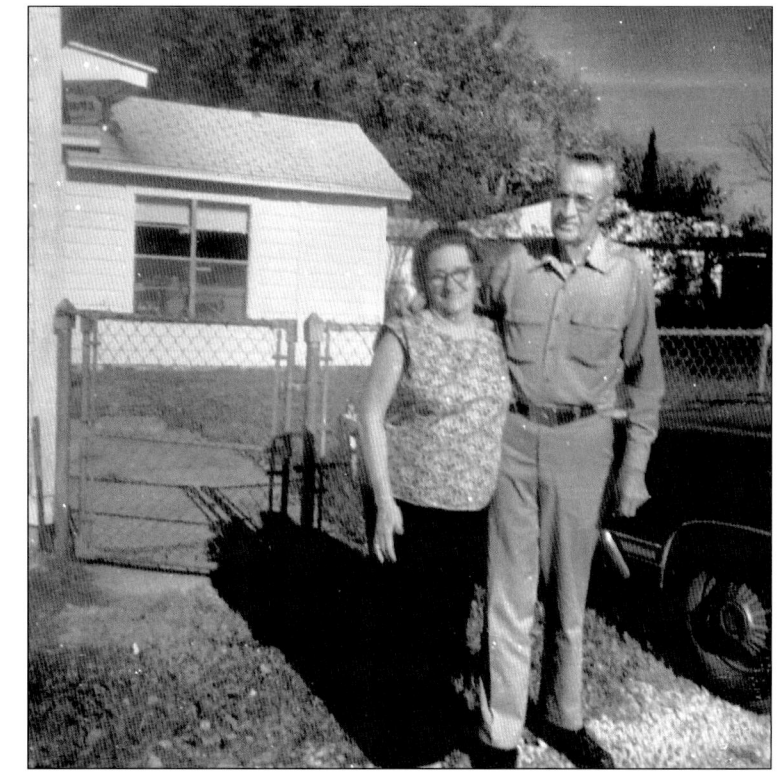

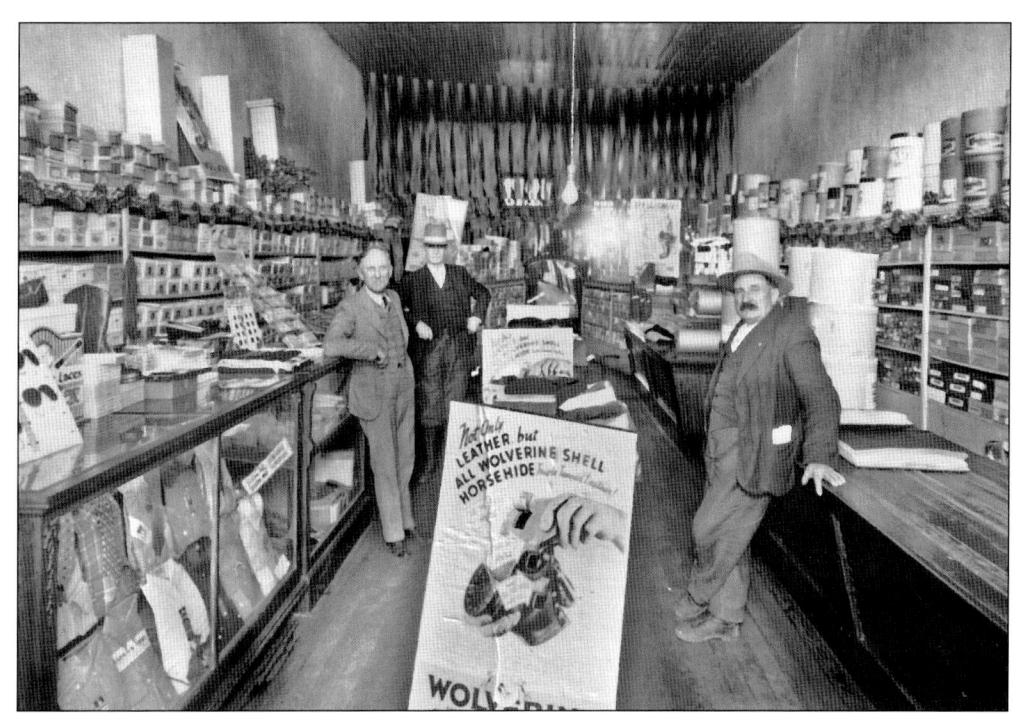

Hise Seagraves Sr. (left) is shown in his dry-goods store on Oak Street; however, the other two men are unidentified. Seagraves came to Roanoke with his father, Byram, arriving with siblings James, Henry, Lucy Ann, and Amanda Susan. Seagraves worked as a cowhand at Berry Hood's cattle ranch as a youngster, and then gravitated to Smith's Dry Goods Store. He also was an officer at the Continental State Bank. (Courtesy of HSC.)

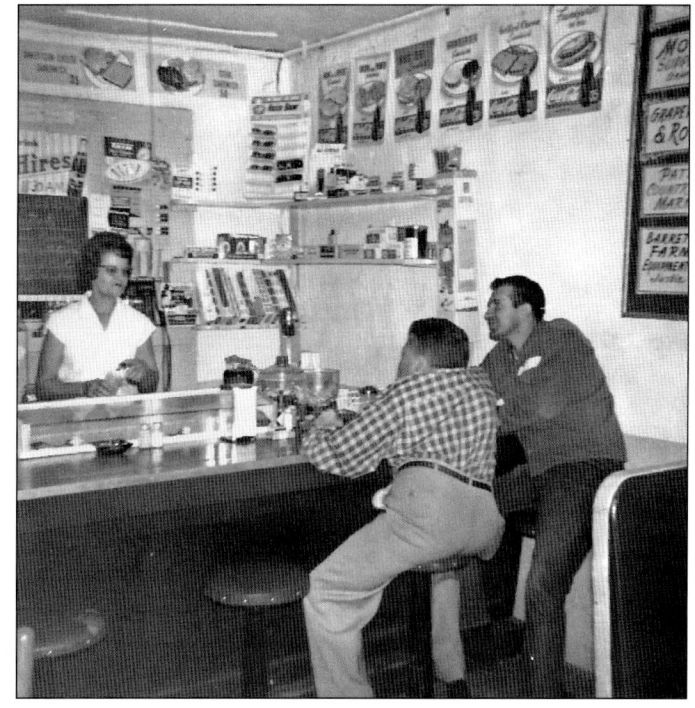

Discussing the day's events in the cafe McPherson ran on Oak Street are, from left to right, Bobby Fay McPherson, Grant Owens, and Kermit Jackson. McPherson and her husband, Watt, had a farm on Roanoke-Haslet Road, and Grant Owens managed the Roanoke Credit Union. (Courtesy of HSC.)

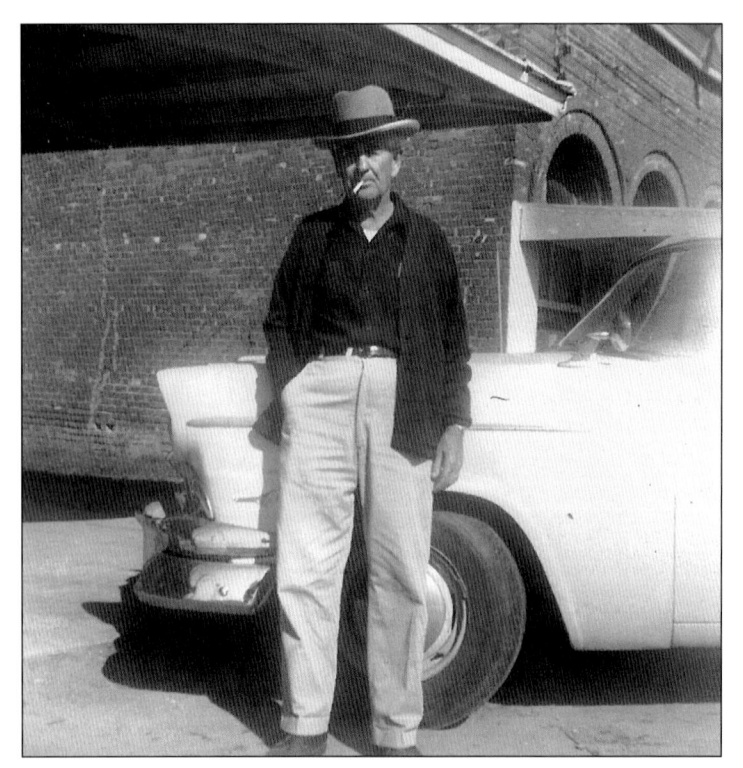

Claud Raibourn, shown here, lived with his parents in the Pacific Hotel, which they owned. It was a wooden, 15-room structure located on the northwest corner of Main and Oak Streets. The Pickett family had previously owned the hotel. The structure was damaged by fire in Roanoke's early days, and it was remodeled into a family home by Claud. After the death of his mother, Claud lived there with his wife, Beulah, and daughter, Mozelle. In recent years, the old hotel has been moved to a new location and once again renovated. (Courtesy of HSC.)

Pictured from left to right, Ritchie Simmons, Hise Seagraves Sr., and Ernest Manire had stores adjoining each other on Oak Street. Simmons had a variety store, Seagraves operated a dry-goods store catering to men, and Manire owned a grocery store that was established in 1916, which was in the same location for 49 years when it closed upon Manire's death. (Courtesy of HSC.)

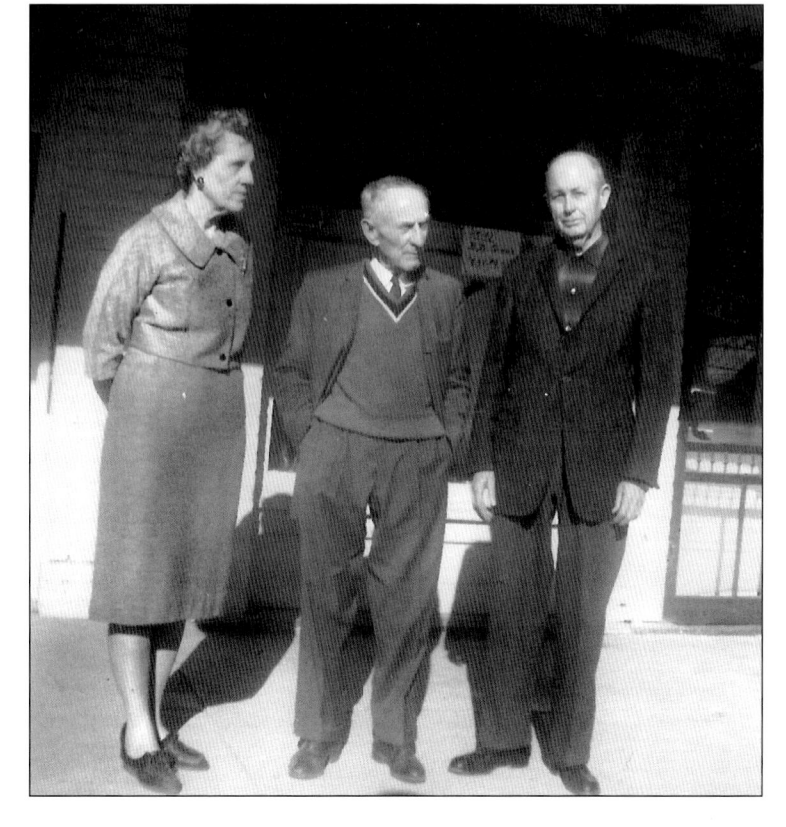

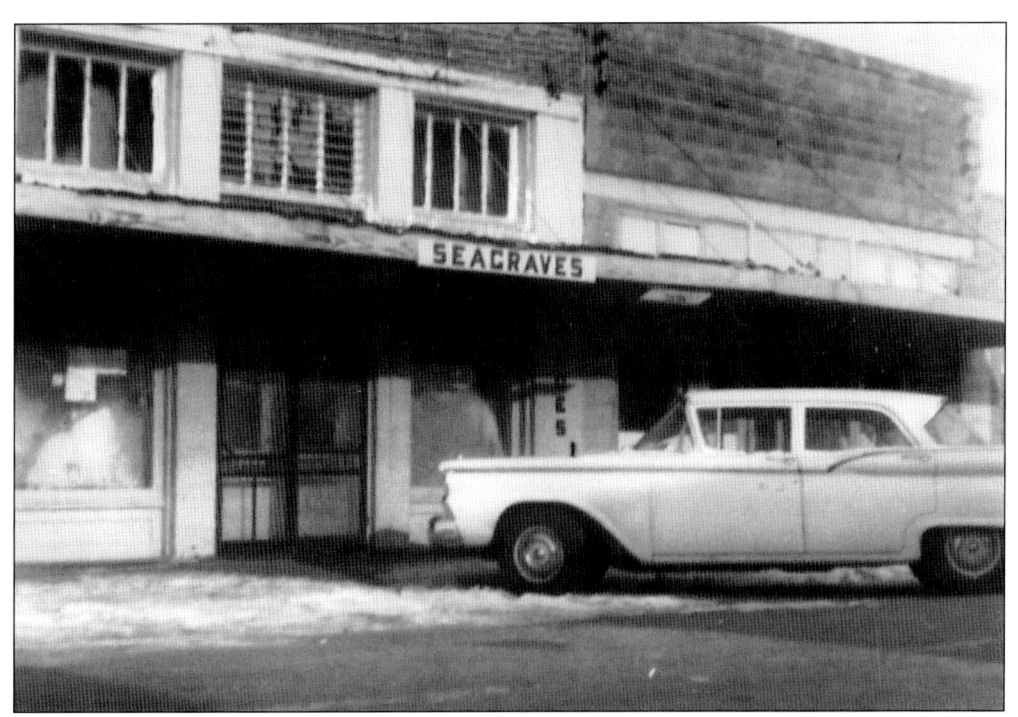

Hise Seagraves Sr. was a leading citizen of Roanoke. He came to Roanoke in 1885 with his father, Byram, who soon began to practice medicine. Hise went to Tennessee to pursue a medical education; however, he returned after one semester. The fact that he had only nine months of formal education may have hampered his success in medicine, but he had a successful dry-goods store, pictured above in 1962, after returning to Roanoke. In almost everything else he did, he excelled. (Courtesy of HSC.)

Ida Cade, a daughter of William G. Patterson, owned a store next to Hise Seagraves Sr. for more than 40 years. Her husband, John R. Cade, sold caskets in the back of her store. Patterson owned the store previously, but he turned it over to his daughter, Ida, when he returned to Missouri. Cade's Dry Goods was later sold to Ritchie Simmons. (Courtesy of HSC.)

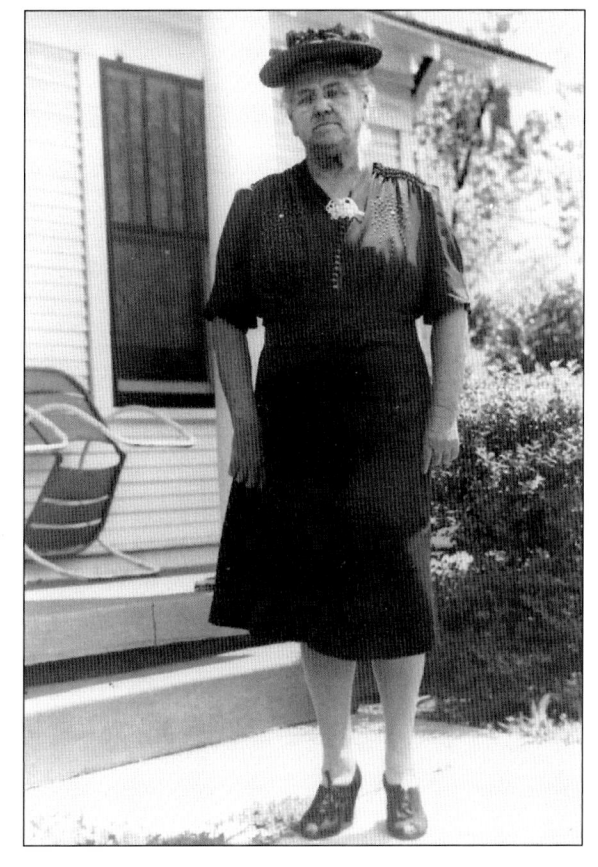

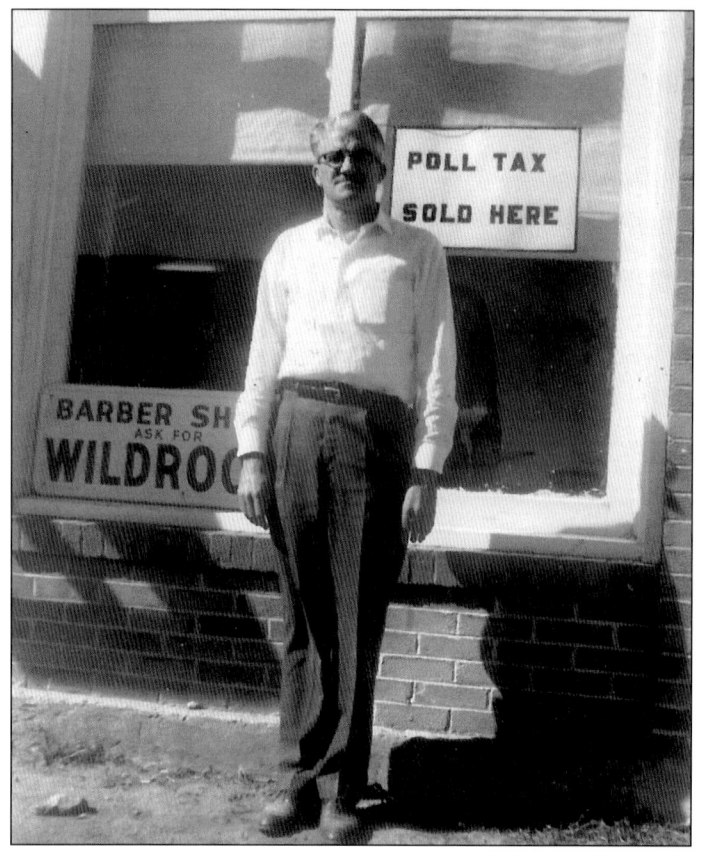

John "Toots" Tidwell is shown standing in front of his barbershop on Oak Street, which prominently displays a poll-tax sign in the window. Tidwell was not only a barber, but he also served as a postmaster, school board member, and mayor of Roanoke. In addition, he served on the board of the Northwest Bank in Roanoke, and most recently a school was named for him in the Northwest School District. Tidwell (below, at far left) is shown inside his shop with some of his customers. (Left, courtesy of HSC; below, courtesy of RVCM.)

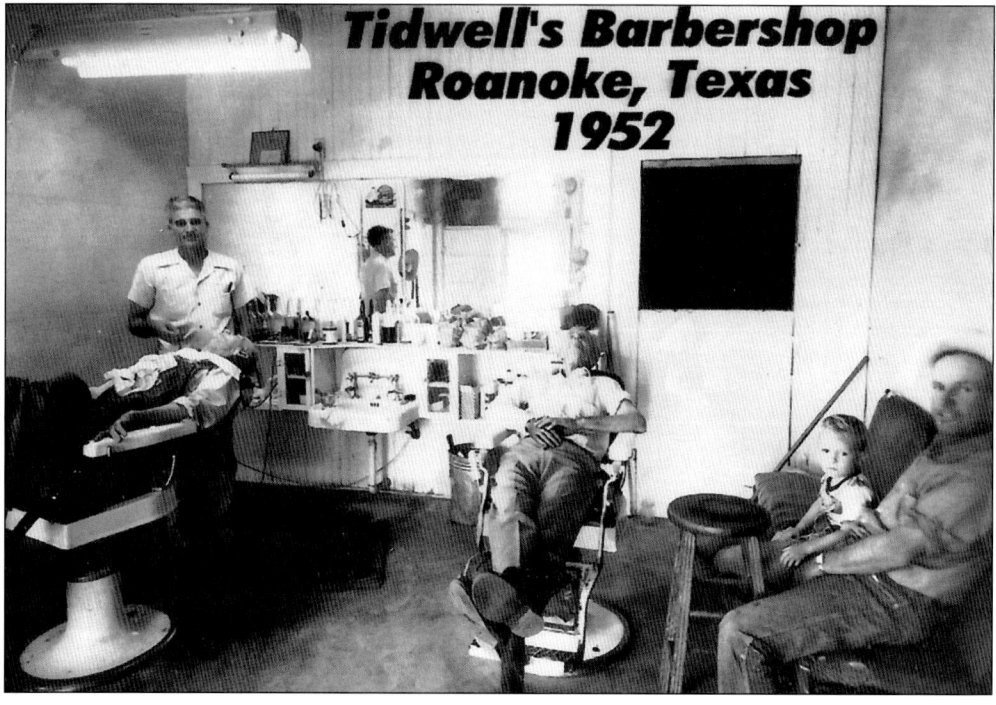

In the photograph at right, Gerald Ward (left) and Clint (C. A.) Cowan Jr. are standing at the podium to address a Roanoke reunion group on June 19, 1976, as part of a bicentennial celebration. Ward, a former Roanoke resident, was superintendent of the Fort Worth public schools and a recipient of a Silver Star for his service in World War II in the South Pacific. Cowan was a classmate who had suffered a sudden high fever as a youngster, leaving him unable to speak, though he was most adept at making himself understood. In the photograph below, from left to right, Conway Peterson, Inez Howe, and Henry "Mc" Howe are enjoying a laugh, reminiscing about school days. Conway, while recovering from surgery, once dug a grave for his former classmate, Willie George Lee, to ensure he was buried near his family. (Both, courtesy of Conway and Calvin Peterson.)

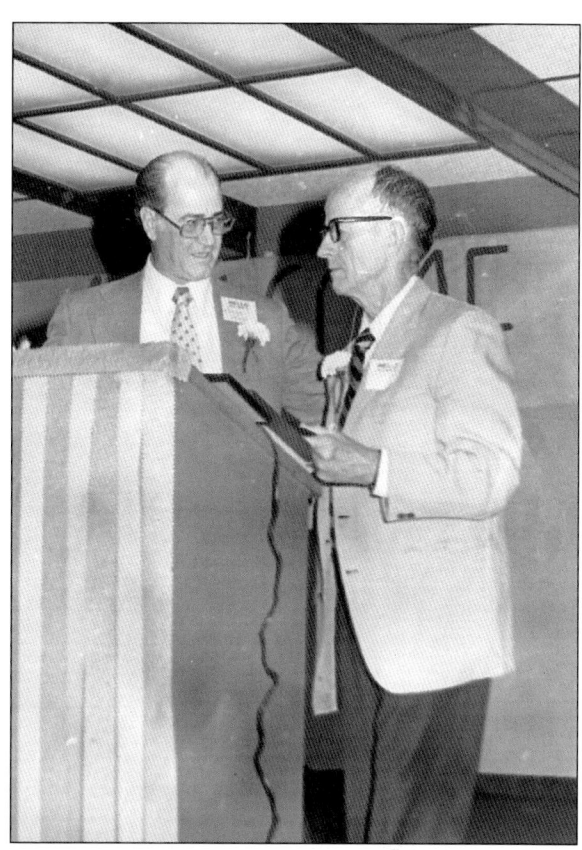

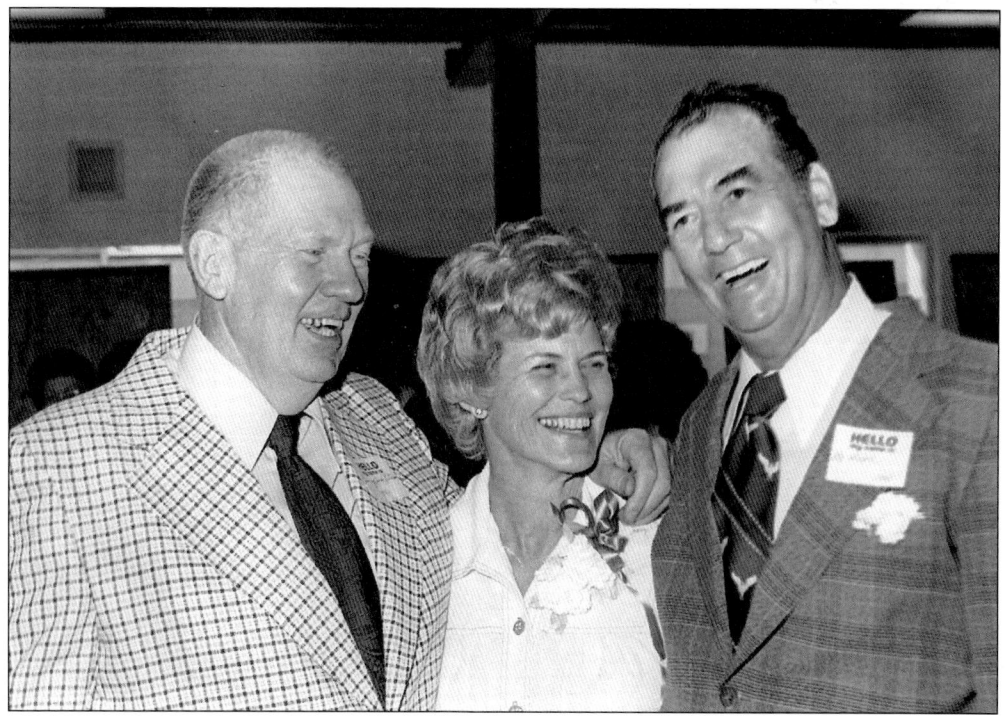

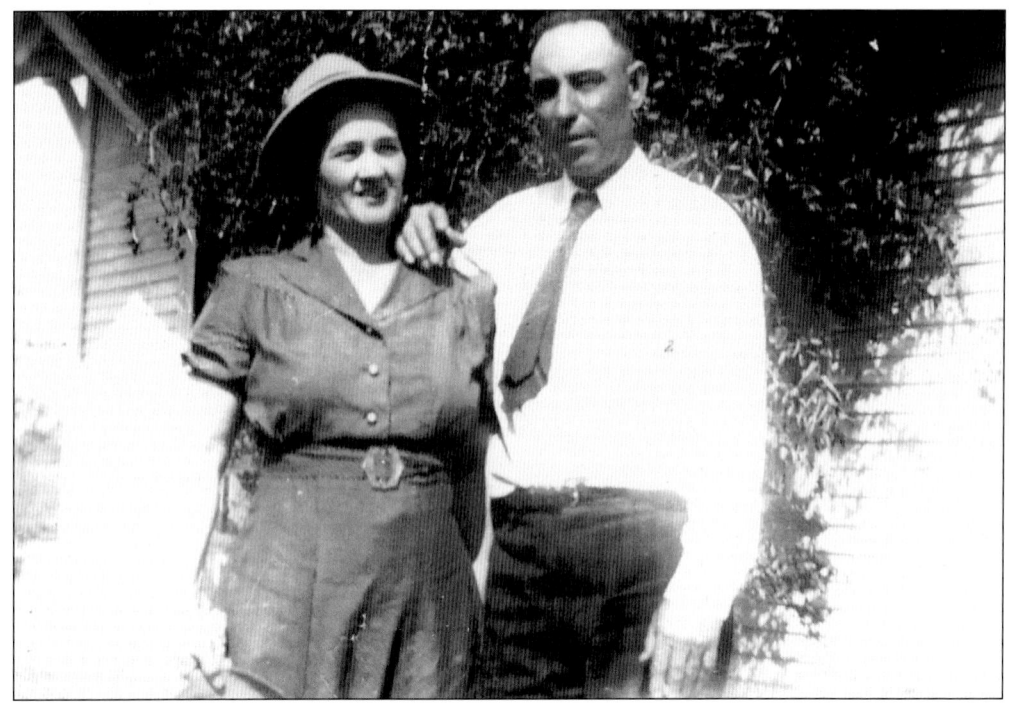

Shown here are Odle Lee Thomas and his wife, Mary Lee Cryer. Odle moved to Denton County in 1897 with his family. He married Mary Lee, born in 1900, and they lived in Gribble Springs, Texas, where all four of their children were born. The boys were James, Ernest, Alfred, and Billy Joe. They moved to Roanoke in the early 1930s, where the elder Thomas sharecropped on the Samuel Reynolds ranch. (Courtesy of Billy Joe Thomas.)

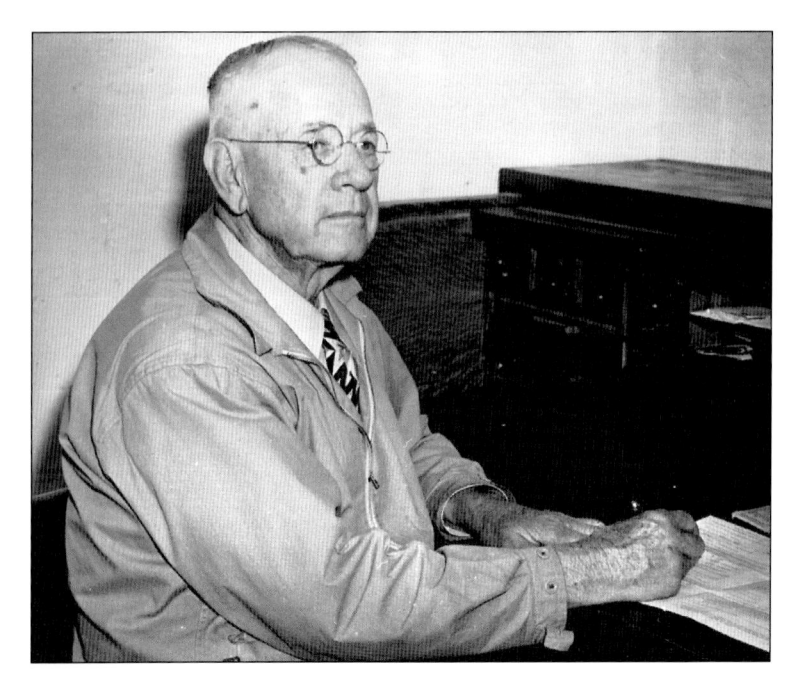

Clint Cowan, justice of the peace and city judge, is shown at his desk. He also worked as a rural mail carrier for years. Two other members of the Cowan family worked for the U.S. Post Office as well. The Cowans came to Texas by train in 1878 and moved to Roanoke in 1879, paying $175 for their property. (Courtesy of HSC.)

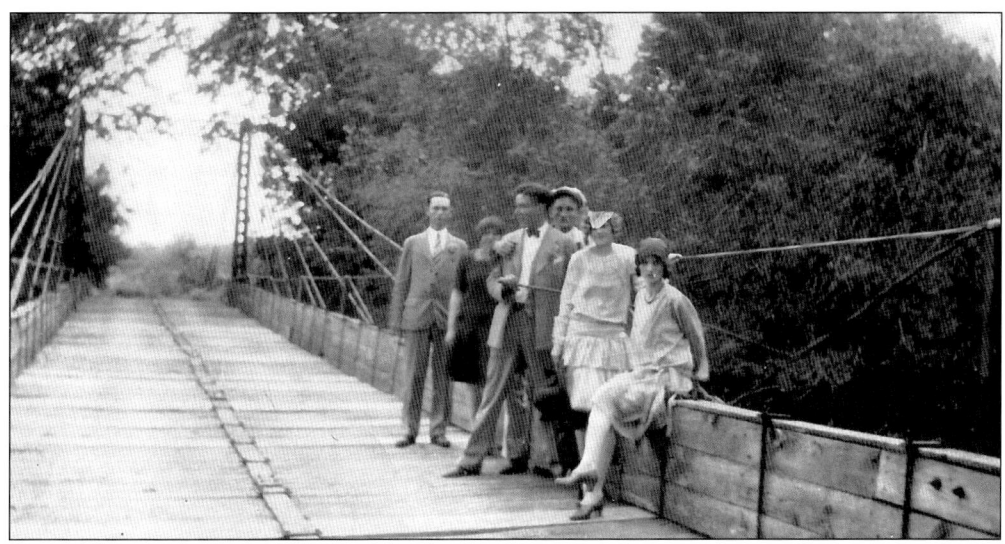

Gathered on the old wire bridge are, from left to right, ? Wilson (the pastor), Pauline Ragsdale, George Jones, "Gumby" Andrews, Joe Kelly, and Murl Kelly. This bridge was later replaced by a safer, more reliable version. Around this bridge is where the young people would gather for picnics, a day of fun, and, of course, photographs. One school class skipped school on April Fool's Day to attend a picnic here sanctioned by the principal, who accompanied them. A new group of young adults (at right) is enjoying the new bridge, which some still called the "wire bridge." Pictured here are, from left to right, Eddie Jack King, Mary Louise Graham, Margie Garner, and Edward Crites. Neither bridge is in existence today, as Grapevine Lake took over the site. (Above, courtesy of Emily Ragsdale; right, courtesy of Edward Crites.)

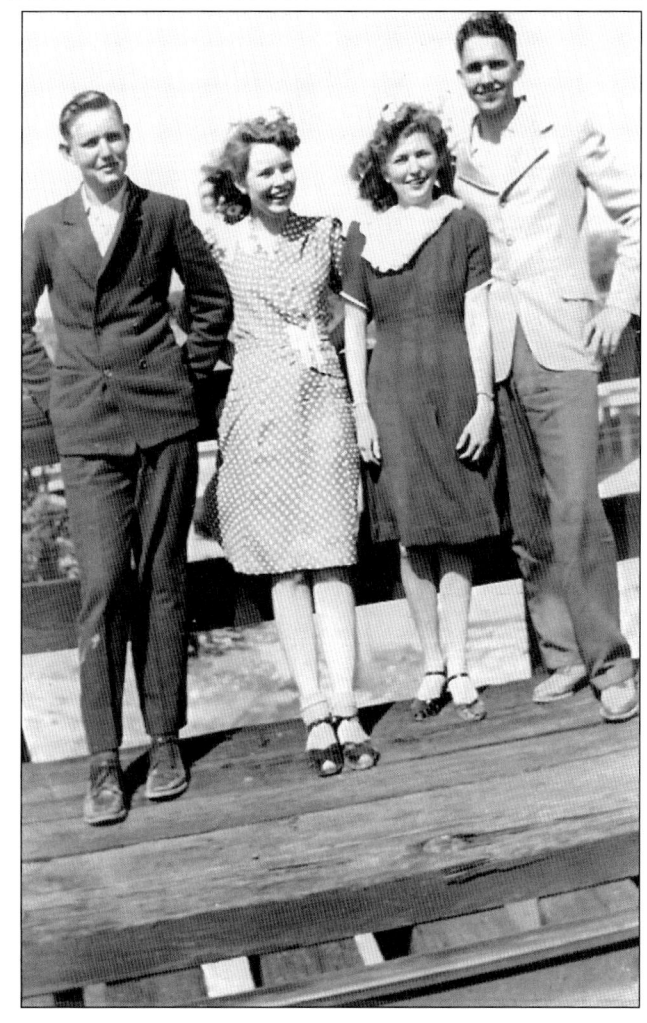

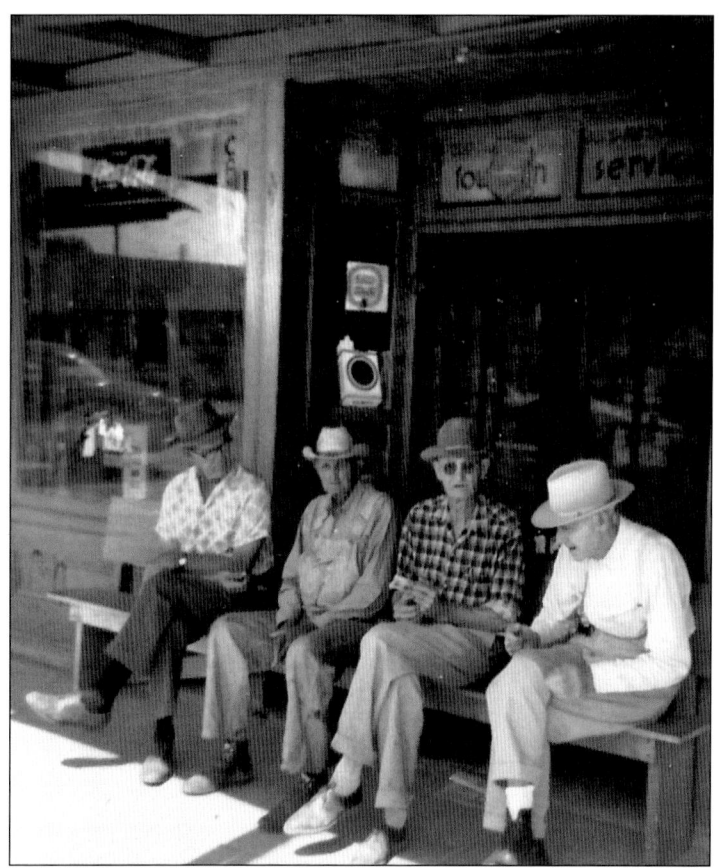

Pictured in this c. 1962 photograph on one of the benches on the west side of Oak Street are, from left to right, Aubrey Carpenter, Sam Ottinger, John Crosby, and Charlie Blackburn. The benches on Oak Street were always filled as friends met to talk over the events of the day. The occupants of the bench in the picture below are, from left to right, W. W. Prewitt, Richard Crites, ? Hayes, Bill Taylor, Lonnie Crosby, and ? Causey. They are most likely in town with their families and have stopped to visit. Many of the men waited here while their wives shopped or visited at Simmons Dry Goods. (Both, courtesy of HSC.)

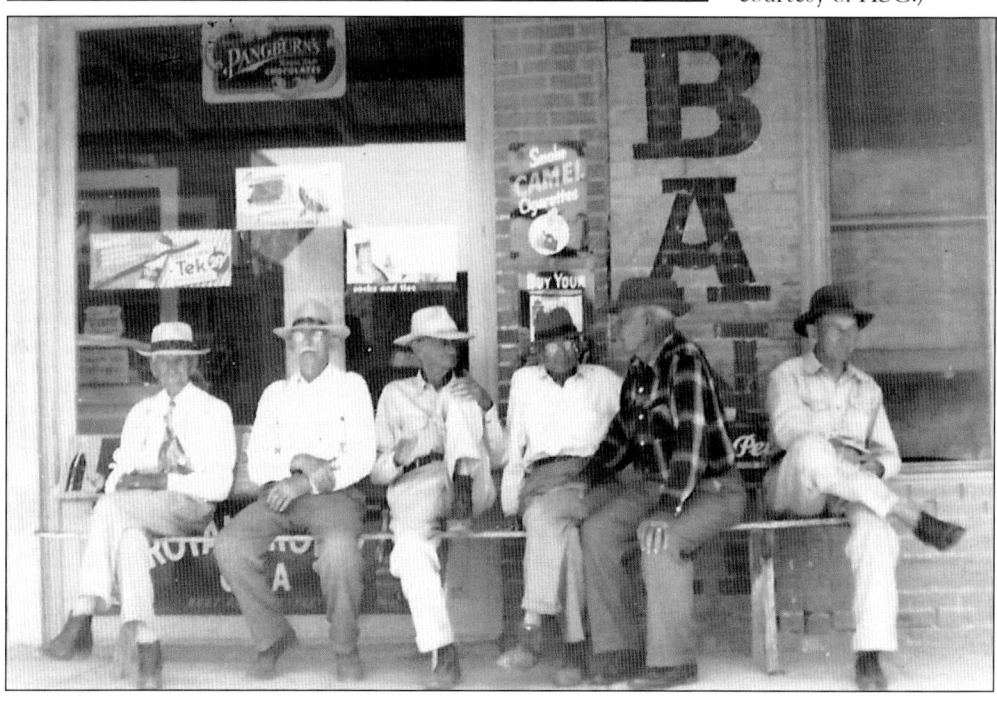

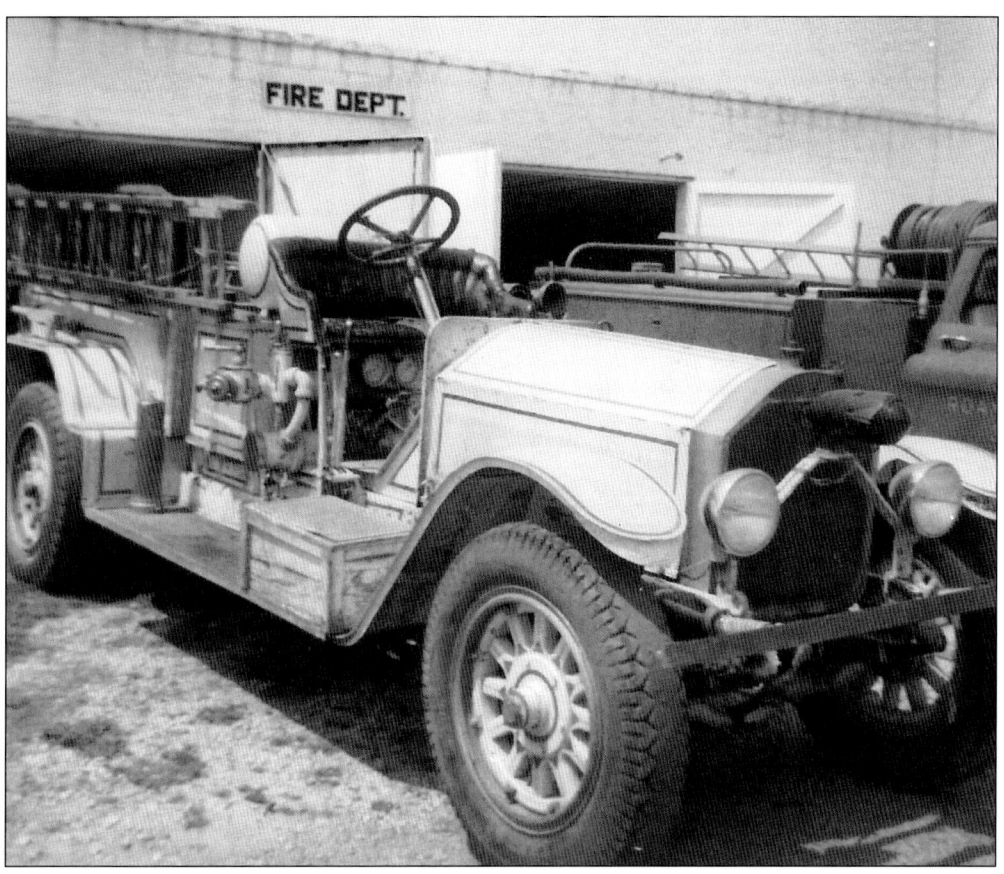

This 1923 LaFrance fire truck was purchased used from the City of Fort Worth in 1948. It served the volunteer fire department in Roanoke for many years. During some years, there were not enough men at home during the day to answer the fire phones, which were in private homes, so the women of Roanoke took over the firefighting under the leadership of Martha Watson, the assistant fire chief. The picture below shows the fire truck that the fire department restored with the help of donations from citizens. The truck in earlier years was white; however, the red was deemed more appropriate when it was restored. This truck is featured in a small fire museum at the corner of Oak and Main Streets. (Above, courtesy of HSC; below, courtesy of RVCM.)

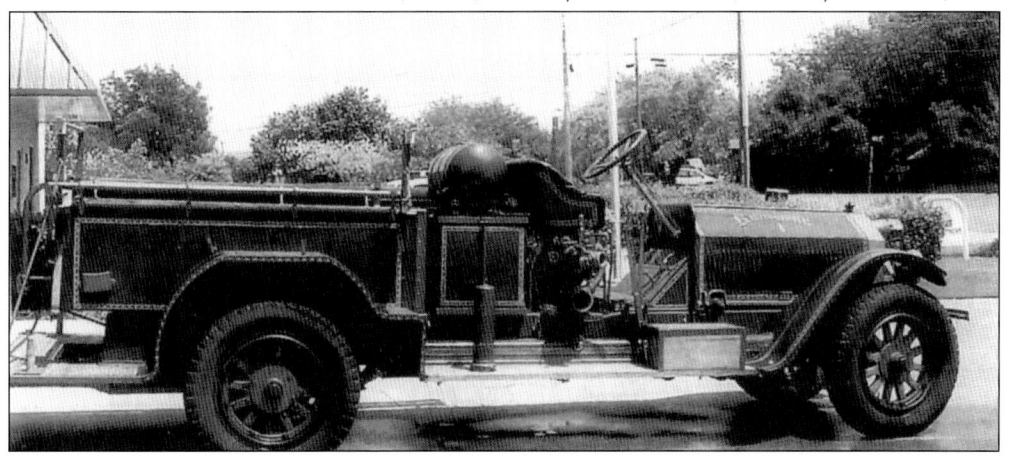

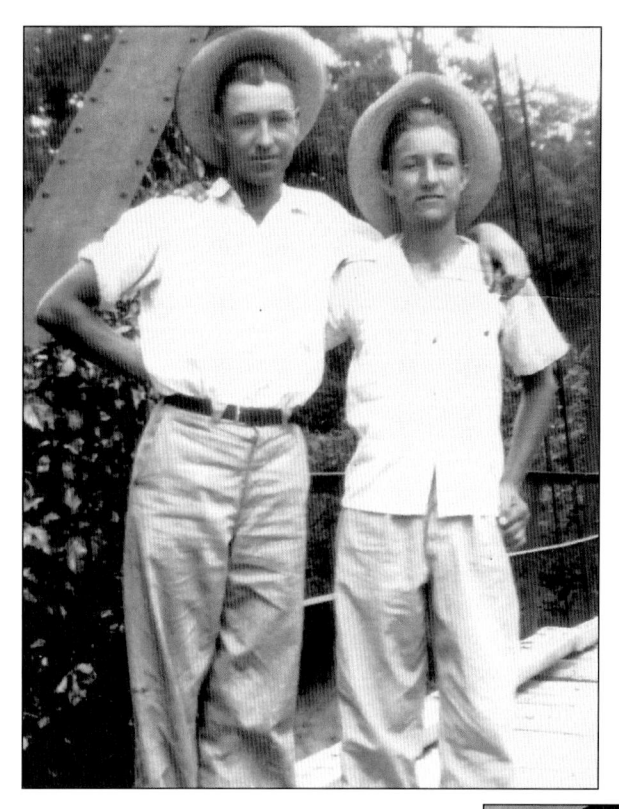

Hollis Lee (left) and Earl Kelley Jr. are shown on the old wire bridge in this 1940s photograph. Lee lived on the Ed Olson farm west of Roanoke, where the Texas Motor Speedway is located. His family worked on the Olson farm. Kelley was a member of the Future Farmers of America while in school. He married a young woman from Weatherford, Texas, in California when he was 29 years old, and they adopted three children. (Courtesy of Evalena Kelley Morris.)

Frank Leon Fanning, shown at the podium in this c. 1976 photograph, grew up in Roanoke, the son of Nell and Claude "Buster" Fanning. He retired as a captain from the U.S. Navy. He has been actively collecting information and pictures from old town Roanoke families for years to be used in a book on Roanoke's history. Fanning was responsible for having the old Continental State Bank named to the National Register of Historic Places. He is the current owner of the building, though a beauty salon occupies the space, which still boasts the original walls and safe. (Courtesy of Conway and Calvin Peterson.)

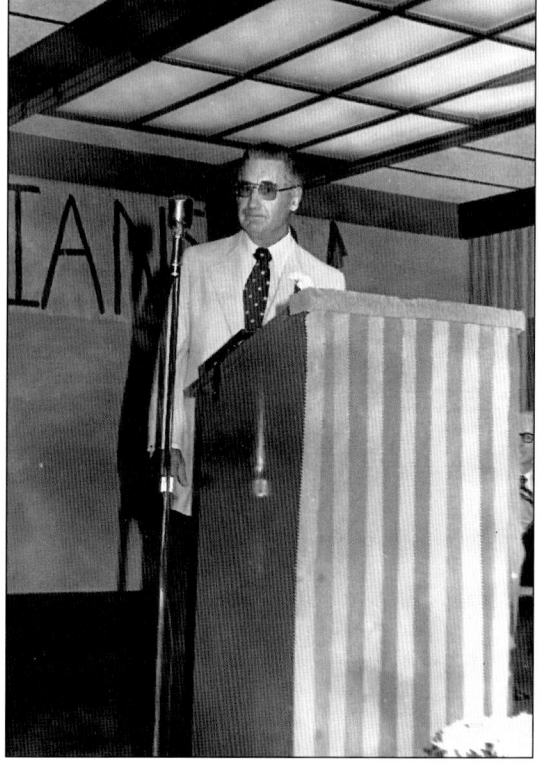

Howard Guy McDonald was transferred to Roanoke by the railroad from a tower station in Bells, Texas, to become the stationmaster. McDonald served for more than 30 years in that capacity and was the last person to hold that position in Roanoke. The McDonald family lived for many years on Oak Street. (Courtesy of Vance McDonald.)

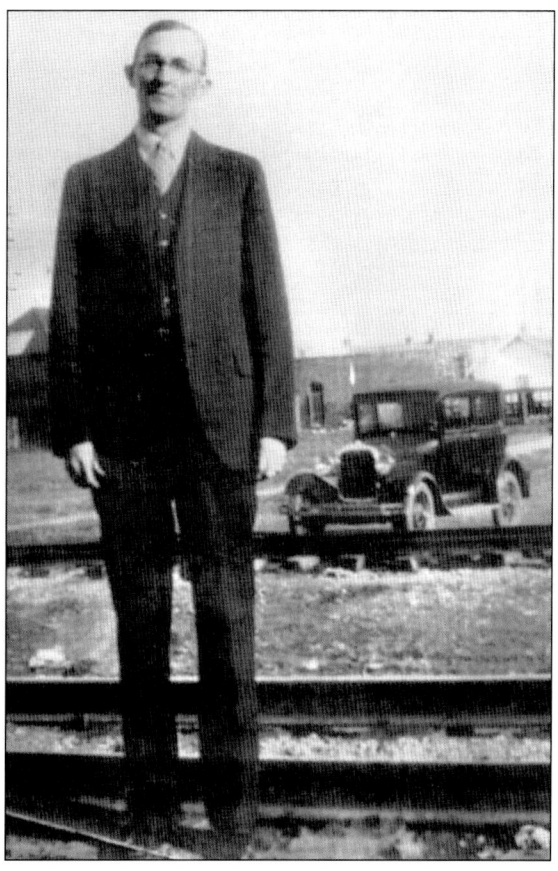

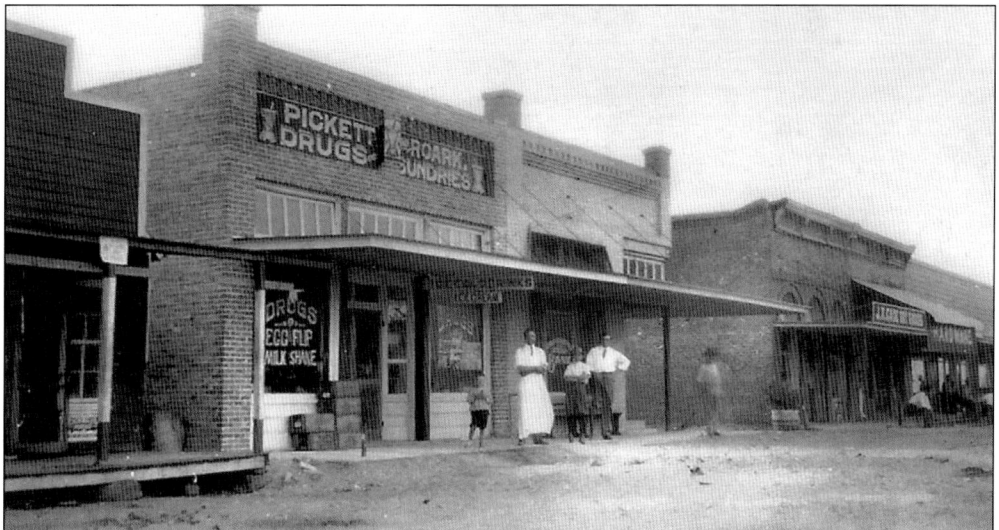

The Pickett Drugstore was on the west side of Oak Street. The Pickett family lived west of Roanoke on Litsey Road. Harry Pickett played in the community band, and a member of the Pickett family owned the Pacific Hotel prior to it being sold to Mitchell Raibourn. Ben Pickett owned a blacksmith shop on Oak Street, which was later owned by Andy Alexander. (Courtesy of Inez and Henry M. Howe.)

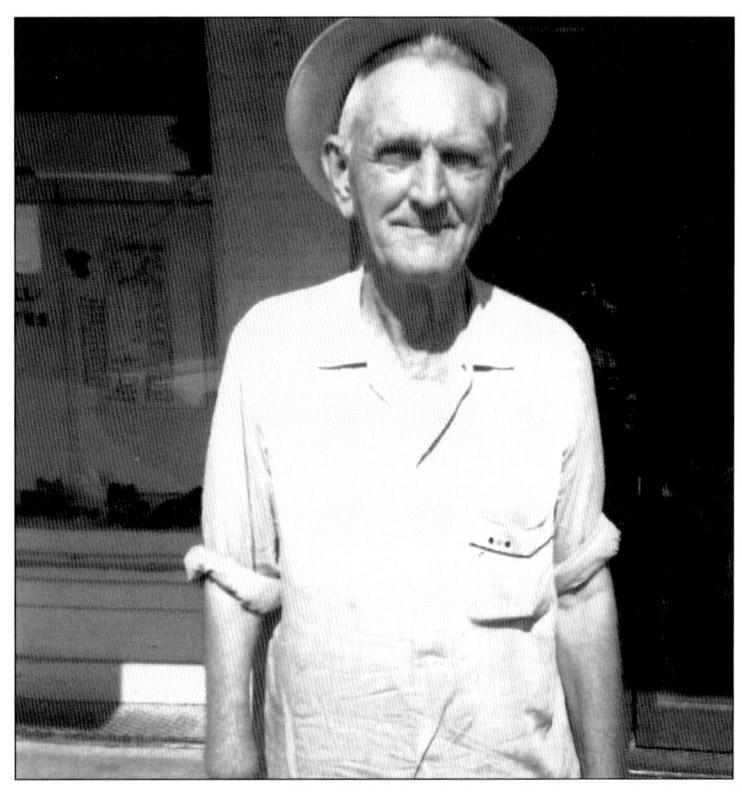

Dave Ottinger, pictured at left in 1962, lost part of his arm in a 1910 gin explosion. In later years, Ottinger operated a dry-cleaning business. In the photograph below, Ottinger (left) is seen playing dominoes with barber John "Toots" Tidwell. An abandoned building was once turned into a domino hall, as playing dominoes was a favorite pastime. In fact, several of the younger men often went to surrounding communities to participate in tournaments. (Both, courtesy of HSC.)

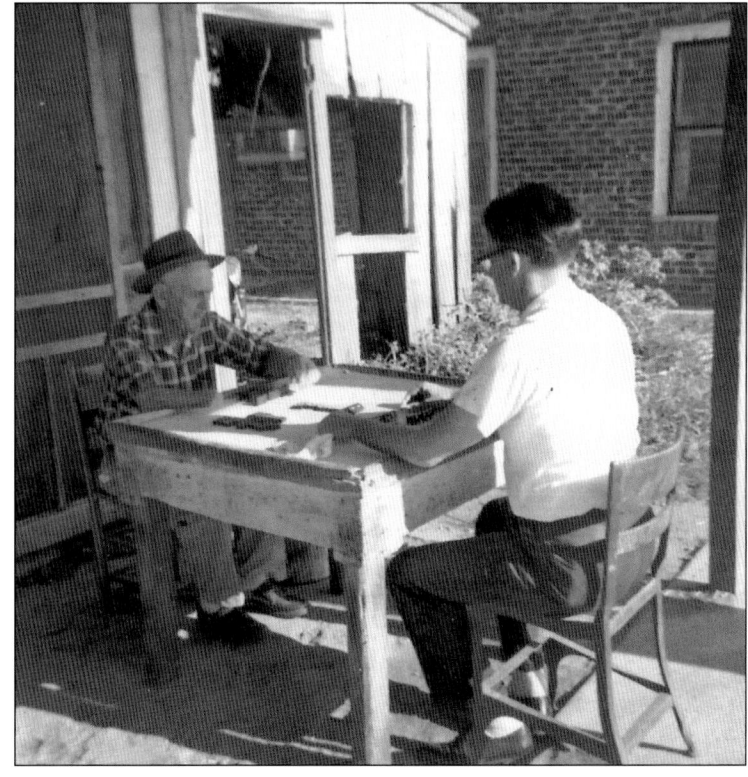

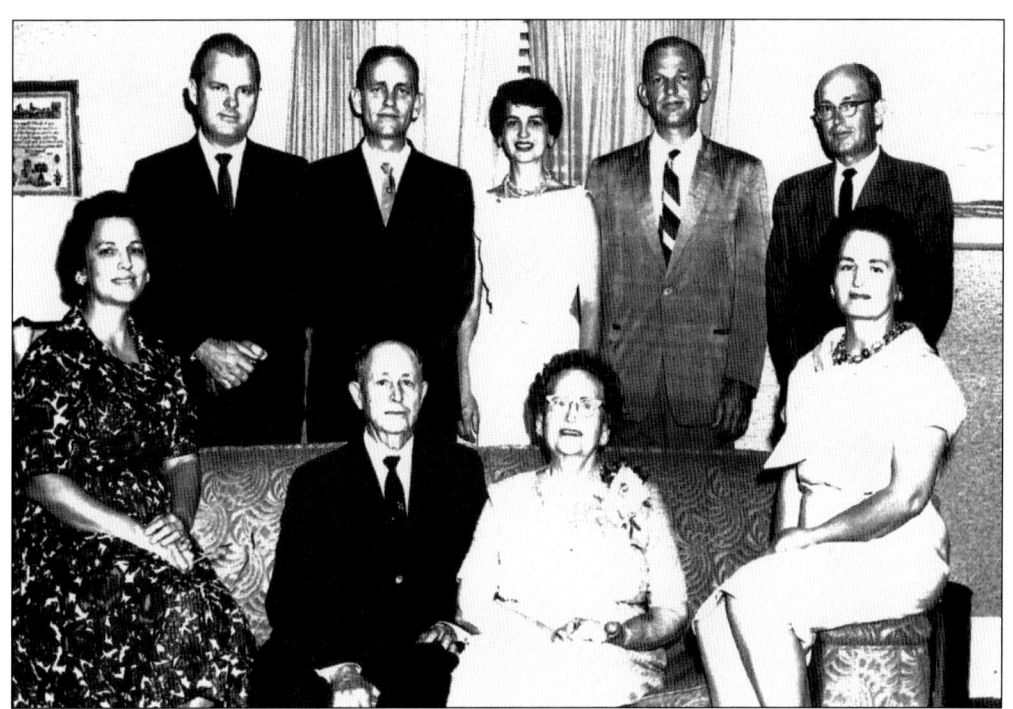

The Manire family members pictured here are, from left to right, (first row) Katherine, Ernest Lawrence, Zera, and Lois; (second row) Phillip, Bill, Nancy, Robert, and Ernest Lawrence Jr. The elder Manire owned a grocery store on Oak Street next to Hise Seagraves's dry-goods store. The family was well respected in the community and were members of the Church of Christ. All of the Manire children were college graduates; quite an accomplishment for a small town family. (Courtesy of William Manire.)

Manuel "Buster" and Emily Bogart were the children of Charles and Ada Bogart. Manuel served in World War II in the Seabees and was stationed in Oahu, Hawaii. Manuel and Emily grew up on the Cartwright farm south of Roanoke, so they walked 1.5 miles to school in Roanoke everyday. There were plenty of neighbor children who accompanied them, including Tony and Juanita Underwood, who had a horse-drawn cart that they rode into school everyday. (Courtesy of Emily Ragsdale.)

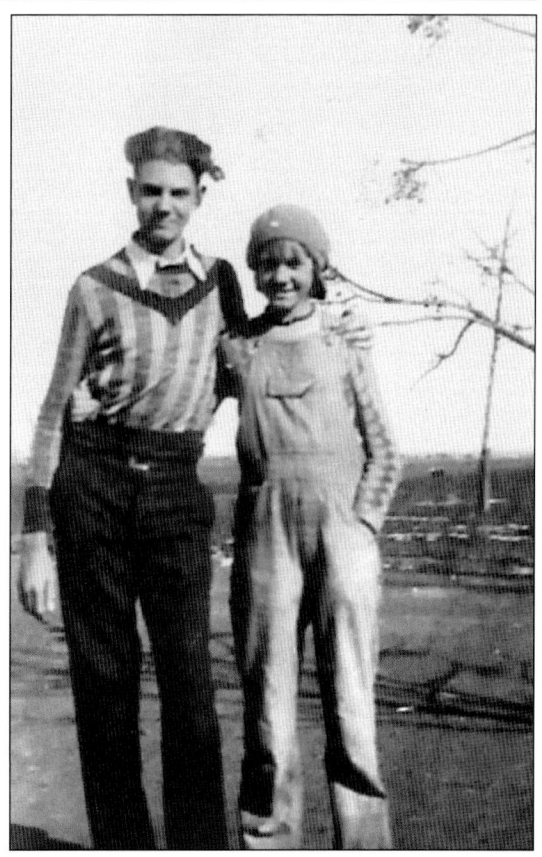

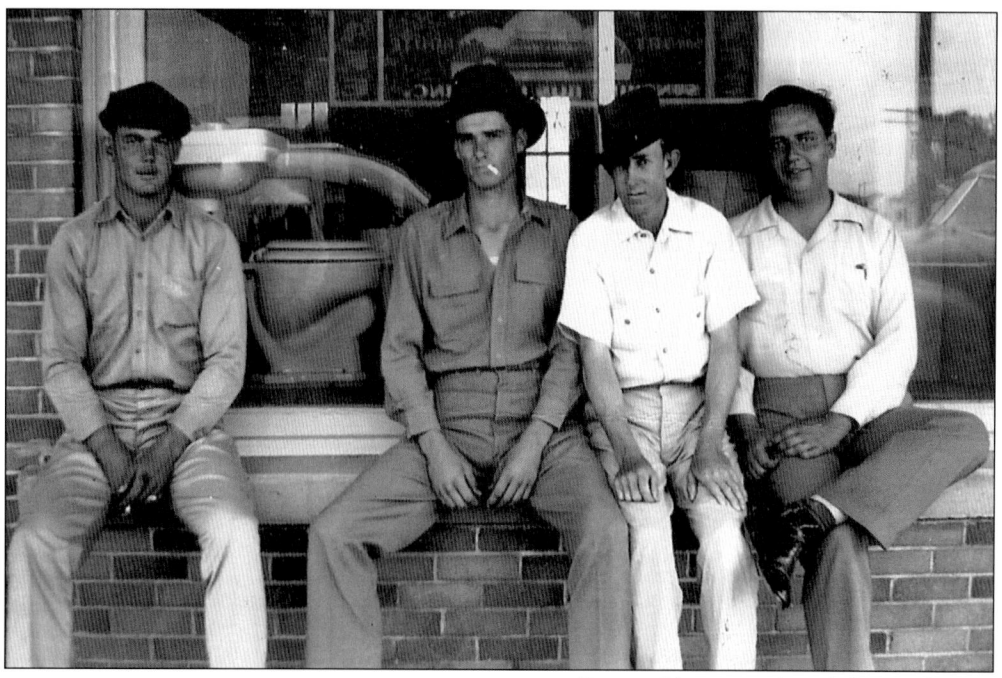

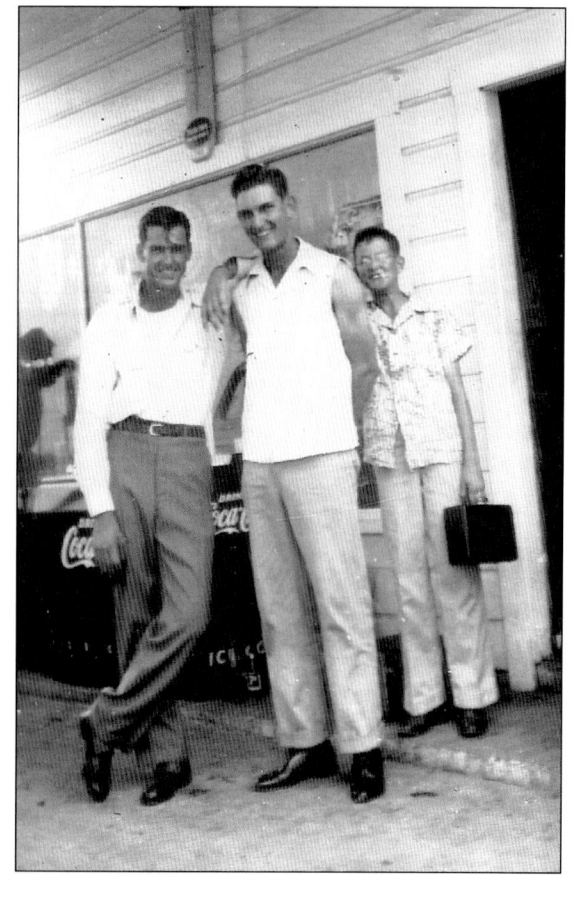

Pictured here are, from left to right, Gordon Stephenson Jr., Edward "Blackie" Blevins, Weldon Mundy, and Willie George Lee, all sitting on the window ledge of the plumbing business on Oak Street. Notice how the young men are sitting on the ledge to ensure that the commode can be clearly seen through the window. (Courtesy of HSC.)

These young men are, from left to right, Tal Tidwell, Grover Malone, and Dick Lipsey. They are standing in front of one of the service stations in town, which was a fairly common sight, as service stations were popular meeting places for the young men in Roanoke. (Courtesy of Vertalee and John Coleman.)

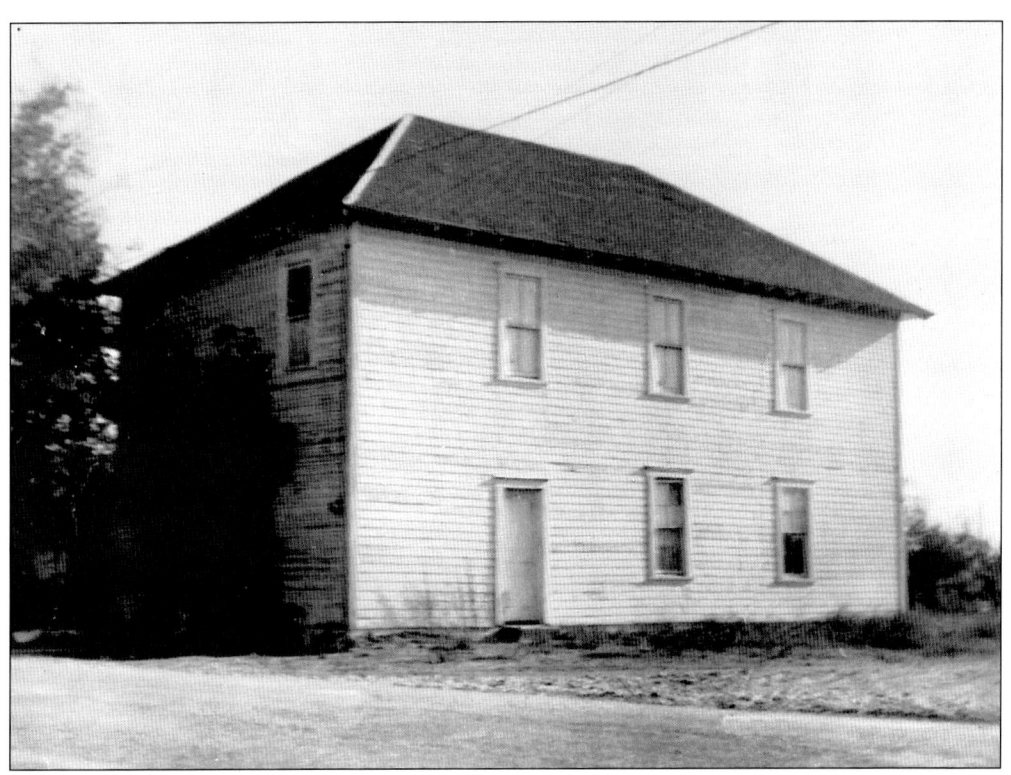

The Masonic lodge, pictured above in 1952, is shown in its original position very close to Oak Street. During the days before Roanoke had a police force, vandals consistently broke out the windows, so during a renovation the members boarded the windows with siding before the building was moved to the back of the lot. The Masonic lodge (at right) is shown as it appears today. Many townspeople referred to this building as the community center. The lodge moved to Roanoke in 1883, meeting in various places until this building was constructed in 1908 as the permanent home. This is still an active lodge with a Texas Historical Subject Marker. (Above, courtesy of HSC; right, courtesy of Ann Clark.)

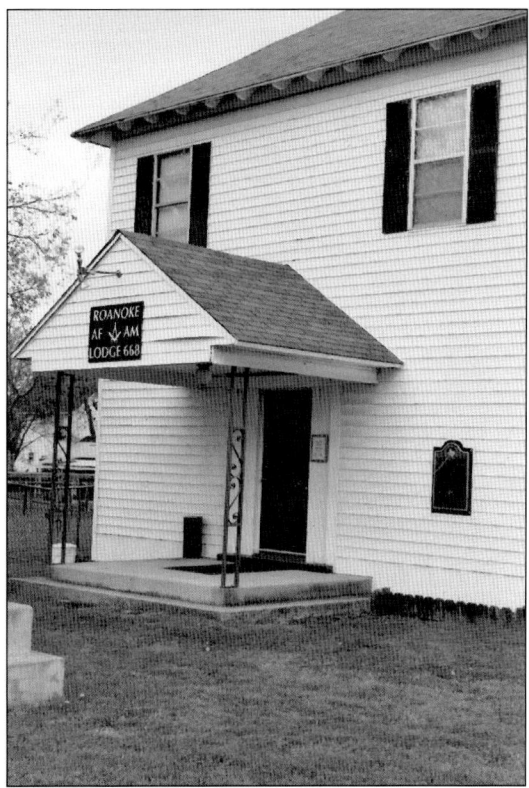

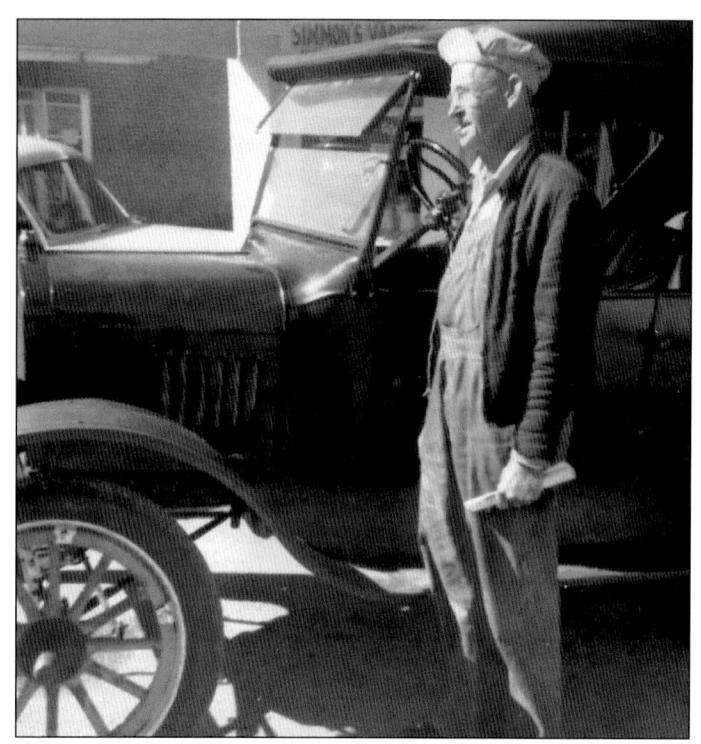

Andy Alexander, pictured in both photographs, had a garage that featured an old forge he used into the 1960s. The young men of the community were constant visitors to the garage, and the word around town was that he could fix anything. Andy did not take fools lightly. If anyone said they were in a hurry to get something done, he would tell them they should have started earlier. (Both, courtesy of HSC.)

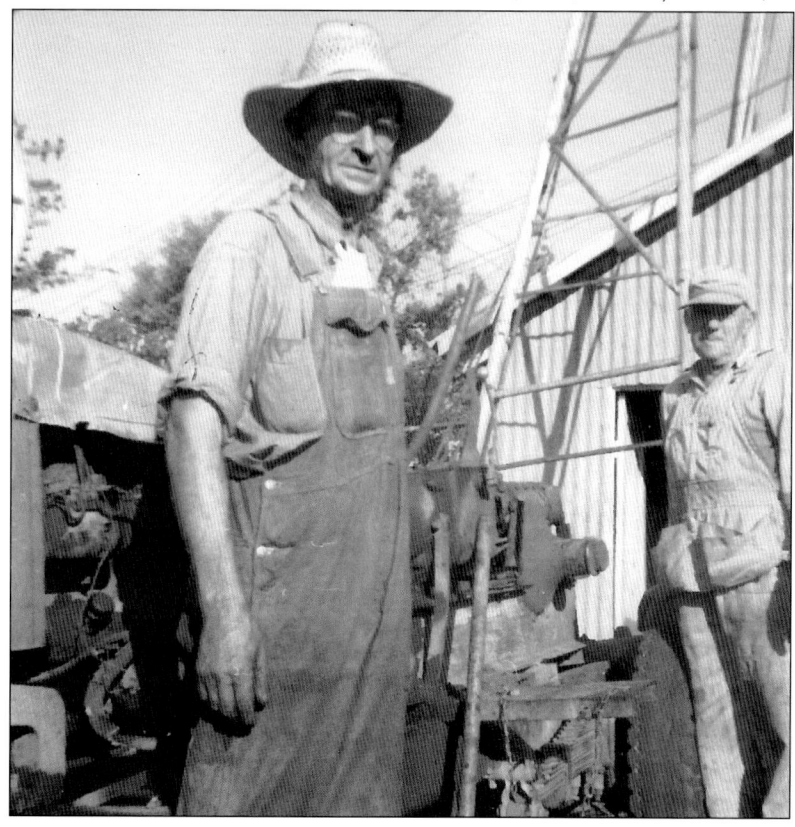

The Coleman family (pictured at right) are, from left to right, Ruby Feemster Coleman holding son Derle; her husband, John Sr.; and their other son, John Jr. (standing). Their son John Jr. and his wife, Vertalee, are shown in the photograph below. John Coleman Jr. and Vertalee Brock, who were in the same class in Roanoke, married shortly after World War II in 1949. John is an active member of the Roanoke Masonic lodge, and Vertalee is well-known for the interesting quilts she constructs. Most recently she has made several quilts featuring vintage Roanoke photographs. Additionally, she and several others have completed quilts made from squares drawn by the Roanoke Elementary third-grade classes, one of which hangs at the Roanoke Visitor Center and Museum and the other at the Roanoke Elementary School. The couple has three children, Estelle, John Alan, and Dale. (Both, courtesy of Vertalee and John Coleman.)

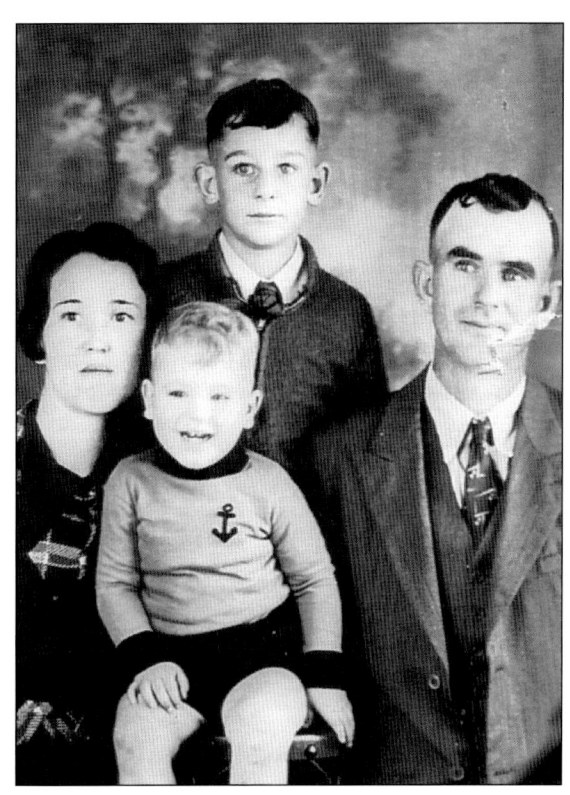

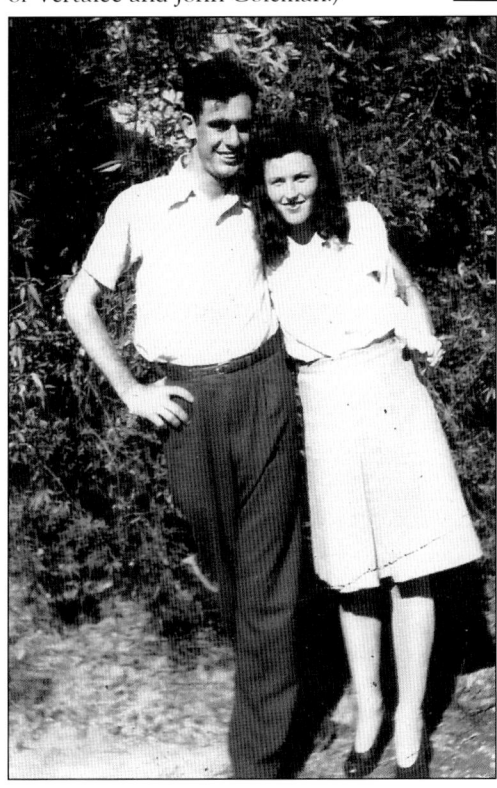

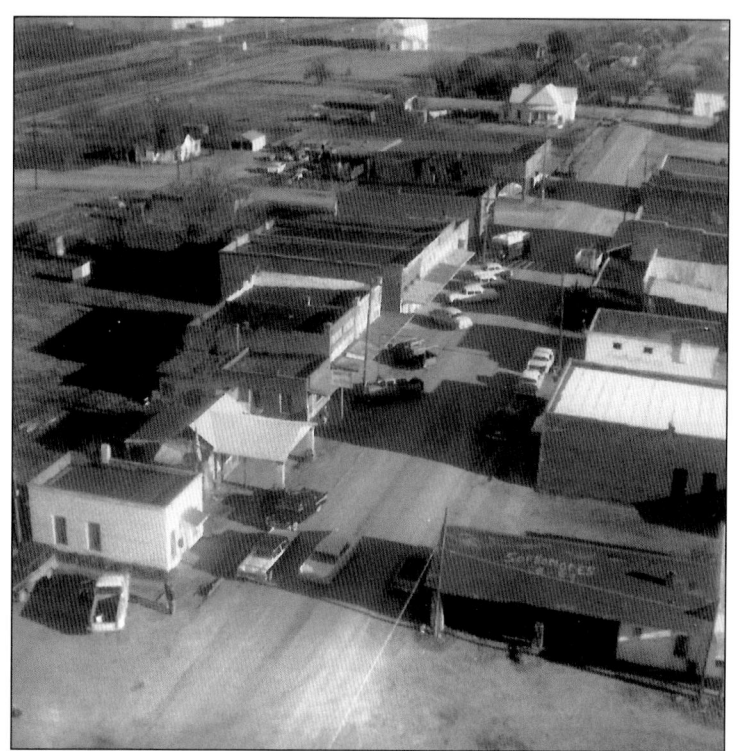

This view of Oak Street to the north was taken on January 31, 1962, by Bob Carruth from the top of the downtown water tower, which is still standing, although it is no longer in use. Climbing the water tower was a dangerous feat for many of the boys in town. One boy, who scared his friends, slid off the side but was able to stop before falling to the ground. Years later, Mayor Tony Smith continued to defy gravity by climbing the tower to make repairs. (Courtesy of HSC.)

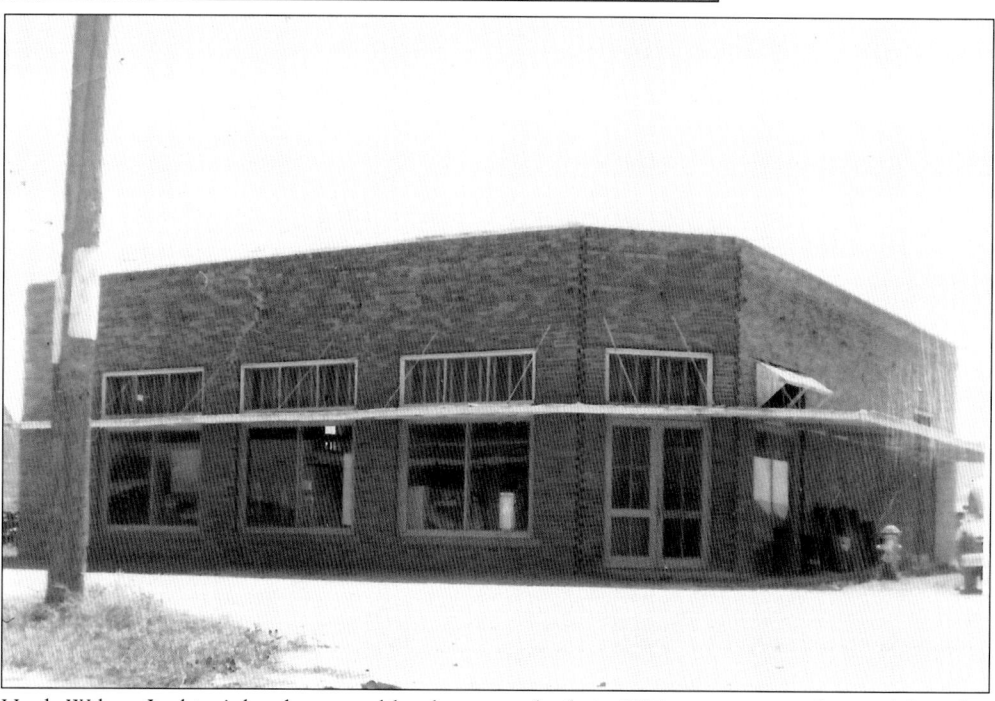

Hugh Wilson Jenkins's hardware and lumber store, built in 1916 on property obtained from his second wife's family, was still active into the 1950s. This building still stands; however, at this time it is the delight of customers craving Mexican food. The building has been embellished and painted in vibrant colors, but the structure of the building remains unchanged. (Courtesy of HSC.)

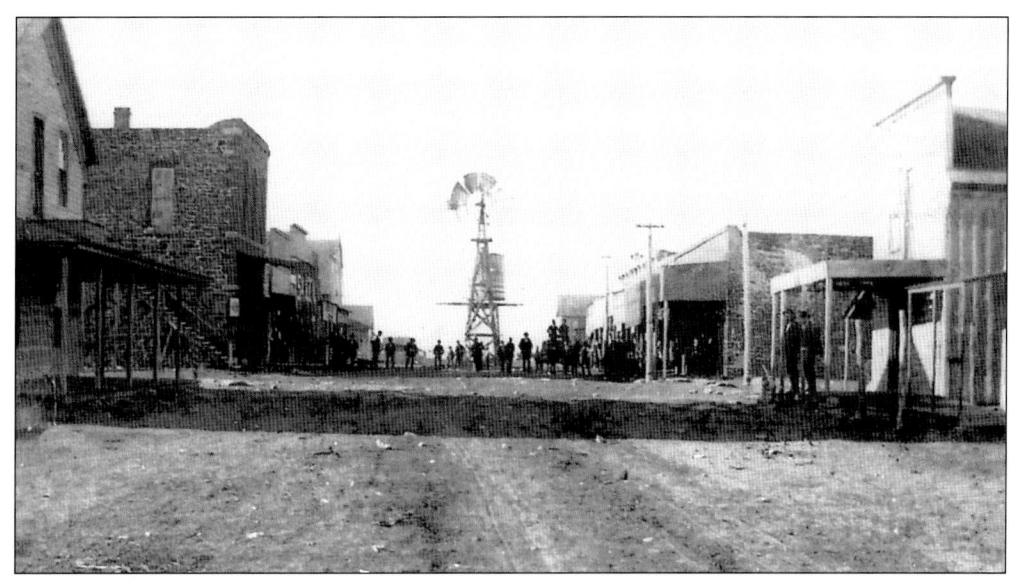

In the early 1900s, Roanoke was a typical Western town, complete with a windmill-powered water system in the middle of Oak Street. In this photograph, at left is the Eureka Hotel, owned by Thomas and Elizabeth Brand, and next to it is the Silver Spur Saloon, owned originally by Burrell and Robert Snead, who had it built. The saloon had an outdoor staircase to the second floor, which is barely visible in this picture. (Courtesy of Inez and Henry "Mc" Howe.)

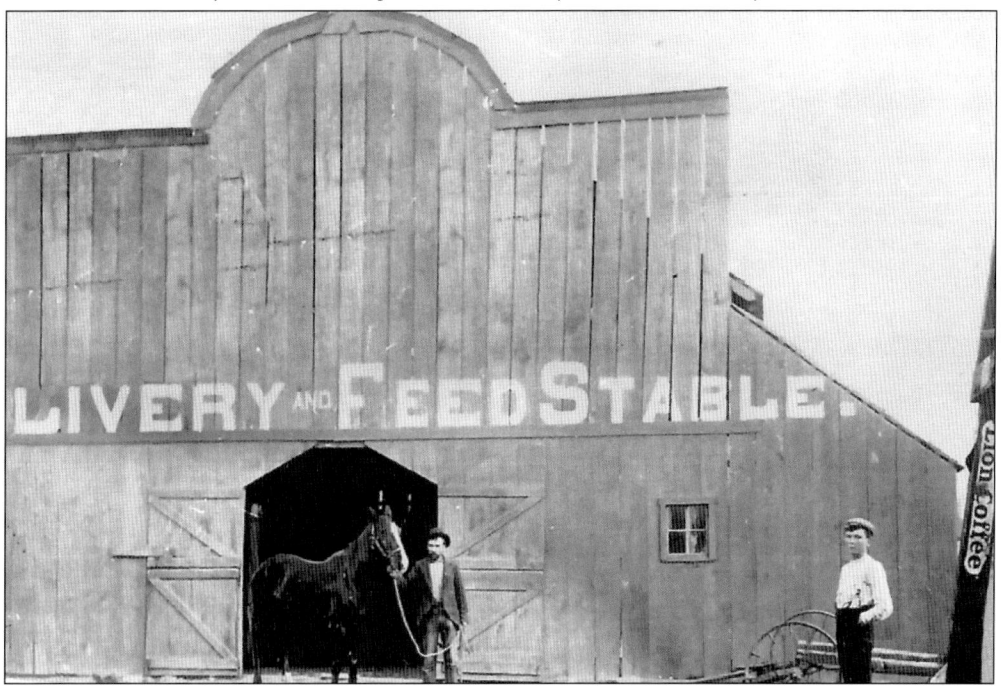

This livery stable appears to be located on Oak Street; however, in about 1900, Joe Selby owned a livery stable that was located one block east of Oak Street, directly behind the building south of the Silver Spur Saloon. Many people coming to Roanoke by horseback to spend the night in the hotel or visit the Silver Spur Saloon could feed and board their horses at this livery stable. (Courtesy of Emily Ragsdale.)

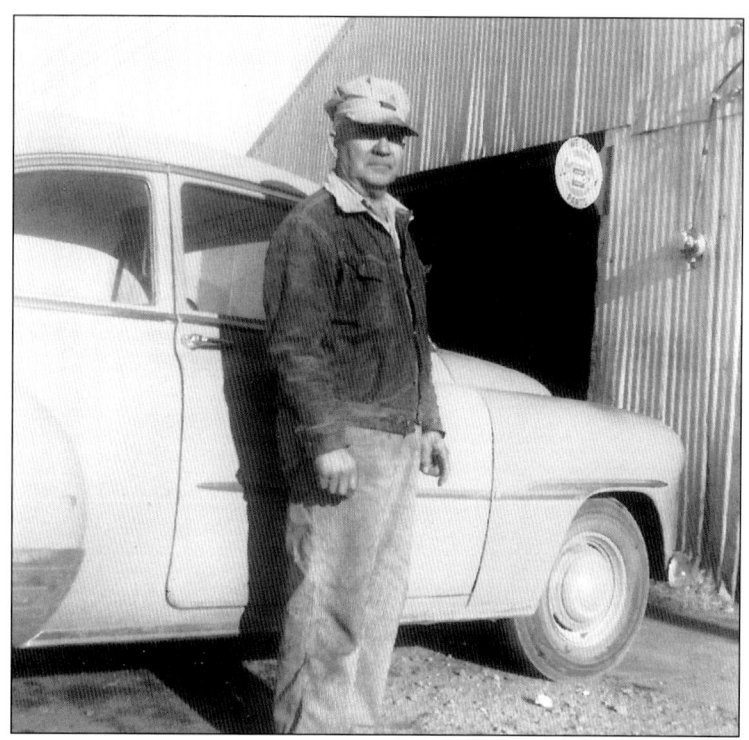

Eric Lassen, shown in front of his garage on Main Street, was an inventor, ambidextrous, and was considered to be a very intelligent man. The photograph below shows another view of the Lassen garage, which is still standing and in remarkable condition, considering its age. Lassen and his family lived on Lamar Street, located in old town Roanoke. (Both, courtesy of HSC.)

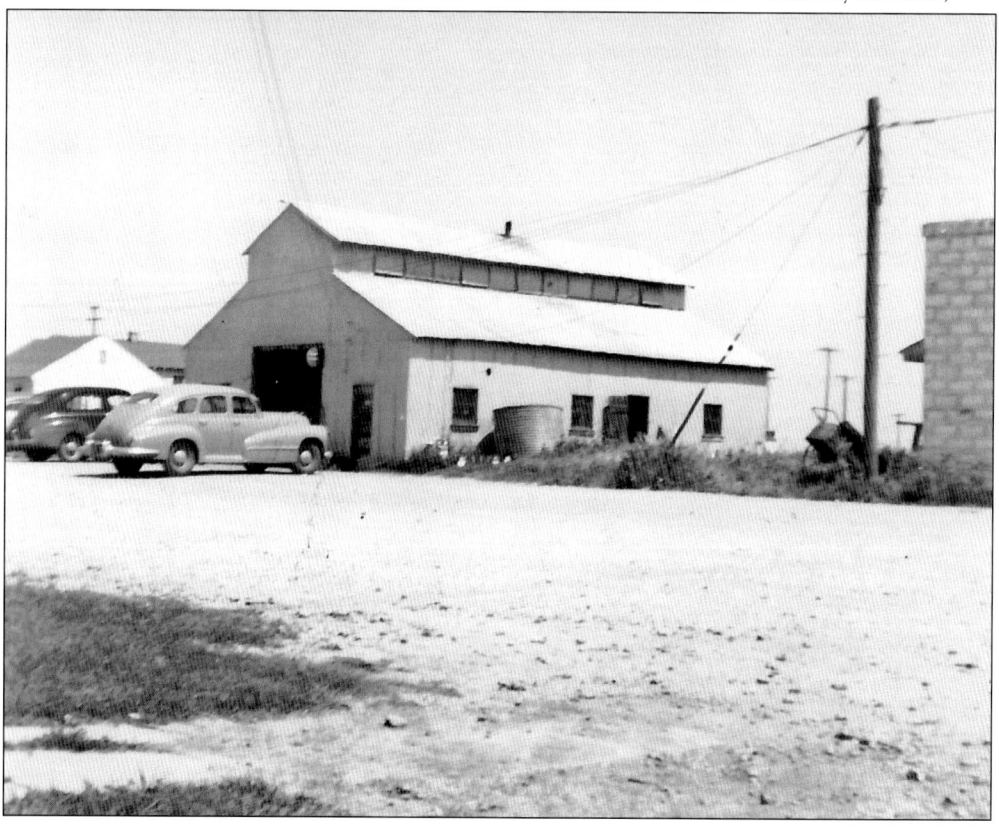

Four
SCHOOLS AND CHURCHES

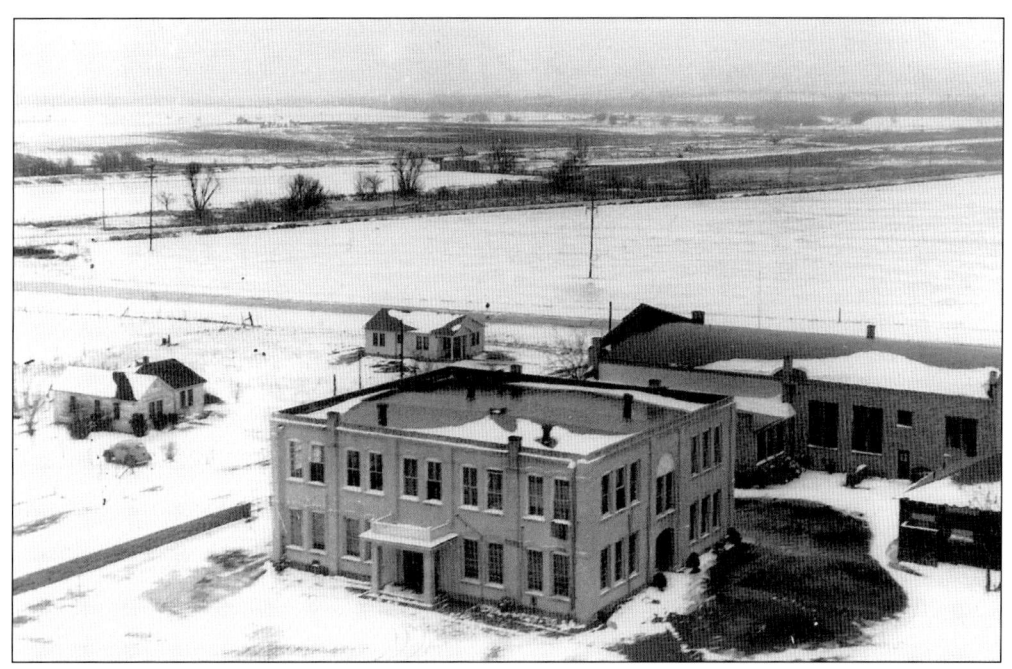

The two-story Roanoke School building shown here was built in 1912 to replace the first Roanoke school, constructed in 1887. The bottom floor housed elementary students in the first through eighth grades, with two classes in each room. The high school students and the principal's office were upstairs. After a new high school building was constructed next door in 1935, the upstairs of this building was used as a lunchroom. Prior to that children brought their own lunches. (Courtesy of Conway Peterson.)

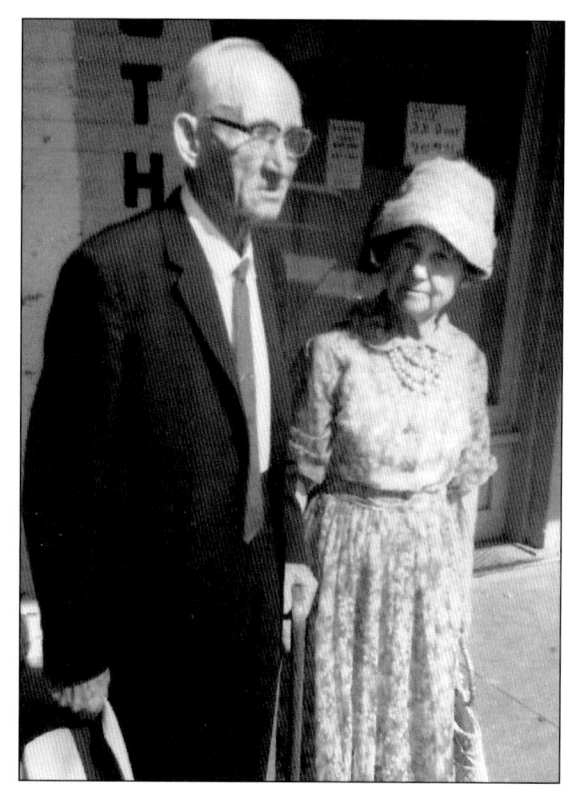

In this c. 1962 photograph, educators Idelle and Rodney Love are strolling on Oak Street. Idelle, known as Miss Love, taught first and second grade for years and then concentrated only on first-grade students. She always referred to the students as her "little folks." Her husband was known as Professor Love and served as the superintendent of schools. Absolutely nothing kept Idelle Love from getting to school, sometimes crossing the creek in her boots or riding to school on horseback. (Courtesy of HSC.)

Ruby Lassen was a first-grade teacher at Roanoke Elementary School and the wife of Eric Lassen, who owned a garage in town. They were the parents of Frederick, Gretchen, Gertrude, Hady Marie, and Carl. Lassen interrupted her teaching career to rear her children but resumed it later, and she worked until retirement. (Courtesy of HSC.)

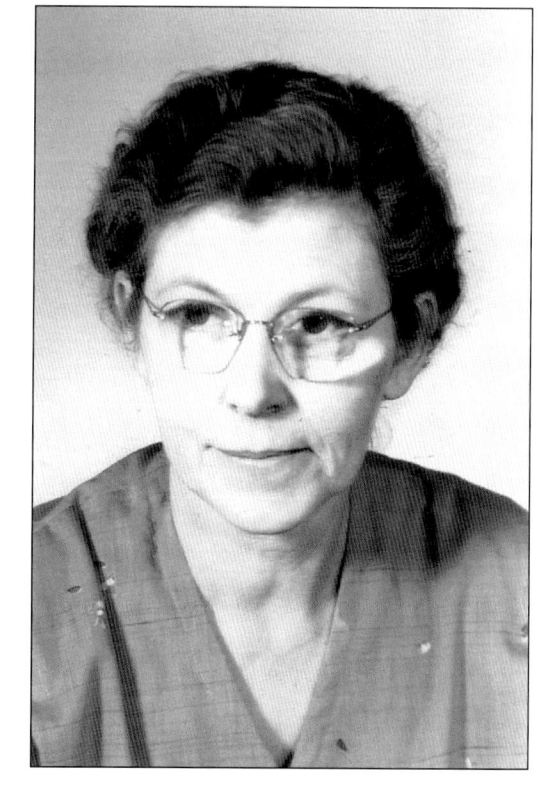

Curtis Turner (left) and Charles Stephenson were childhood friends who went through school together in Roanoke. Turner, the son of Luther (L. D.) and Edna Turner, lived in town, and Charles, son of Gordon and Valera Stephenson, lived on a dairy farm. Turner still lives in Roanoke, and these two avid golfers still play together once a week. (Courtesy of Marjorie Sturdevant Thomas.)

The girls on this merry-go-round are, from left to right, Nelda Owen, Nancy Manire, Cozette Pinion, Patsy Leyland, and Frances Haynie. This type of playground equipment is seldom seen now. Most of the play equipment was outside until a new school was built, which housed a new gymnasium, enabling students to play basketball or other games during inclement weather. (Courtesy of Marjorie Sturdevant Irick.)

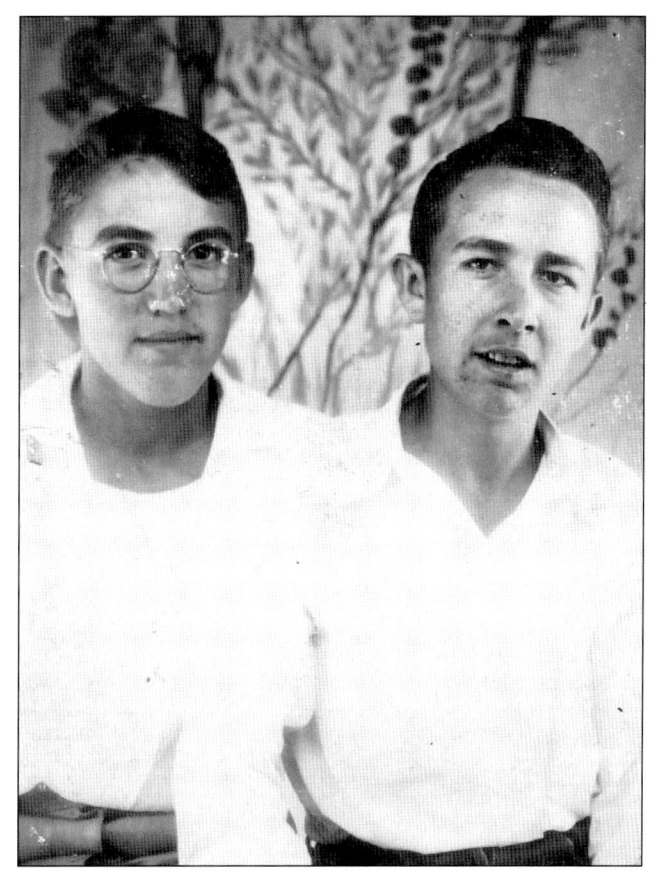

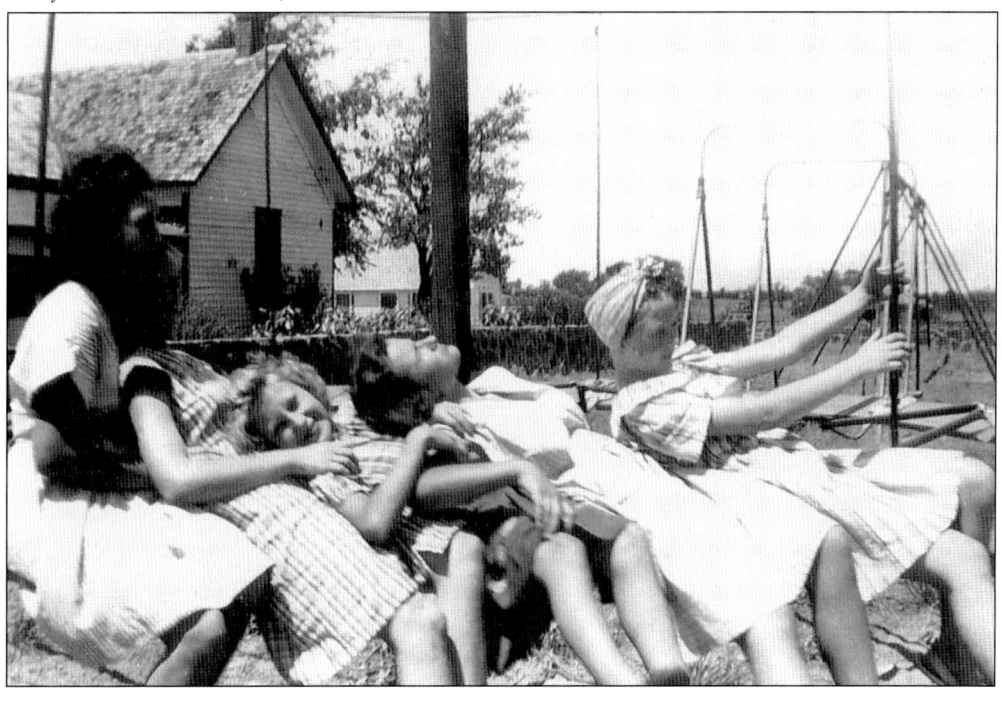

101

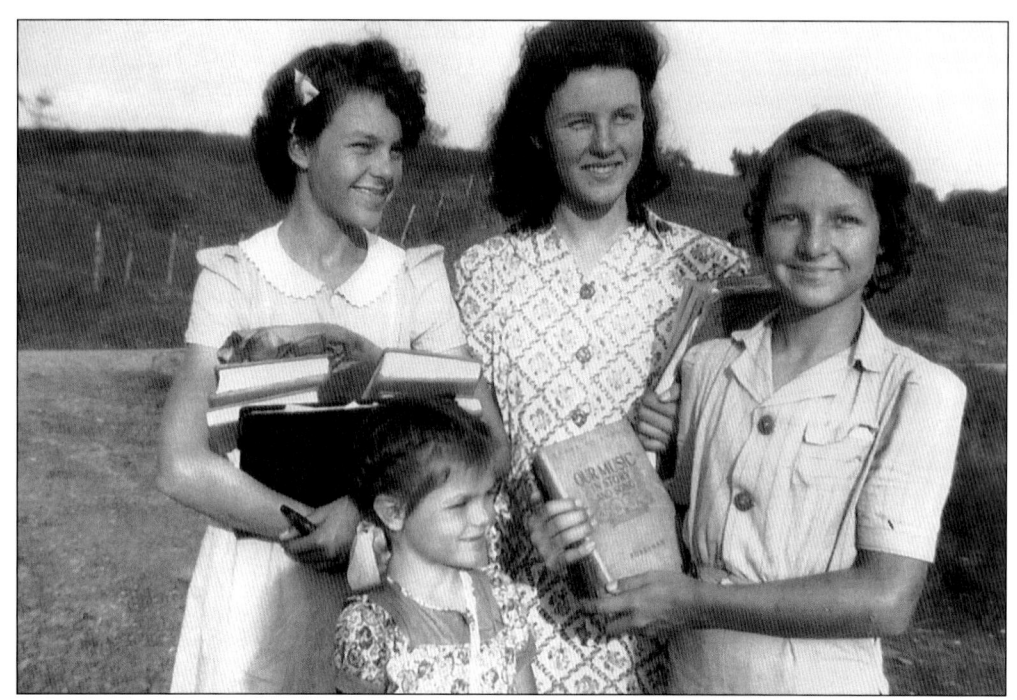

The youngsters pictured here have just returned from school. The older girls are, from left to right, Ellen, Vertalee, and Stella; the younger girl is their sister Jean. Their brother, Ernest Jr. (known as E. C.), was born later. They are all children of Lela and Ernest Brock, who lived in the northwest corner of the area now bordered by the crossing of the Highway 114 bypass and Highway 377. (Courtesy of Vertalee and John Coleman.)

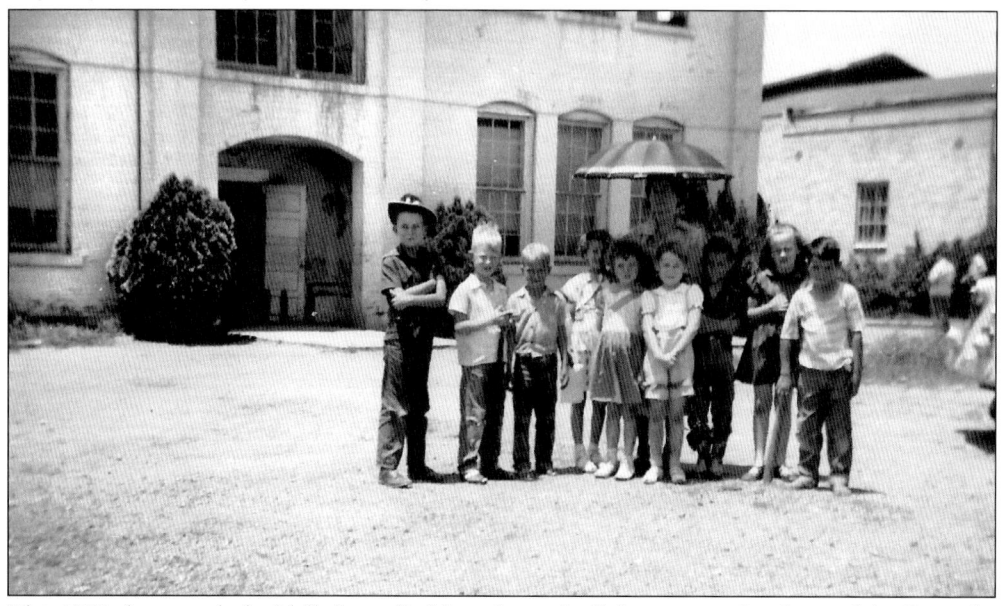

This 1954 class, taught by Idelle Love (holding the umbrella), is pictured in front of the Roanoke school, constructed in 1912. The children are unidentified. Love was probably one of the teachers at this school who had the most longevity, and there are many adults in the community who still talk about her impact on their lives. (Courtesy of Obie "Dub" Wheeler.)

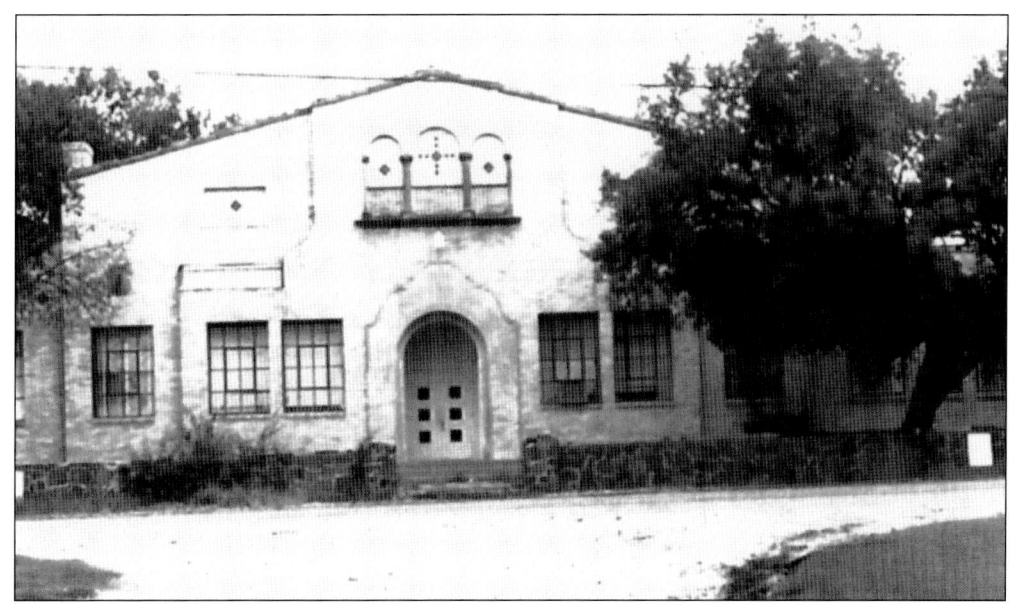

This high school building was constructed in 1935 next to the two-story existing school. This building was demolished in 1996, and a new elementary school was built on the school property. The archway pictured above the door was preserved and set into the original rock fence built by the Works Progress Administration on the school grounds. The rock fence is the only structure left with historic interest on this school property, which has been in use since the late 1800s. (Courtesy of Vertalee and John Coleman.)

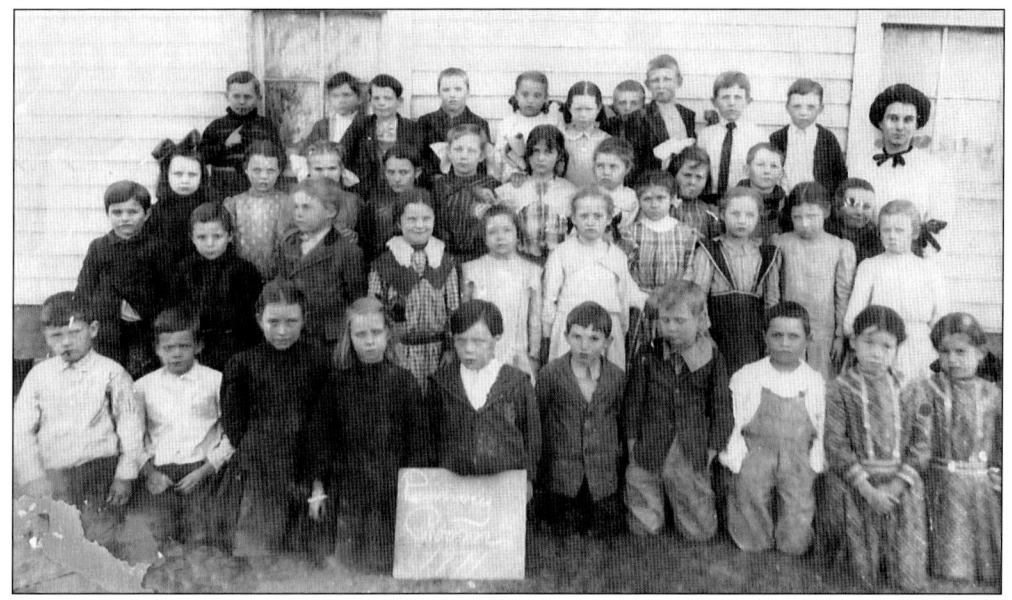

These school children are pictured in front of their frame schoolhouse, which predates the brick and rock buildings that followed. None of these school children have been identified. This is one of the oldest known photographs in existence of early school classes in this area. There are still older people around who attended area schools such as Star, Medlin, Walnut Grove, or others; however, there is little documentation in writing or photographs for younger generations to enjoy. (Courtesy of Mary Carpenter Estate.)

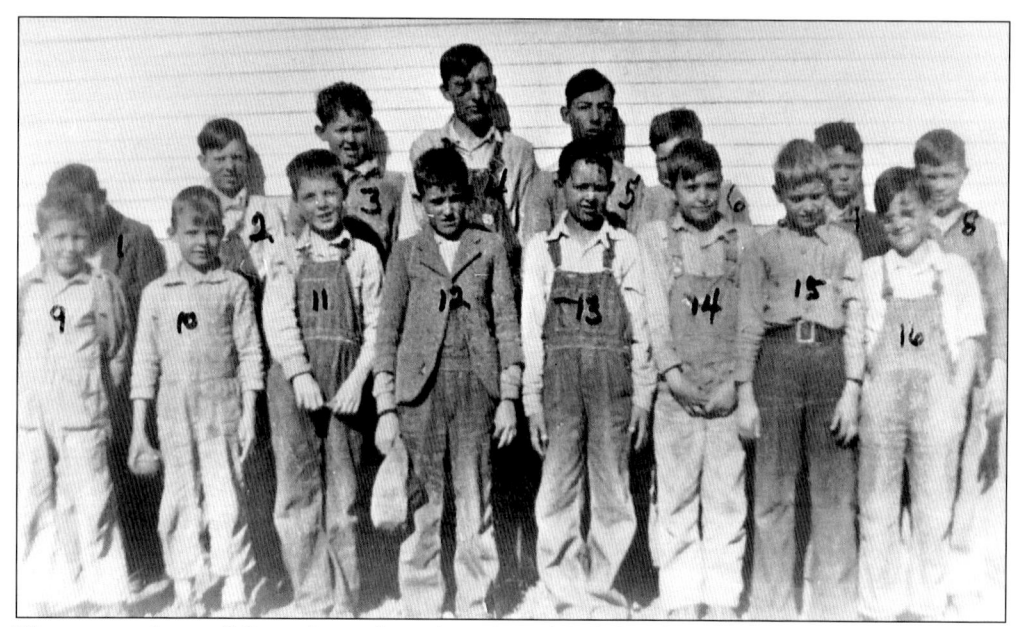

These young boys, all Roanoke students, have been labeled with numbers to assist in identifying them. However, only a few are now readily recognizable, including Norman Crites (3), Glenn Crites (9), Calvin Crites (10), Robert "R. E." Harris (11), Edward Crites (13), ? Johnson (14), and Earl Huffman (15). Lois Manire was their teacher. (Courtesy of Edward Crites.)

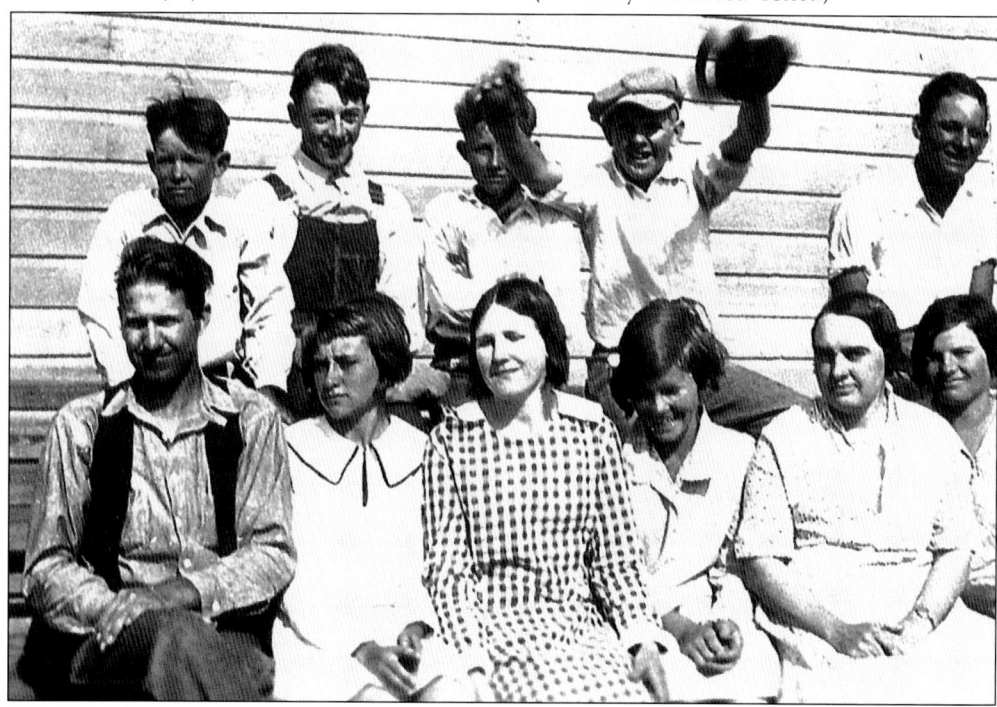

The older children from Elizabeth school and their teacher are sitting on a bench by the school. The only people identified in this photograph are Francis Peterson (second row, far left) and Mamie Holloway (first row, fifth from left). Holloway later married Clint Haynie, and they had two children. (Courtesy of Francis Gay.)

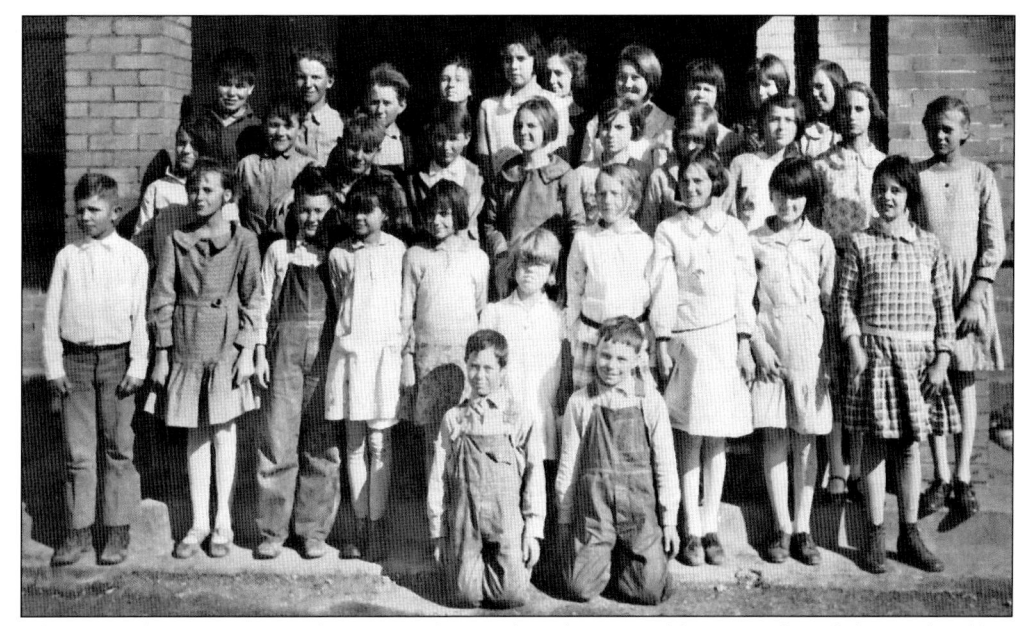

This 1928 class picture may be two grades combined. Pictured here are, from left to right, (first row) E. C. Buell and Charles Fisher; (second row) J. B. Hogan, Marguerite Ragsdale, Morgan Irving, June Gibson, Allene Pippin, Ila Woodson, Ilene Houton, Anna Mays, Dennis Lane, and Omega Gunnels; (third row) Irene Houton, Harvey Newman, Frank Kelley, J. D. Brigman, Johnnie Blakeley, Theresa Fisher, Ilene Love, Reba Attaberry, Nioma Fanning, and Emily Bogart; (fourth row) Levi Webster, Henry Blakeley, Claude Alexander, Maude Alexander, Juanita Marsters, a Miss McCreary, Earleen Carpenter, Margaret Webster, Myrtle Lane, and Lucille Newton. (Courtesy of Emily Ragsdale.)

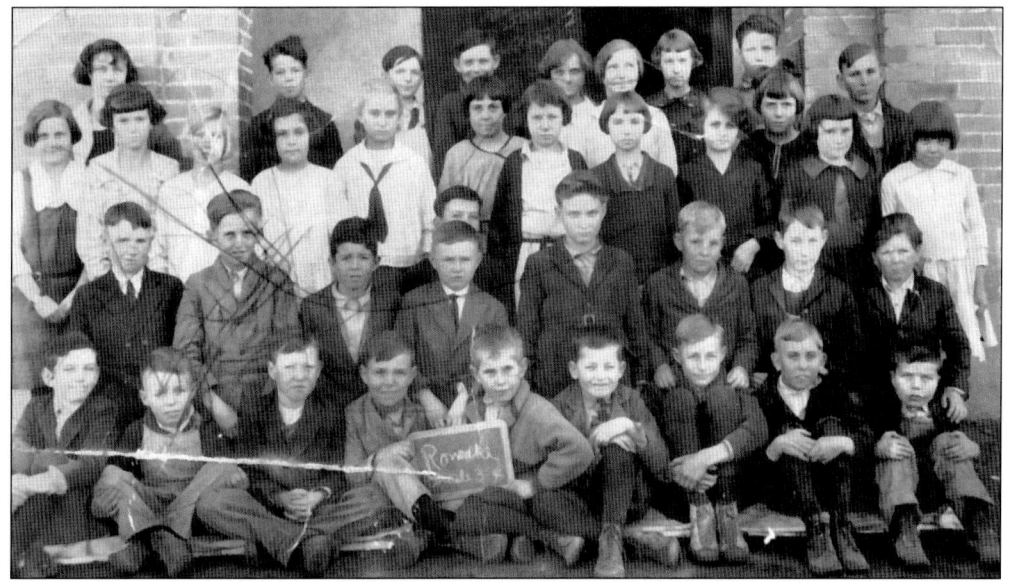

The third and fourth grades at Roanoke School are pictured here in 1922. Unfortunately the only one identified is John Henry Ragsdale, seated in the first row, fifth from left, holding the sign. There are many in the community who have this same picture, but most did not have the foresight to document the student's names for posterity. (Courtesy of Emily Ragsdale.)

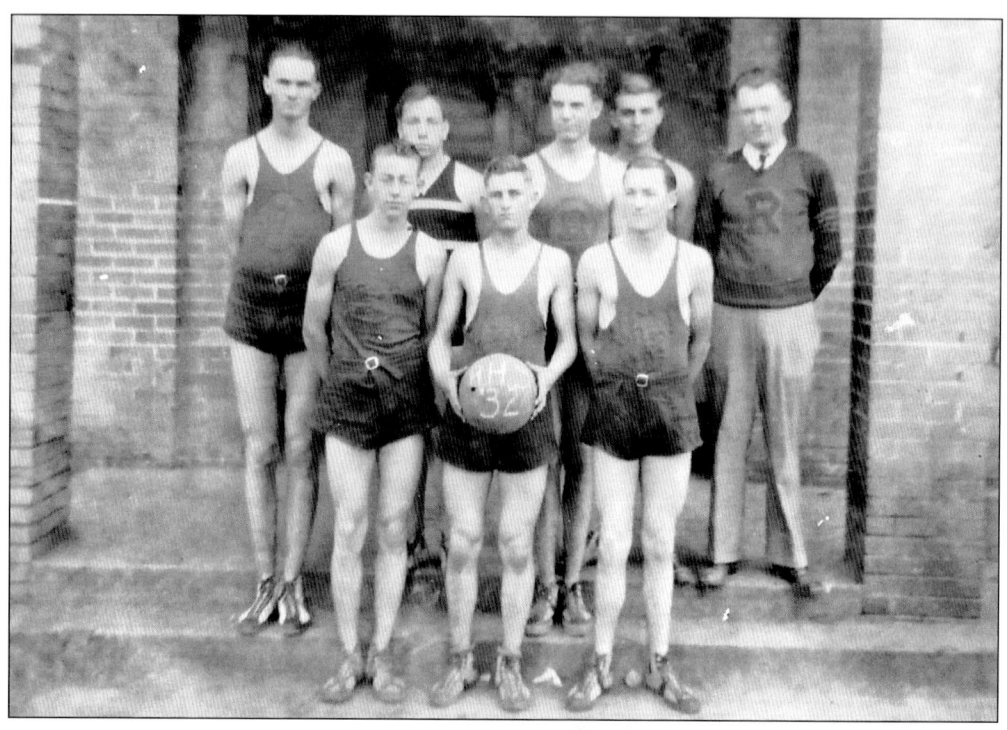

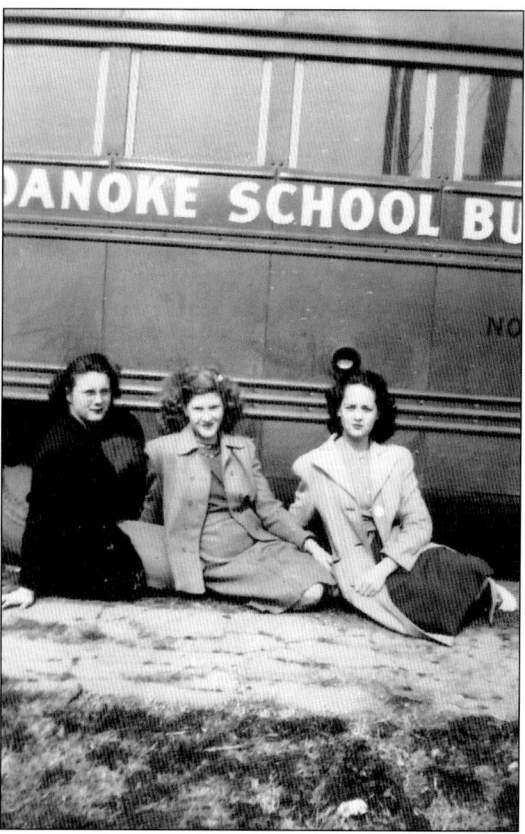

This class "B" championship team of Denton County represented Roanoke in 1932. They are, from left to right, (first row) John Martindale, Bernie Luttrell, and Coy McElroy; (second row) Robert Carpenter, Leroy Crouch, Manuel Bogart, John D. Ottinger, and coach Roy Cloud. Unfortunately this was at the beginning of the Depression, when many of the students who were about to graduate were unable to find outside employment; however, many were able to work on their family's farm. (Courtesy of Emily Ragsdale.)

Pictured in front of the Roanoke school bus are, from left to right, Marilou Harris, Marjorie Sturdivant, and Nancy Manire. Marilou was in the class of 1948, and Marjorie and Nancy graduated in 1949. Many students rode the bus to school. Entire families came to Roanoke on Trade Days or when other events were planned. (Courtesy of Marjorie Thomas.)

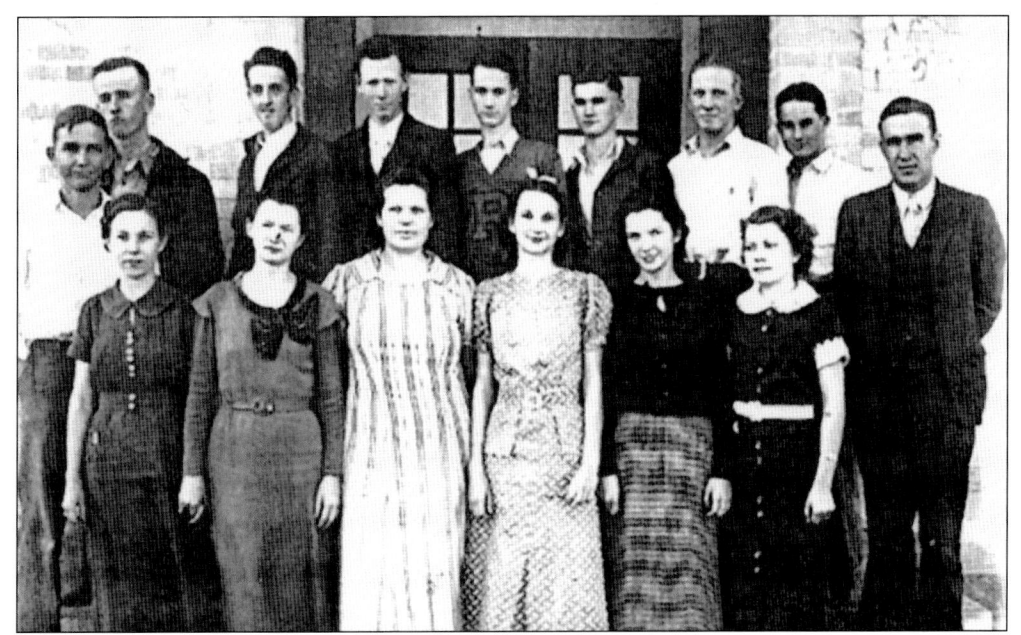

Pictured here are students of Roanoke High School From left to right are (first row) Mineola Luttrell, Dola Huffman, Pauline Martindale, Katherine Isles, Rose Shelton, and Faye Parish; (second row) Emmett Lee, and Lester Jameson; (third row) Clint Cowan Jr., John Thompson, John Fisher, Gerald Ward, L. J. Lee, Randolph Peterson, and Sam Lee. Rosella Lee and Paul Irwin were also in this class, but they were absent the day the photograph was taken. (Courtesy of Calvin Peterson.)

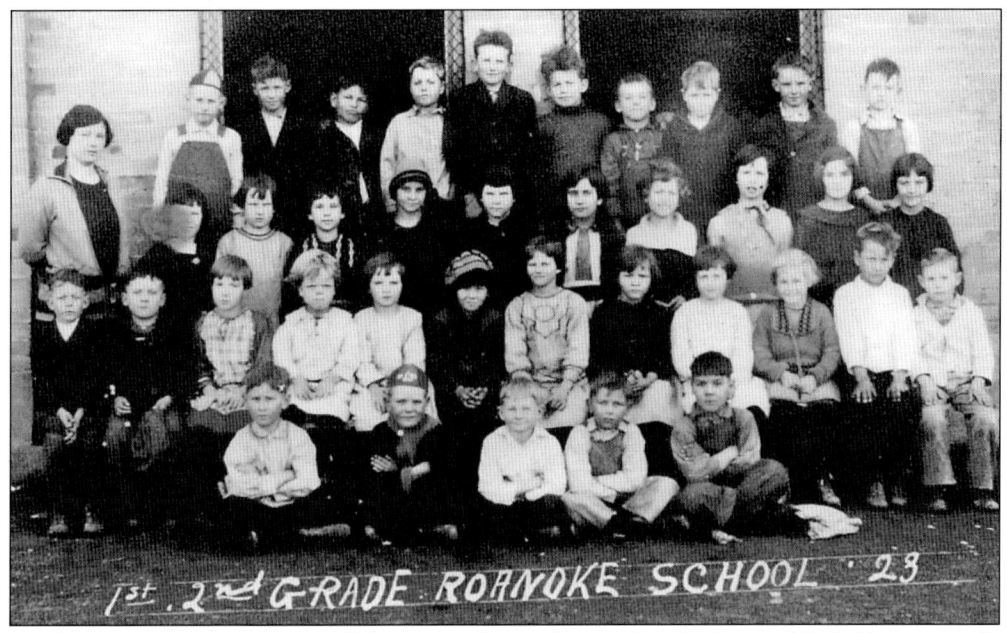

Lucille King is shown standing at left with her first and second grade classes of 1923. Unfortunately space does not permit listing all of the members; however, the Medlin, Blackburn, Blakely, Alexander, Luttrell, Bogart, Kelley, McDonald, Newman, and many other families were represented in these two classes. (Courtesy of Emily Ragsdale.)

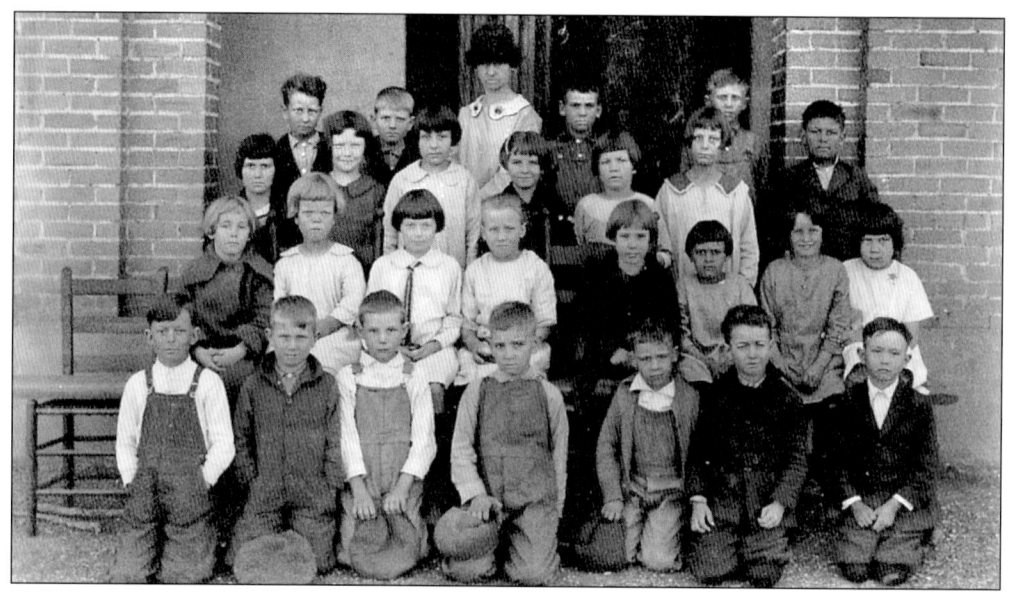

Idelle Love, wearing the hat, is shown with her first and second grade classes of 1924. Students shown are, from left to right, (first row) Jesse Ashlock, Vergil Bourland, Earl Clifton, Floyd Strickland, Clay Whitewell, Morgan Irving, and Osbourn Neeley; (second row) Marguerite Ragsdale, Ila Woodson, Dorothy Cowan, Emily Bogart, Mineola Luttrell, Francis Attaberry, Estelle Coffman, and Juanette Medlin; (third row) Zelma Pippin, Dorothy Medlin, Ethel Hooten, Johnnye Blakely, Margaret Webster, ? Hailey, and Levi Webster; (fourth row) Raymond Shockey, Frank Kelley, Idelle Love, Bill Luttrell, and Odell Williams. (Courtesy of Emily Ragsdale.)

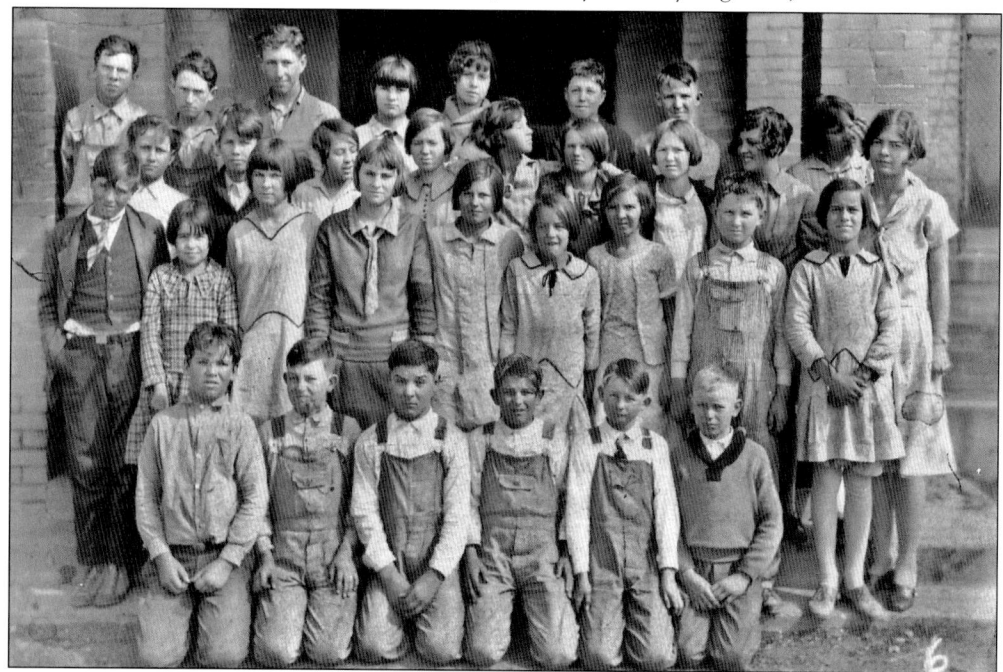

The fifth and sixth grade classes of 1928 are shown here with their teacher, ? Graham. Mary Luttrell Carpenter saved this picture, but the only names on it are hers and the teacher. The rest of the students' names are unavailable. (Courtesy of Mary Carpenter Estate.)

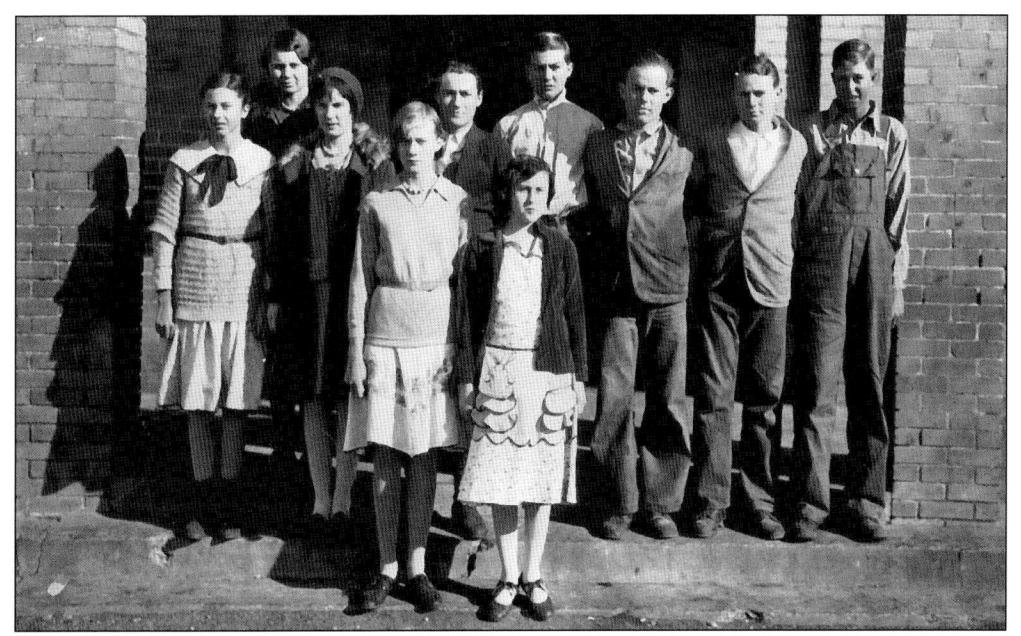

The students of the eighth grade class shown here are, from left to right, (first row) Emily Bogart and Marie Pinion; (second row) Mary Alice Dunton, Gladys Wheeler, Coy McElroy, Orland Horton, Rogan Mahaffey, and Lanier Mundy; (third row) Ester Grace Barr (teacher) and John D. Ottinger. (Courtesy of Emily Ragsdale.)

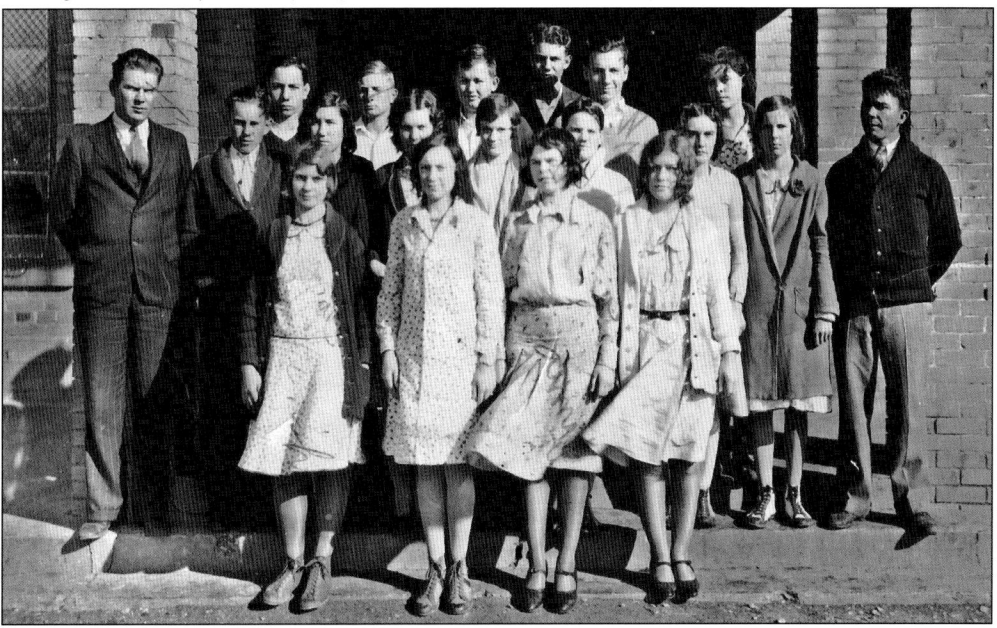

The 1930 junior and senior classes at Roanoke High School are pictured here with their teacher. From left to right are (first row) Louise Lee, Odessa Samsill, Anna Jones, and Opal Parish; (second row) ? Rockett (the teacher), Avis Schooling, Tom Gibbons, Winnie Tidwell, Juanita Underwood, Mozelle Raibourn, Marian Buell, and John Ragsdale; (third row) ? Finley, Jo Clark Rutledge, W. T. Crouch, Manuel Bogart, Ernest Manire, ? Mahaffey, and Leroy Crouch. (Courtesy of Emily Ragsdale.)

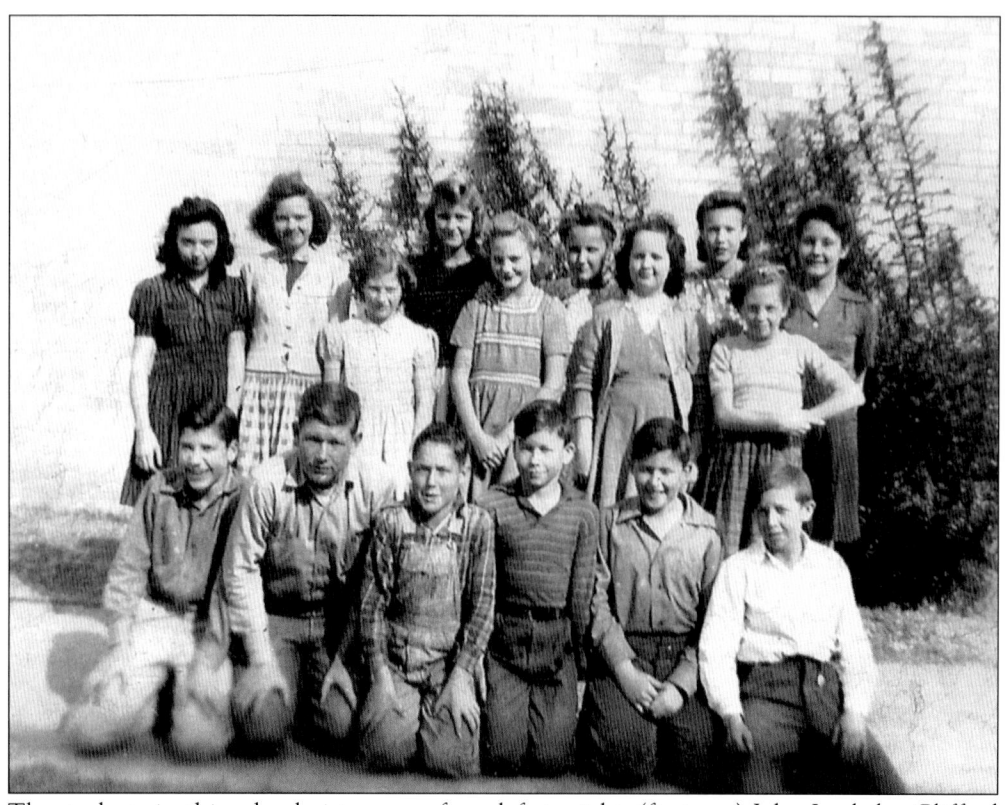

The students in this school picture are, from left to right, (first row) John Lockaby, Clifford Thompson, Billy Joe Thomas, John Clark, David Vanderpool, and Charles Stephenson; (second row) Marjorie Sturdevant, Bonnie Parish, Nancy Manire, and Margaret Mitchell; (third row) unidentified, Louise Crites, Valena Payton, Joyce Flanagan, Penelope "Opal" Roberts, and Nelda Owens. (Courtesy of Marjorie Sturdevant Irick.)

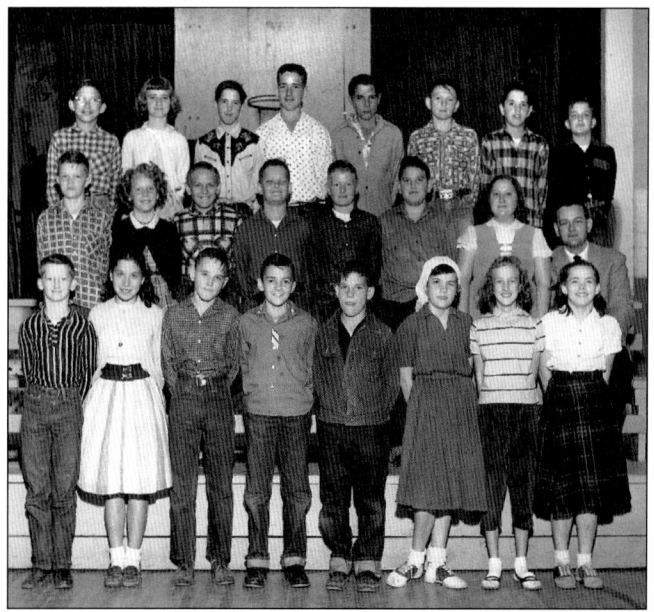

Roanoke Elementary students, standing on the stage in the gymnasium, are, from left to right, (first row) James Garrett, Virginia Edington, Charles Endsley, Jack Fisher, Johnny Huffman, Freda Huffman, Sue Peterson, and Loretta Shockey; (second row) Billy Daniel, Barbara Gray, Jerry Holland, Gene Roach, David McPherson, Bobby Ward, Lucille Williams, and principal ? Kilmer; (third row) Joe Blackburn, Carolyn Brown, Charlie Cook, Allen Knowles, Harold Bruedigam, Tommy Jones, Sterling Paddack, and James Redwine. (Courtesy of James Redwine.)

The Ladies Bible Class of the Church of Christ included, from left to right, (first row) Faye McPherson, Mayna Peterson, and Ruby Lassen; (second row) Edith Parish, Ellen Strickland, and Pearl Brown; (third row) Mary Carpenter, Zula Terrell, Bonnie Miller, Bea Howell, and unidentified. (Courtesy of Dorothy Brown.)

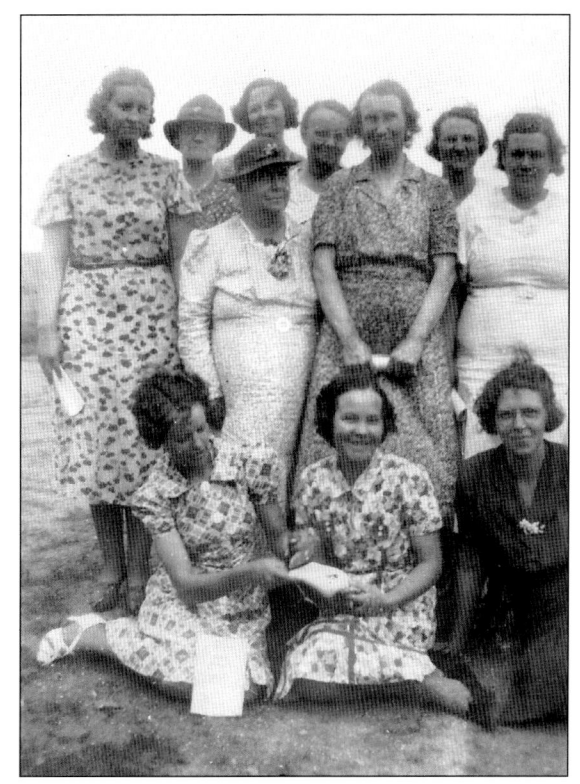

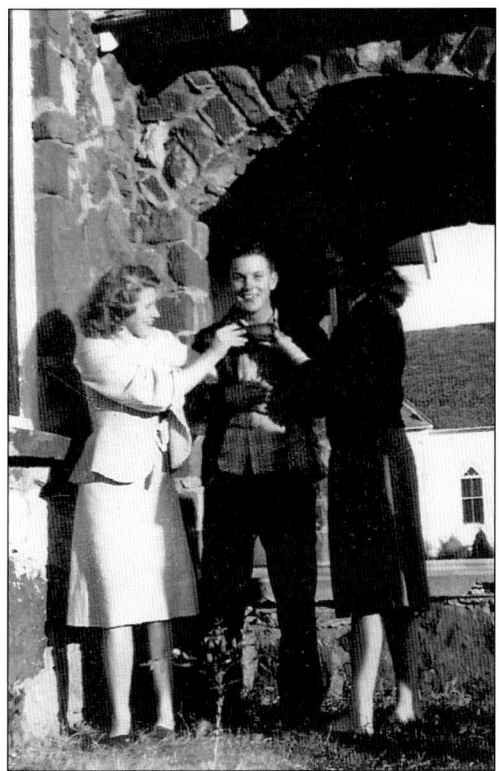

In this c. 1949 photograph, in front of the rock Church of Christ building are, from left to right, Marjorie Sturdevant, George Vaughn, and Nancy Manire. The white church seen through the arch is the Methodist Church, which has since been moved several times; the building is now a wedding chapel in Trophy Club. The Church of Christ occupies the site where the first church in Roanoke, the Union Church, stood at the corner of Rusk and Walnut Streets. (Courtesy of Marjorie Sturdevant Irick.)

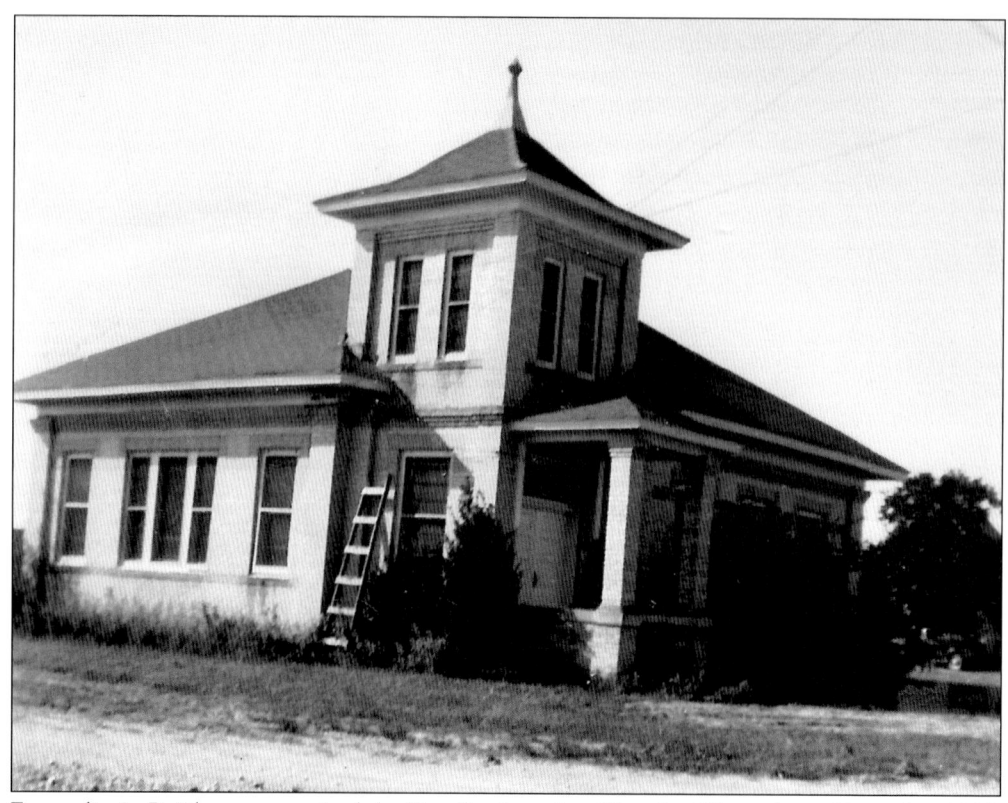

Evangelist L. B. Chaney organized the First Presbyterian Church of Roanoke in December 1883. Prior to this, services were held by all denominations in the schoolhouse located north of what is now Highway 114. In 1917, the church, pictured around 1953, was built on Oak Street. One of the founding members was Elizabeth Brand, who often took granddaughter Alberta Maher to services with her, much to the chagrin of the pastor who was not amused by Alberta's balance beam act on the railing separating the congregation from the minister. The Presbyterian congregation is shown below. (Above, courtesy of HSC; below, courtesy of Alberta Lincecum.)

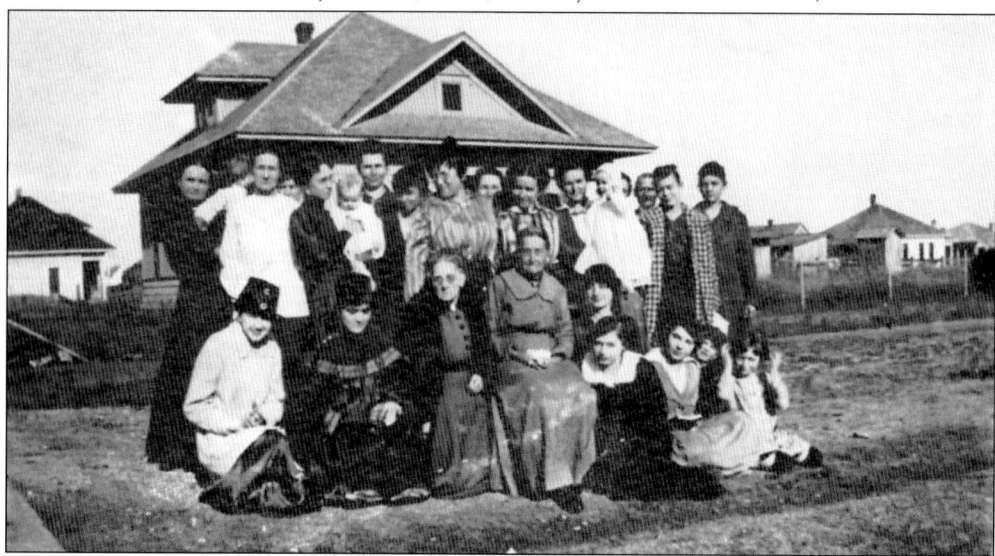

The Methodist church was organized in 1900 after a community revival. The new church was known as the Episcopal Methodist Church, South. Church members supported the construction, and many community members donated time and materials to start building the church in 1906. Peter Lassen was responsible for the construction of the steeple, which housed the bell that rang each Sunday and for other community events. In 1939, the church became known simply as the Methodist Church. (Courtesy of Vertalee and John Coleman.)

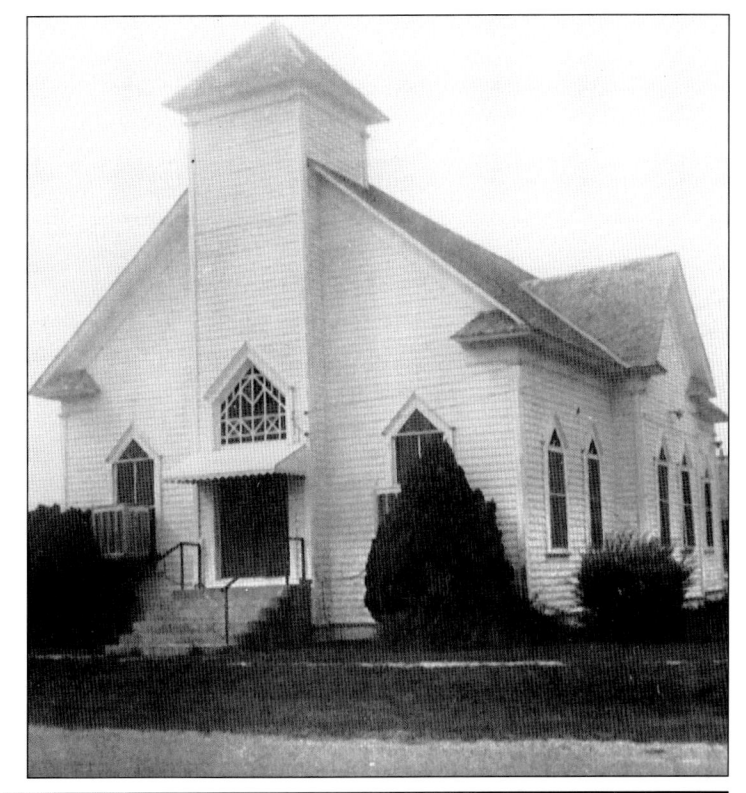

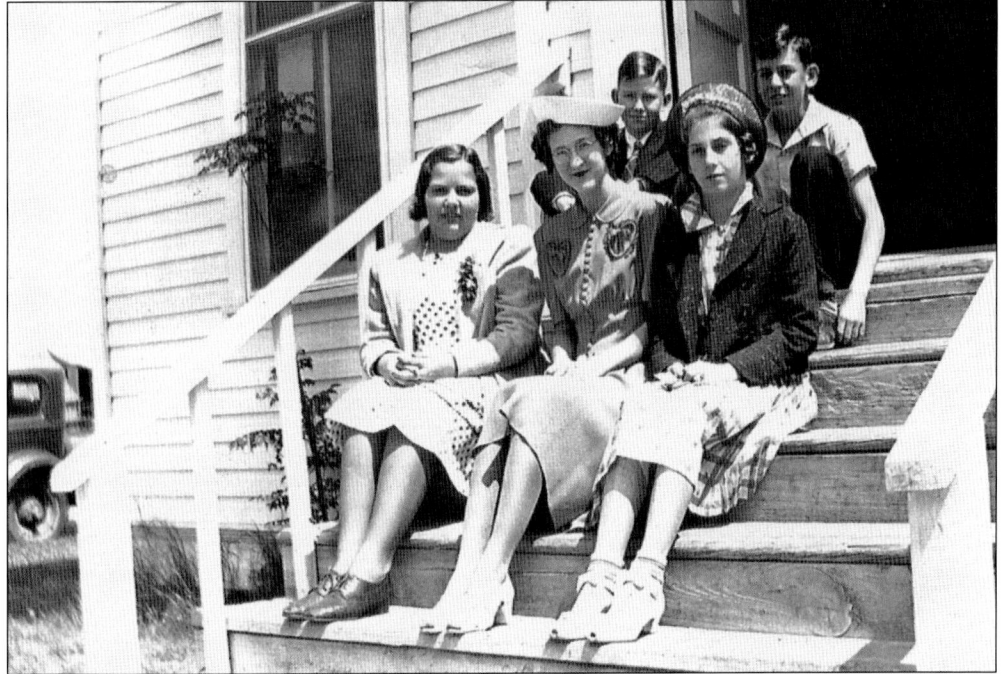

The church members sitting on the wooden steps are, from left to right, (first row) Jane Boyer, Mary Crouch, and Mary Ann Mitchell; (second row) Fred Usry and John A. Coleman Jr. (Courtesy of Vertalee and John Coleman.)

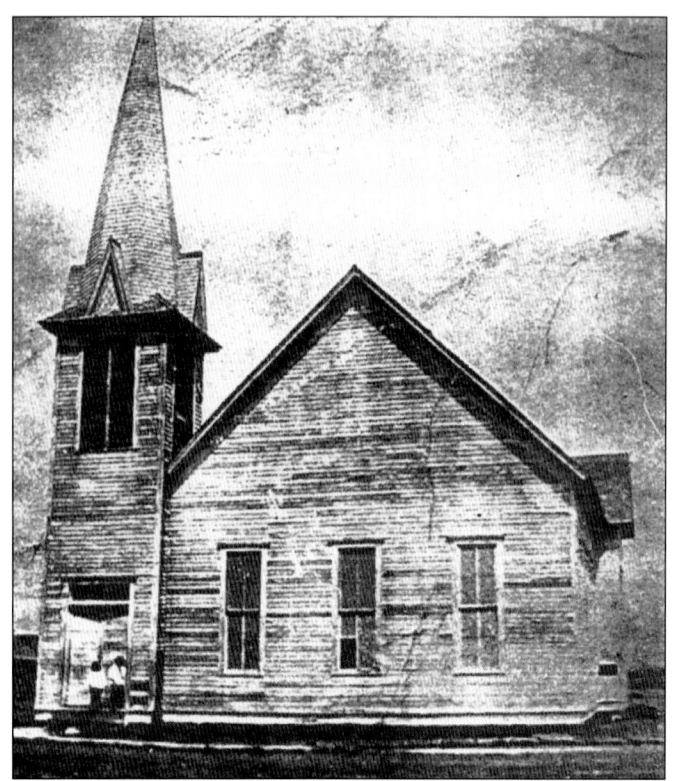

The Union Church was located at the corner of Rusk and Walnut Streets to serve the community's spiritual needs. The Episcopal Methodist, the Presbyterian, the Baptist, and the Church of Christ all met here. Each denomination used the church building on alternate Sundays until they built their own building, except the Church of Christ, which remained. Later the women of the Church of Christ decided they needed a new sanctuary, so they started removing boards one by one, and they were soon joined by others who helped build a new sanctuary using some of the original lumber. (Courtesy of Dorothy Skidmore)

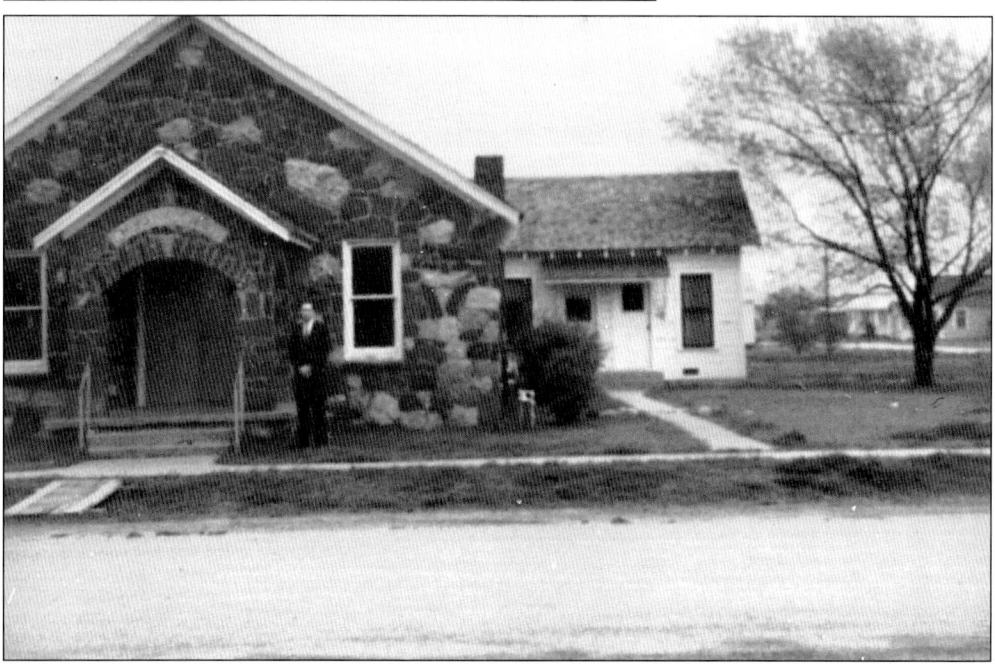

The Church of Christ was built in the 1930s on the same site as the Union Church. It was built of native stone and featured a sign over the arch made of petrified wood, prompting one youngster to refer to it as the petrified church. This building was replaced in the 1960s, and a larger, more modern building is now in this location. (Courtesy of Pat Turner.)

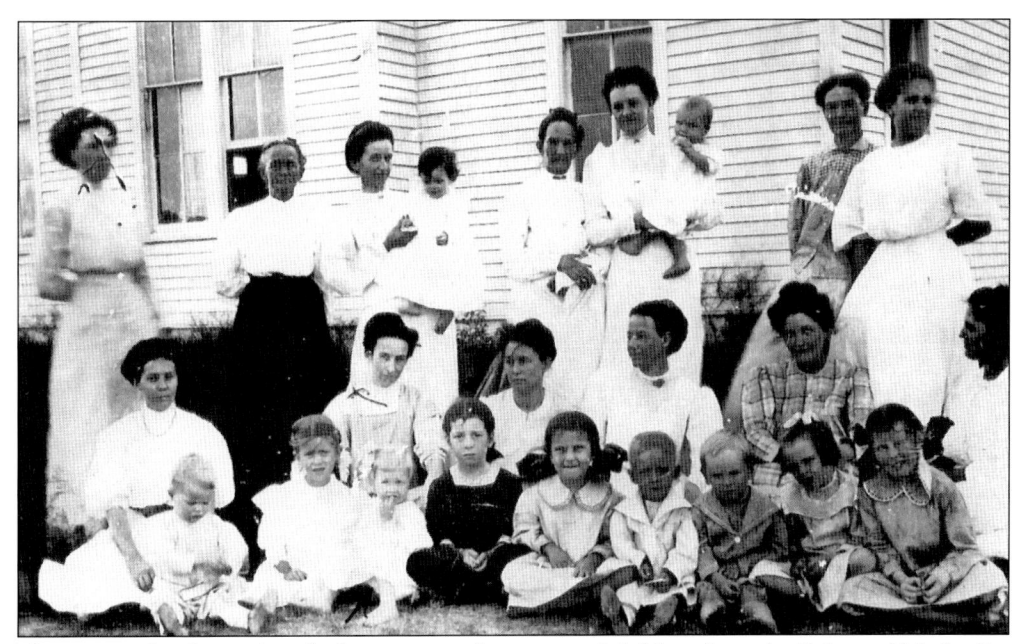

This picture has been identified as a group of women and children from the Episcopal Methodist Church, South members. However, the only participant identified is Lucy Manire Elsea, a member of the Church of Christ. She appears at the left of the photograph (standing, second from left, wearing a black skirt). It was common for Roanoke residents to attend Bible study or revivals at churches other than their own. (Courtesy of RVCM.)

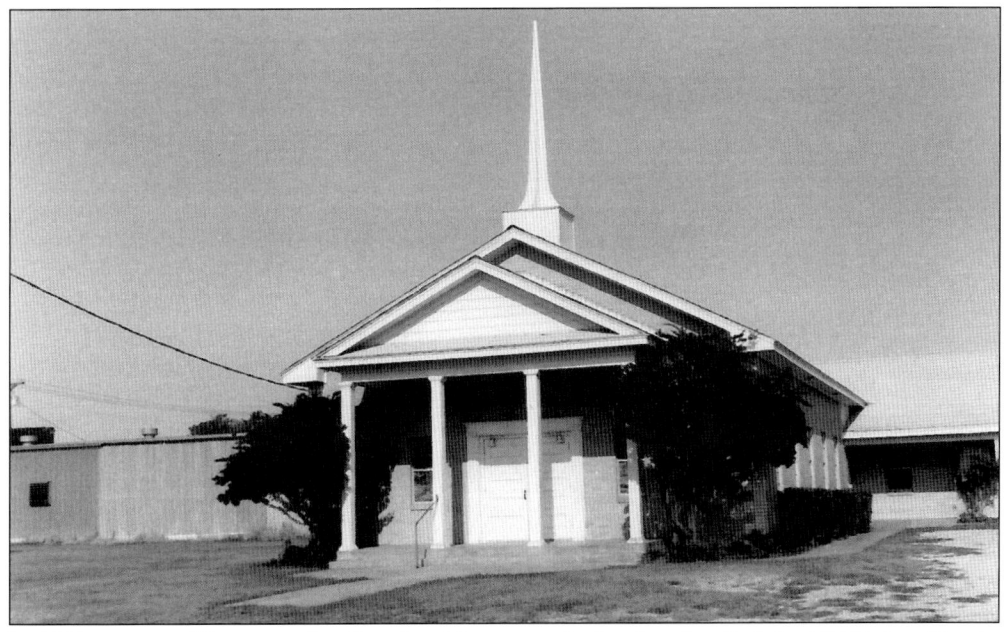

In 1874, a group of Baptist settlers from Louisiana organized a church called the Old Colony Baptist Church, which met at Medlin Mound School. In 1881, the congregation joined with other denominations to build a community church known as the Union Church. The Baptists left that building in 1910 to build a church of their own. The First Baptist Church (pictured here) is the newest church, though some of the older buildings are still on church property. (Courtesy of Wanda Smith.)

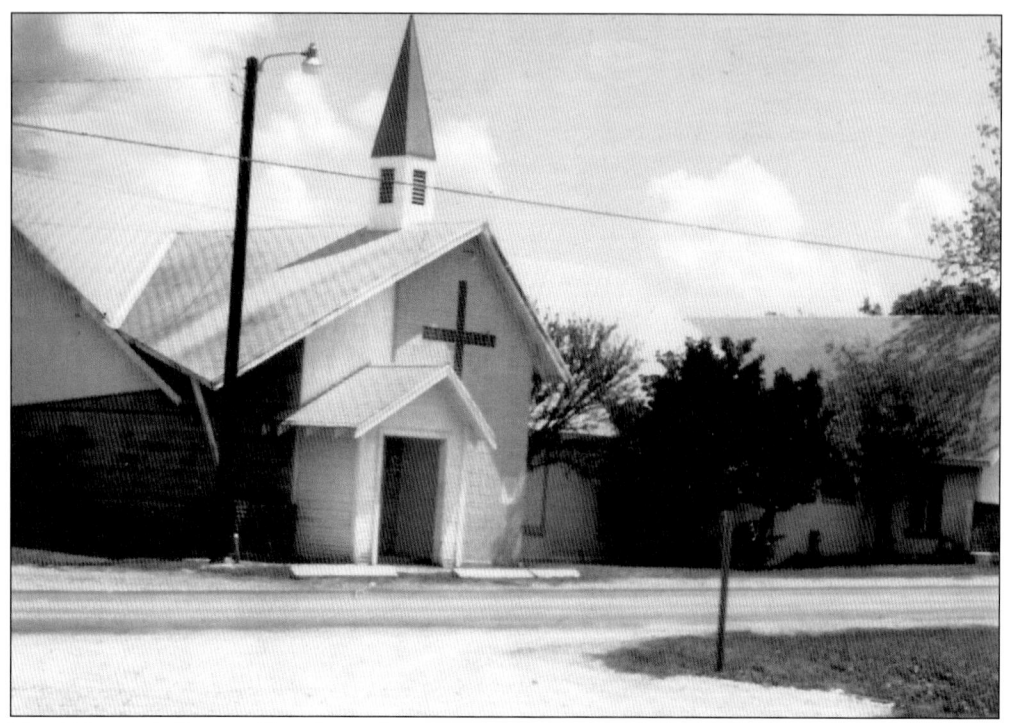

This Tabernacle Baptist Church was designed and constructed by Jake Parsley Jr. next to an already-existing auditorium. The church was built in 1957 and had a dedication conducted by the Reverend Sherman Morgan in October of that same year. (Courtesy of Barbara Medlin Langston.)

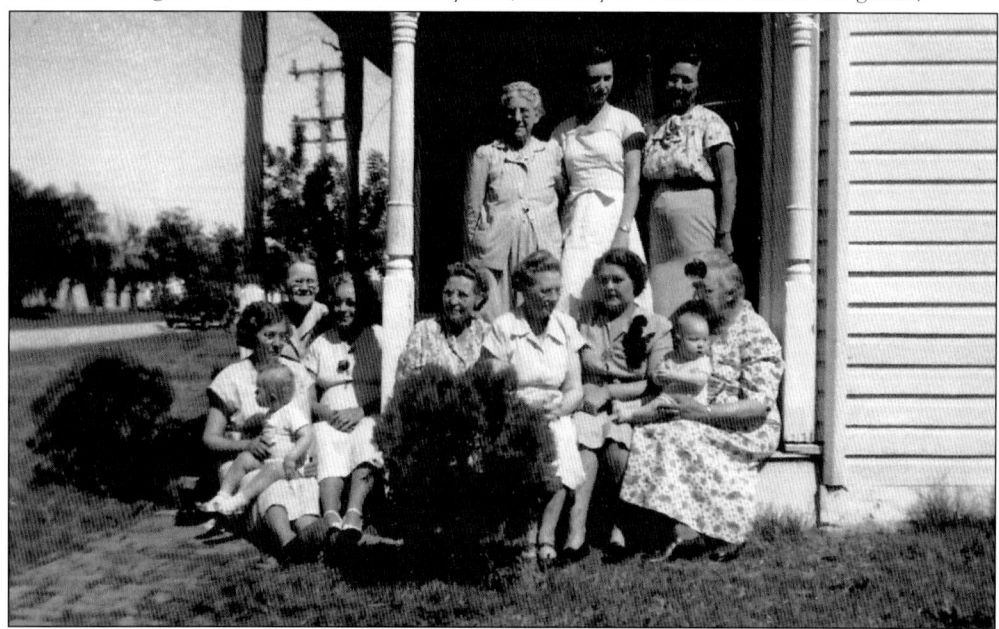

The Methodist women pictured, identified by their married names, are, from left to right, (first row) Mrs. T. A. Malone, Jimma Belle Ragsdale, Mrs. W. R. Roberts, Mrs. Phil Holley, unidentified, Mrs. Otis Woodruff, and Frances Haynie; (second row) Mrs. ? Barnes-Wilson, Gertrude Hawthorne, and Faye McDonald. The two young children are unidentified. (Courtesy of Emily Ragsdale.)

Five

FARMS AND RANCHES

A cook shack, a cooking shanty on wheels, was essential to the survival of early cowboys and others who worked away from home in the fields. The wagon pictured here is a cook shack available to a threshing crew near Roanoke. Male cooks ran most of the Western cook shacks; however, in later years, women came to the fields to cook for the workers. Though the original cowboys may not have waxed poetic about the original cook shack, the name is still popularly used on many restaurants throughout the West. (Courtesy of Alberta Lincecum.)

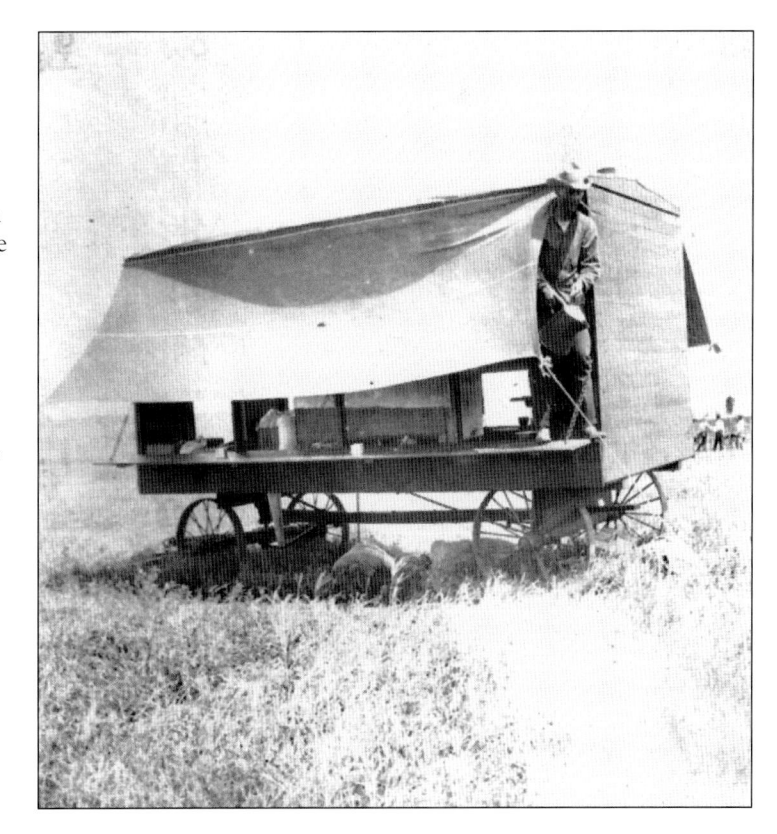

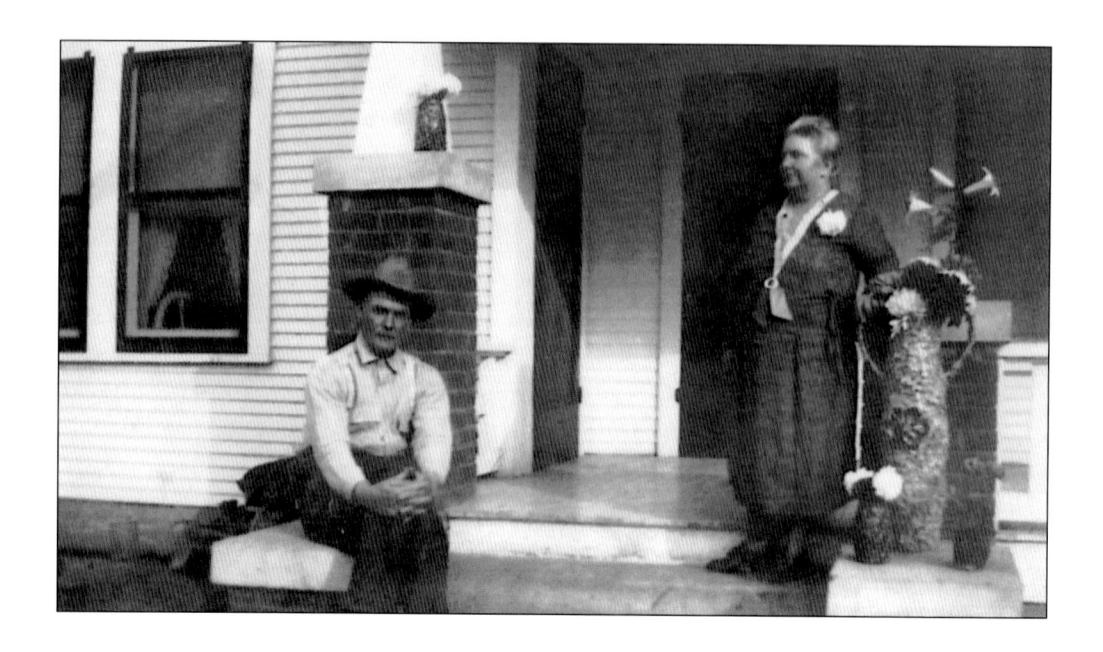

Thomas Parish (March 27, 1877–October 4, 1945) and Edith Parish (March 12, 1878–January 24, 1950), pictured above, are standing on the front porch of the home they built when they moved to Roanoke in the 1930s. They were forced to sell their farm in Azle because the back-up waters of Eagle Mountain Lake would cover most of their land. The photograph below features the Buell property, where Van Zandt Parish, a son of Thomas and Edith Parish, lived with his family in 1938, prior to building a more modern home. (Both, courtesy of Bonnie Parish McKee.)

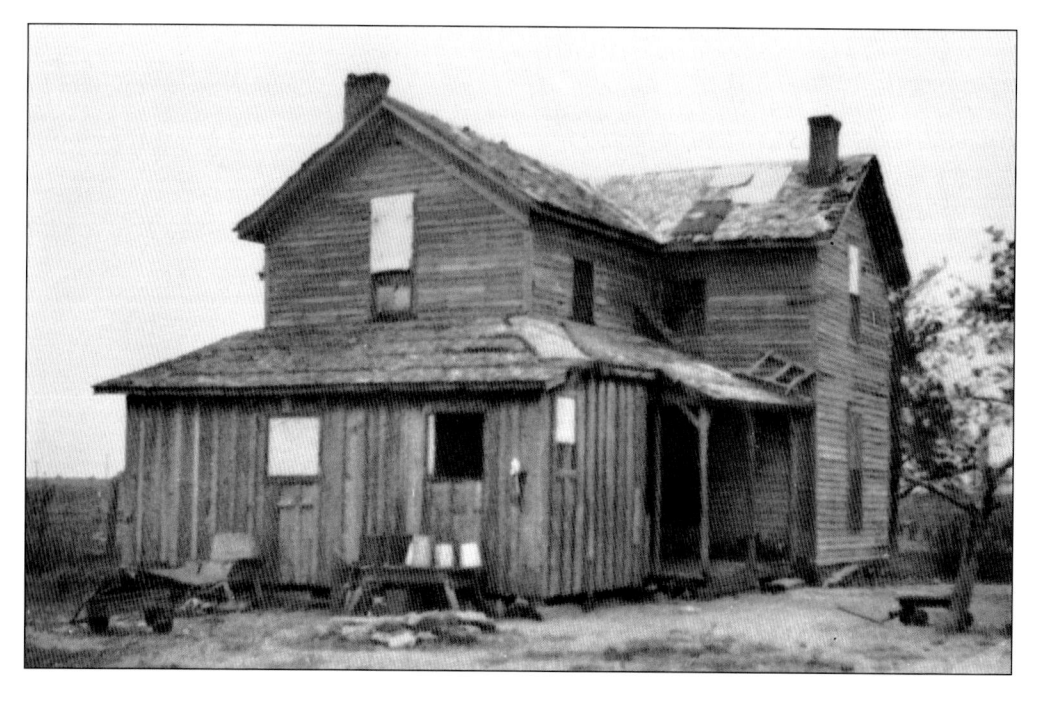

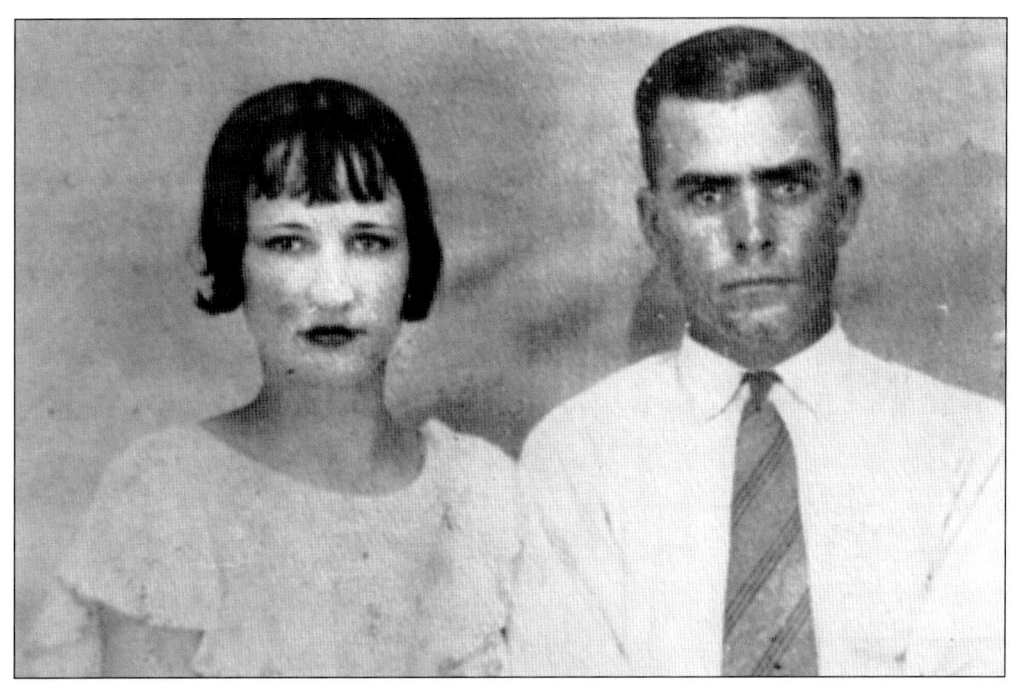

Pictured are Van Zandt Parish (September 1, 1906–February 9, 1994) and Lorene Parish (November 23, 1909–February 11, 1998) shortly after their marriage. The Parish family bought a farm in Roanoke and began to build houses, barns, and other support buildings. Thomas and Edith Parish lived in the main house, and their son, Van Zandt, and his wife, Lorene, lived in a smaller house on the property. Later the younger Parishes moved two farms away from the elder Parishes. Bonnie Parish, their daughter, has written a charming account of an incident that happened during a storm, which flooded the yard in Roanoke. Lorene Parish, Bonnie's mother, raised chickens, which would not live if left out in the inclement weather, so she brought them into the house. Though the storm was scary, the antics of the chickens gave them plenty to laugh about later. One of the chickens jumped on a dresser; when it saw its image reflected in the mirror, the chicken pecked at the mirror, much to the amusement of the children. Van Zandt and Lorene had three children, Bennie, Bonnie, and Darrell. The farm was eventually sold, and the Roanoke Recreation Center is on part of this property. (Both, courtesy of Bonnie Parish McKee.)

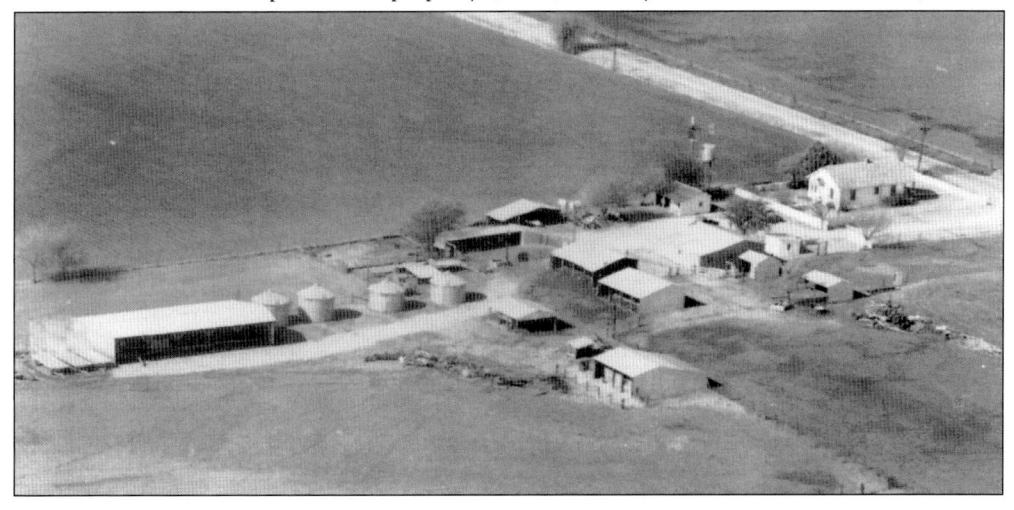

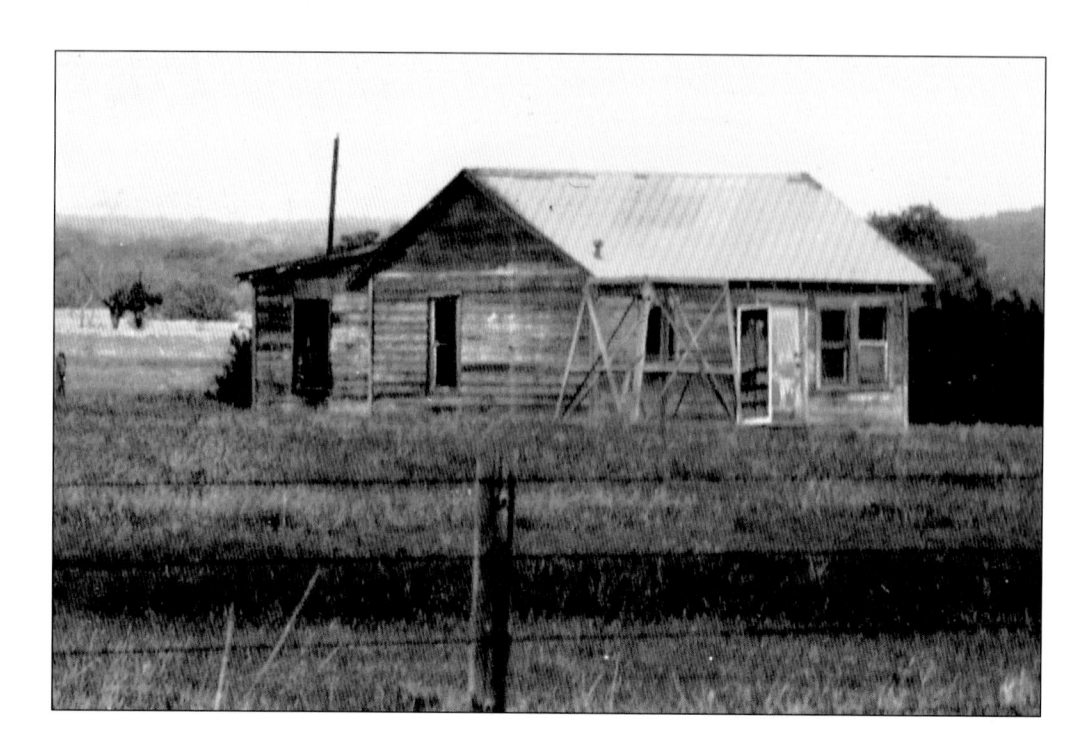

The old house pictured above was once a rental house on the Medlin farm, which was situated on Farm to Market Road 1171, northeast of Roanoke. The property belonged to Jesse James Medlin and his wife, Fannie; however, their son Lonzo and his wife, Edith, also lived there. The Medlin farm on Roanoke-Haslet Road, pictured below, was bought in 1951 when their former farm was endangered by the back-up waters from Grapevine Lake. (Both, courtesy of Barbara Medlin Langston.)

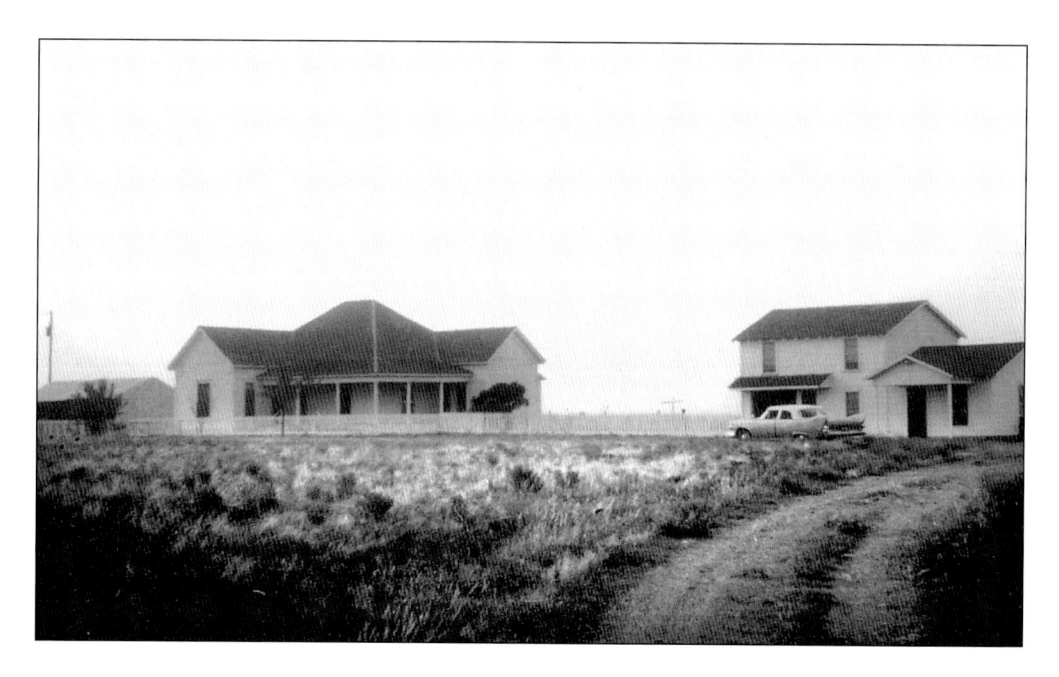

Pictured here are, from left to right, Jesse James Medlin; his wife, Fannie Lee; and his son and daughter-in-law, Lonzo and Edith Wilkerson Medlin. The farm complex pictured below was bought in 1951. Three generations of the Medlin family lived on this property. Barbara Medlin, Lonzo and Edith's daughter, has indicated she led a charmed life and may have been spoiled by her parents and grandparents since she was an only child, like her father. (Both, courtesy of Barbara Medlin Langston.)

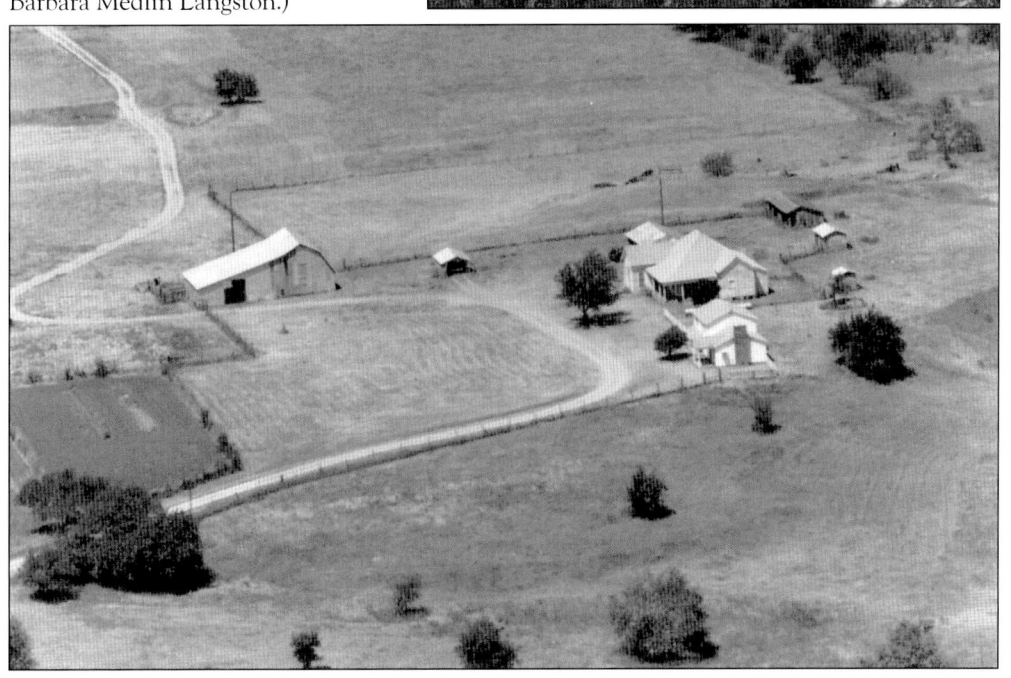

O. B. Ragsdale's Thresher

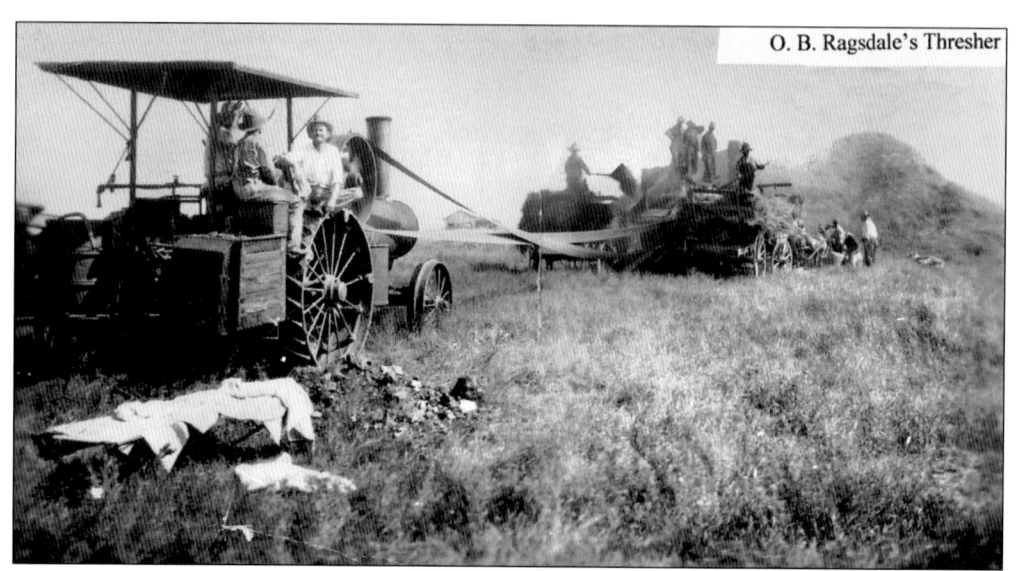

This thresher was owned by Baxter Ragsdale, who provided threshing services to area farmers. Baxter was born in 1885 in Garden Valley. Unfortunately, when he was only three years old, his father died, forcing him, as the oldest of three brothers, to learn to farm and repair machinery. Baxter married Jimma Belle Strickland while still living near Denton Creek; however, after several floods they moved into town. (Courtesy of Emily Ragsdale.)

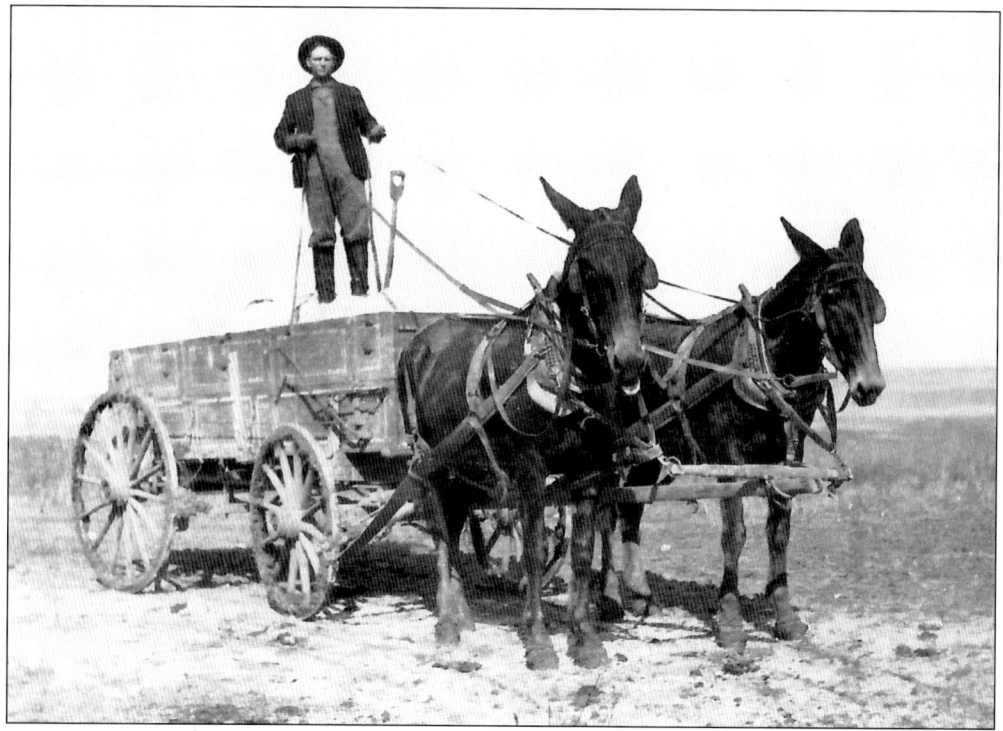

Bill Griffin, aided by mules owned by John Tolan, is driving a wagonload of cotton on the E. D. Farmer ranch in Azle. Farmer was an Englishman who had a farm next to Berry Hood, from Roanoke. Hood often brought workmen from Roanoke to work on his farmland, and they eventually started working on the Farmer property as well. (Courtesy of Alberta Lincecum.)

Valera and Gordon Stephenson Sr. appear solemn on what may have been their wedding day. The Stephensons owned a dairy farm northwest of Roanoke. Gordon also raised coon and bird dogs for hunting. The Stephensons had four children, Gordon L. (G. L.), Charles Ray, Nina Mae, and Wayne. Below, the aerial view of their farm indicates the amount of property they had for the dairy, gardens, and out buildings. One of the older Stephenson children once told an interviewer he did not have time to get into trouble as he got up early to milk, went to school, and then had to be at home in the evening to tend to the chores all over again. (Right, courtesy of Nina Mae Outlaw; below, courtesy of Charles Ray Stephenson.)

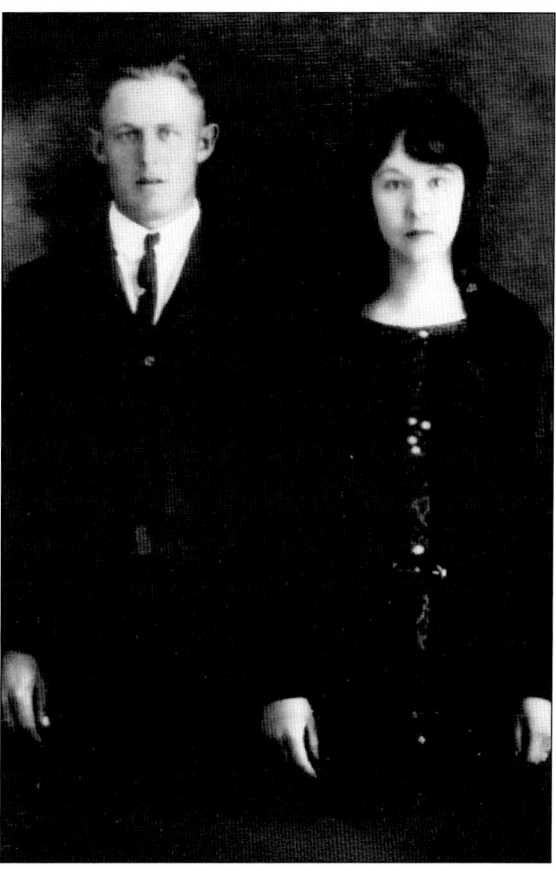

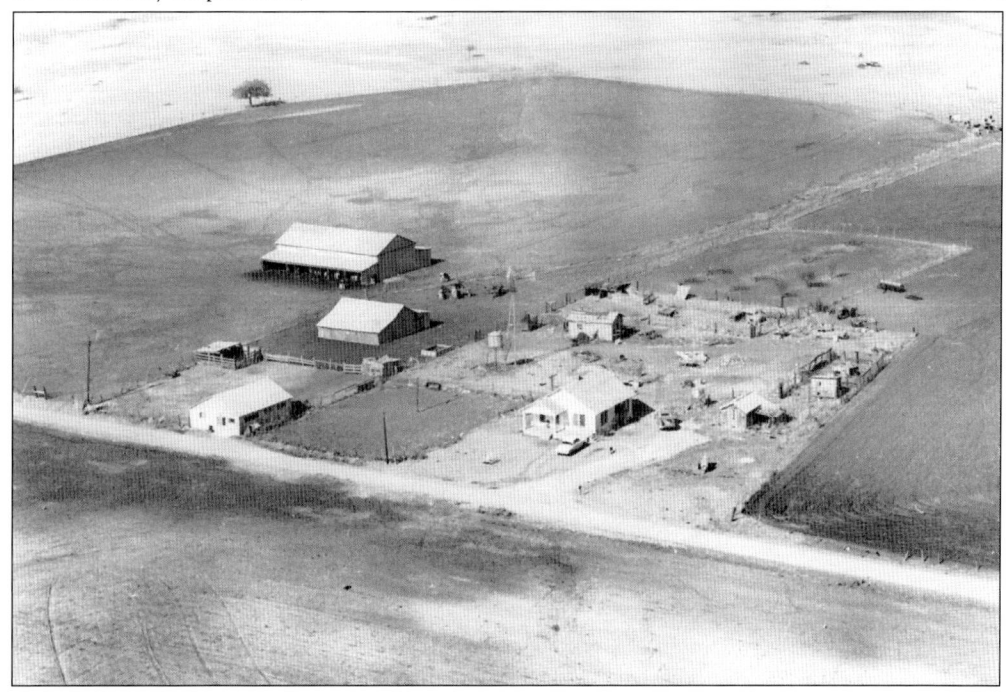

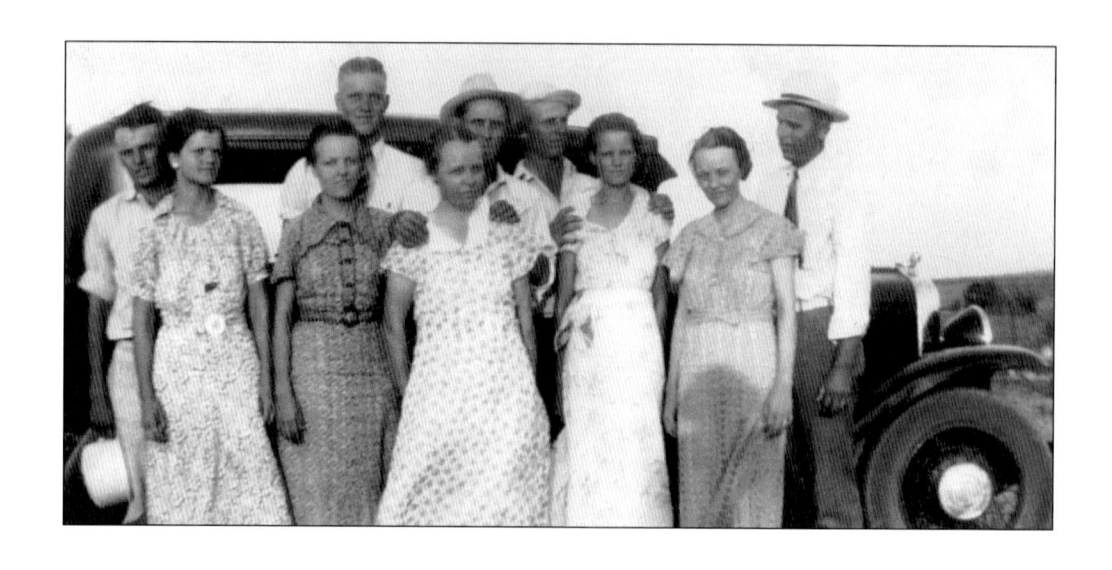

The extended McPherson family is gathered at the farm for this 1940s photograph. They are, from left to right, Wayne and Lorene McPherson, Leamon and Paralee Ragsdale, Dan and Estha Rodgers, Watt and Faye McPherson, and Jodie and Roy Stewart. The Watt McPherson family home, shown below as it looked in 1945, burned in December 1951. (Both, courtesy of Nancy Estill.)

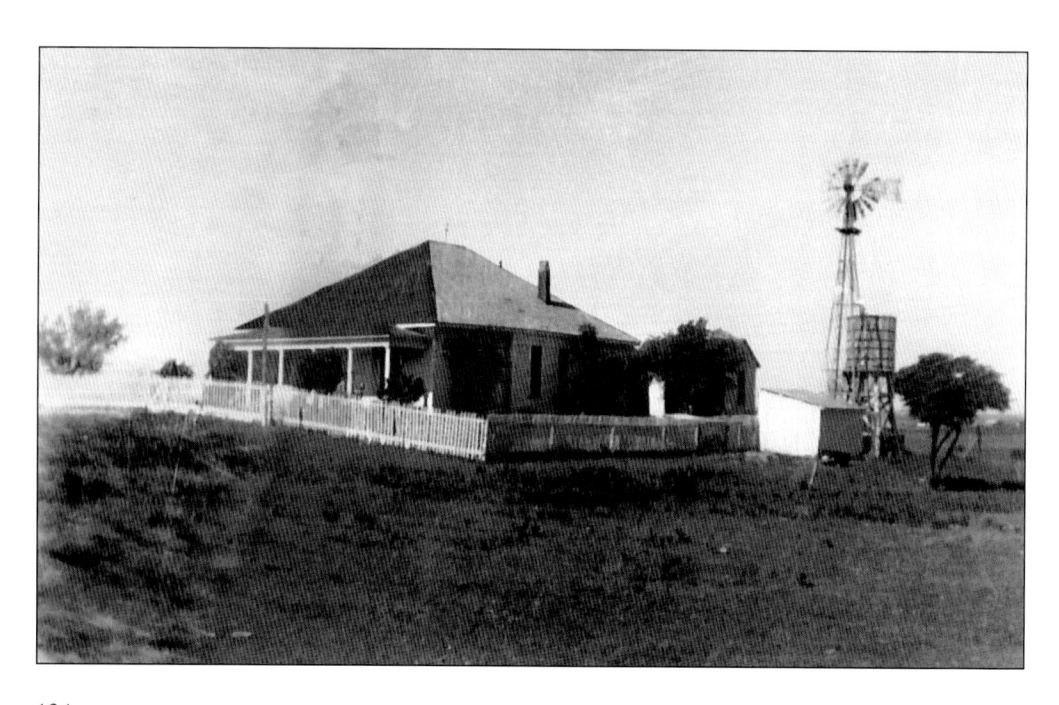

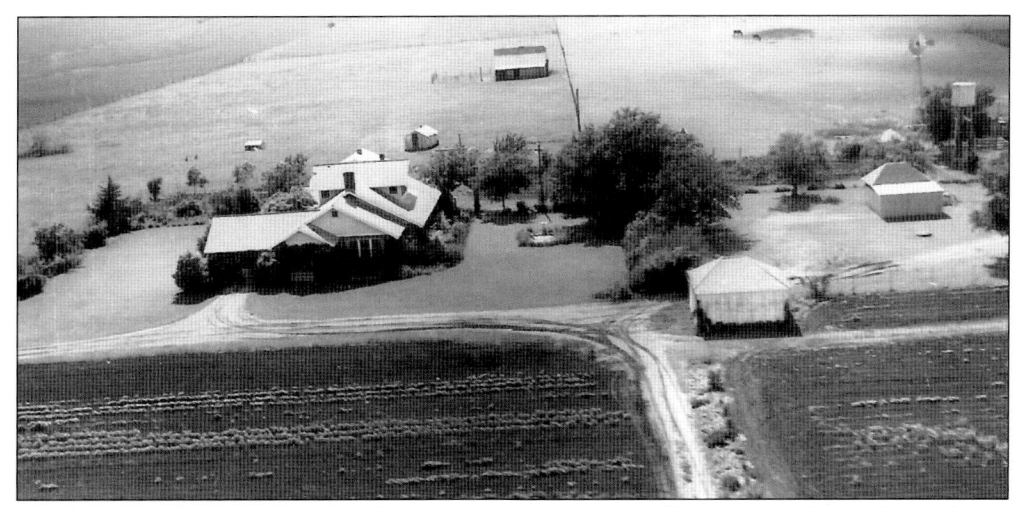

The large farmhouse and surrounding property of the Omas Peterson family was located west of Roanoke. Omas was married to Margaret Francisco, whose name over the years had evolved from the original spelling of Franciscus. Omas not only was an outstanding farmer, but he was also an outstanding citizen, recognized locally, as well as statewide, for his ability to get things done. He is credited with enabling several communities, including Roanoke, to band together to form a consolidated school district called Northwest. Recently, Peterson has been honored by having a school named for him. The five Peterson children pictured below are, from left to right, (first row) Margaret; (second row) her brothers Conway, Calvin, Randolph, and Howard. The building in the center, back of the aerial photograph above is the original farmhouse where all of the Peterson children were born. (Both, courtesy of Calvin Peterson.)

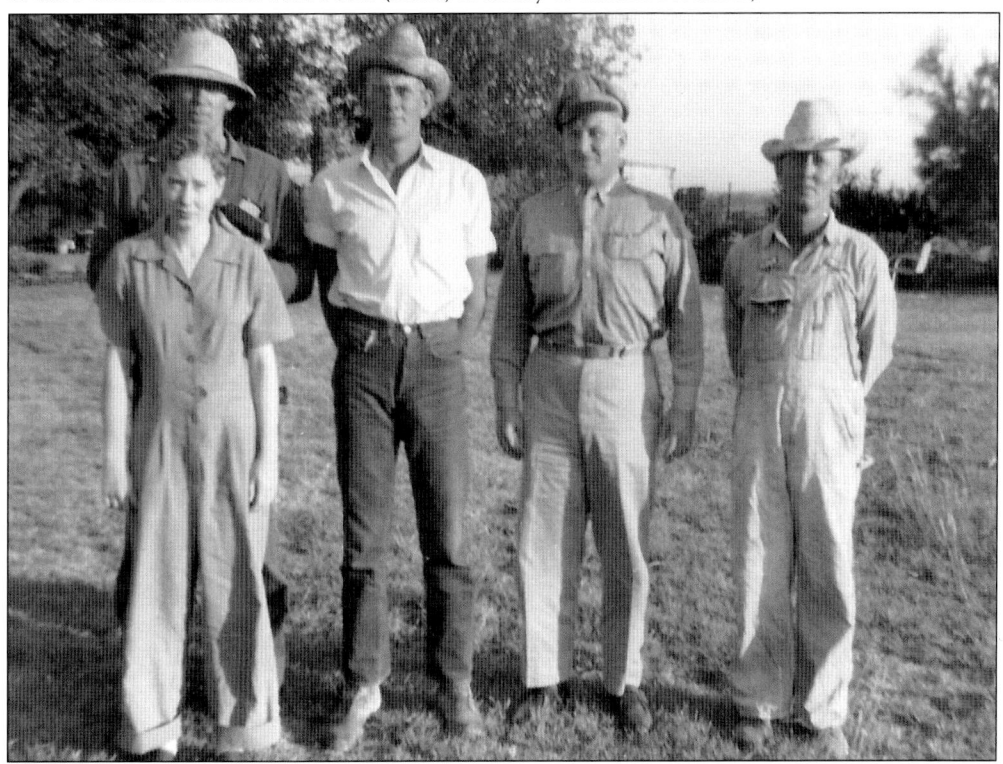

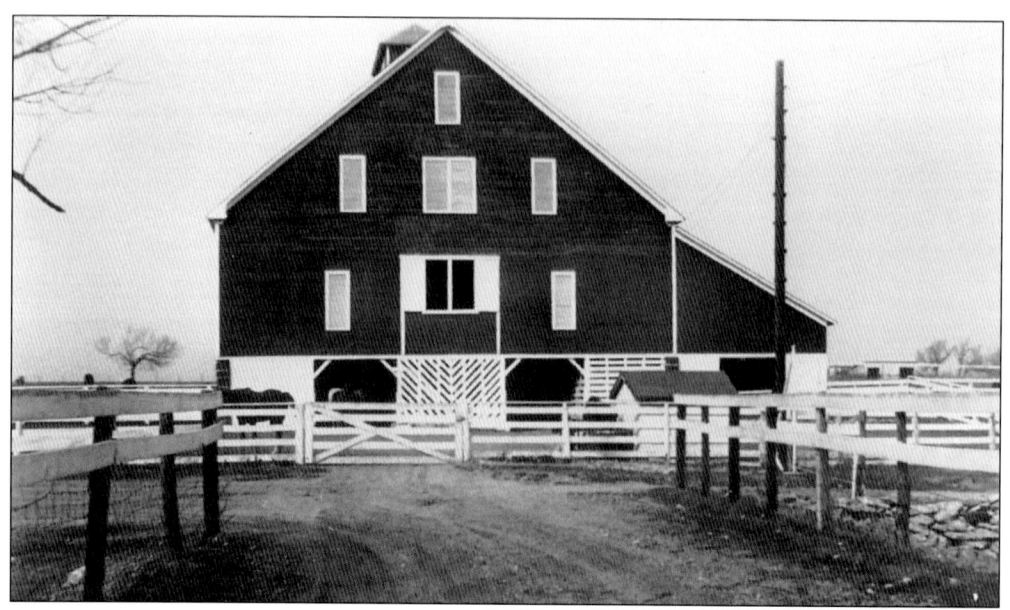

The Medlin barn (shown above) was built for James Medlin after he studied barn designs in many states. A team of mules driving a wagon could drive up to the second level on a dirt embankment, which made it much easier to unload grain or hay. By the time this picture was taken, the barn had passed out of the Medlin family and was owned by a man named Colonel Owsley, who has been described as riding a horse like a cavalry officer. Owsley made few appearances at the farm he named Owsley Bell. (Courtesy of Melvin Walls.)

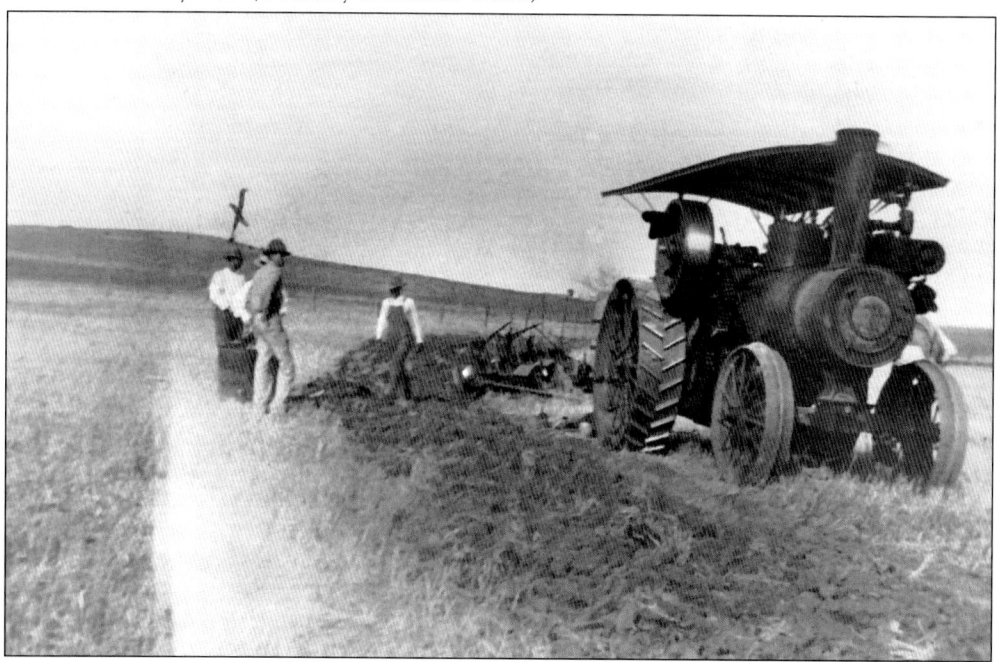

These workmen are plowing a field on Joe Frazier's farm. Frazier was married to Frances Gillespie, whose family was prominent in Roanoke. Frazier and other farmers in the area hired teenage boys to help them in the summer. There are now many older residents who have stories to tell about which farmers they wanted to approach about working for them. (Courtesy of Alberta Lincecum.)

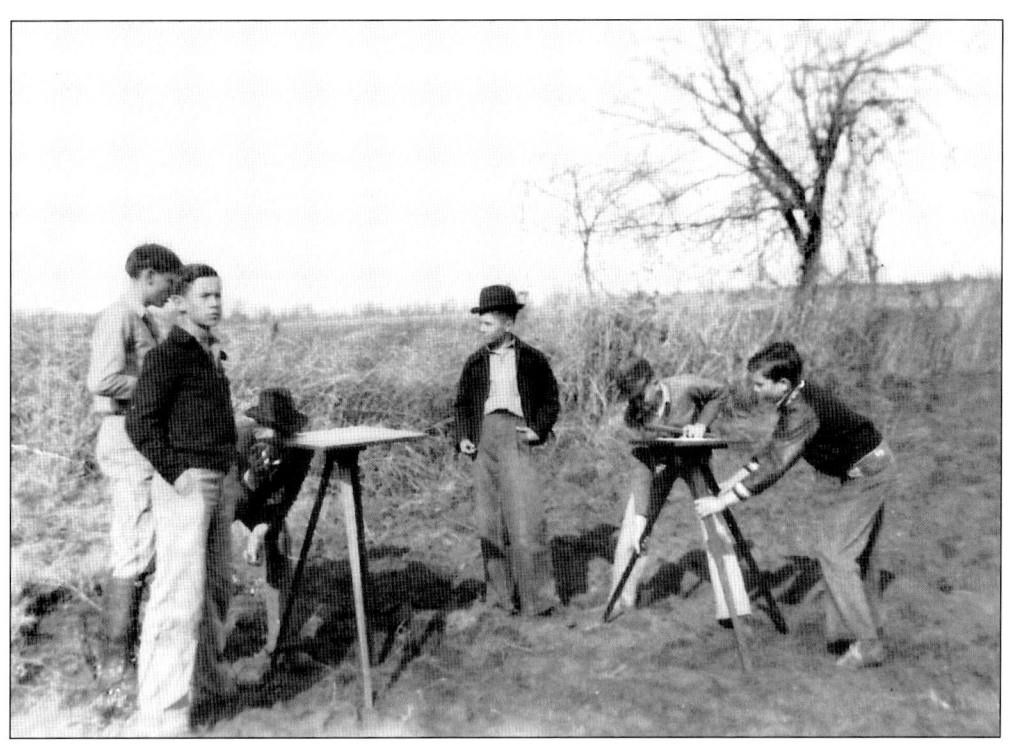

The Roanoke Chapter of the Future Farmers of America 1939–1940 had 34 members, six associate members, and seven honorary members. Most of the youngsters who were members eventually became productive citizens critical to the success of Roanoke. Bill Peterson, pictured above third from left, is the only one of the six youngsters identified. Peterson and the other boys are shown working on a soil and water conservation project. Pictured below are, from left to right, Clayton Mahaffey, Conway Peterson, Calvin Peterson, and Elwin Burgess. The boys attended the Fat Stock Show and the Texas State Fair in Dallas. (Both, courtesy of Calvin Peterson.)

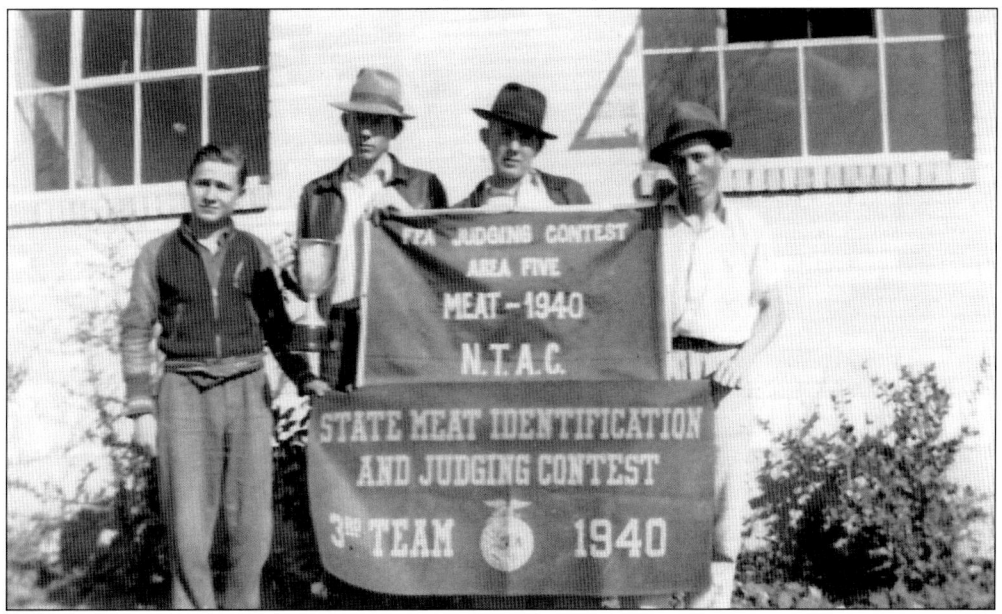

DISCOVER THOUSANDS OF LOCAL HISTORY BOOKS
FEATURING MILLIONS OF VINTAGE IMAGES

Arcadia Publishing, the leading local history publisher in the United States, is committed to making history accessible and meaningful through publishing books that celebrate and preserve the heritage of America's people and places.

Find more books like this at
www.arcadiapublishing.com

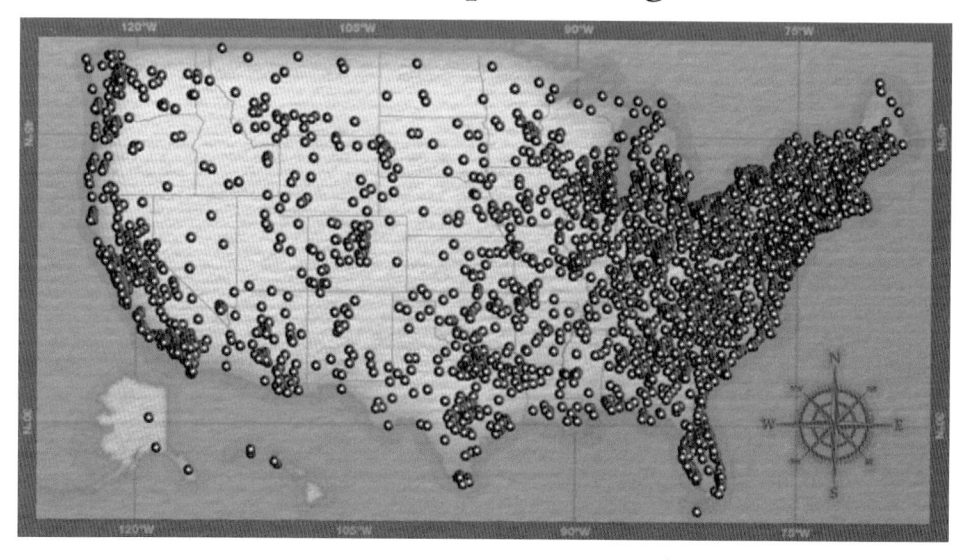

Search for your hometown history, your old stomping grounds, and even your favorite sports team.

Consistent with our mission to preserve history on a local level, this book was printed in South Carolina on American-made paper and manufactured entirely in the United States. Products carrying the accredited Forest Stewardship Council (FSC) label are printed on 100 percent FSC-certified paper.

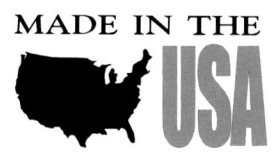

MADE IN THE USA